NICK'S NICKS

This edition published in 2025

Copyright © by Nick Tucker

The right of Nick Tucker to be identified as the author of this book has been asserted in accordance with the Copyright, Design and Patent Act 1988.

All rights reserved. No part of this book may be reproduced in any form or by any electronic or mechanical means, including information storage and retrieval systems, without written permission from the author, except for the use of brief quotations in a book review.

The views and opinions expressed in this book are mine, and mine alone; they do not reflect past, or current policies of Staffordshire Police, or any organisation associated with it.

Author's note

Dear Reader,

All the events in this book are true, although my memory may have failed with regard to details, dates or the order in which they happened.

Some names have been changed to avoid causing offence to former officers or their families.

The word 'shift' appears about three-hundred times in this book, I hope you'll understand the distinction between my referring to either a shift of people, or a day's work.

You may or may not agree with the views and opinions I have expressed, but they are honestly held.

With the passage of the years it's impossible to recall conversations verbatim, (i.e. notes were not made at the same time or as soon as possible afterwards!). I've tried though to preserve the sense of what was said.

I hope nobody is offended by anything in this book, apart from those who deserve to be!

Nick Tucker
February 2025

My thanks to my lovely wife Debbie, an author widow, for her patience, putting up with keys clacking away at her side, and my not paying attention at times.

Thanks also to my friend and former Staffordshire Police colleague, John Pye for his encouragement and guidance.

Dedicated to:

The very many fantastic people that I worked with,

worked for,

and who worked for me.

Those who led from the front,

there were plenty of them,

but nowhere near enough!

Glossary of abbreviations and acronyms.

AFO - Authorised Firearms Officer
ARV – Armed Response Vehicle
ASP - Armament Systems & Procedures
CPS – Crown Prosecution Service
CTG – Central Traffic Group
CMPG – Central Motorway Police Group
FPN – Fixed Penalty Notice
FSU – Force Support Unit
HMI – Her Majesty's Inspector(ate) of Constabulary
NTG – Northern Traffic Group
TSS – Traffic Support South
TSN - Traffic Support North
TSG – Tactical Support Group
VDR – Vehicle Defect Rectification

Nick's Nicks

The extraordinary story of an ordinary policeman

1 - A Good Education

'You've had a good education.'
Words which would follow me around for the next few years.

I'm old enough to have taken and passed the eleven-plus, although my grammar school was absorbed, kicking and screaming into the comprehensive system a couple of years later. I left school with a decent haul of 'O' and 'A' levels, mostly science based, as this was where my teachers felt my talents lay, heading off to Manchester University. I enjoyed the student life but came to realise that my heart wasn't into science after all, I'd learned as much as I wanted to. I lost interest, didn't do enough work and left at the end of two years.

The words at the top of the page came from behind the desk of a Careers Advisor in Stafford – as the job title implies, I was seeking advice. He studied my qualifications and school reports and asked me, quite seriously,
'Have you thought about a career in banking?'
Given the huge bonuses splashed around in that sector today it was probably a mistake to get up in disgust and walk out of the room. My next appointment involved banking anyway – a discussion with an assistant manager of Lloyds' Bank concerning my rapidly growing overdraft.

Inspiration came from the father of a good friend from university, he was an Inspector nearing retirement from West Yorkshire Police. His enthusiasm, sense of justice and compassion, together with a very healthy sense of humour were all things with which I could identify. The literature I received from Staffordshire Police after a telephone enquiry made it clear that I could enjoy a good career with pay which, whilst not great was more than enough for the needs of a young man just out of his teens. I was also attracted by the career prospects, being told that the 'Special Course' at the Police College at Bramshill guaranteed rapid progression through the ranks.

I decided to take the next step and made an appointment with Sergeant Jim Taylor, the 'Liaison Sergeant' at my local police station in Stafford. This was my first experience of police job titles which bore scant resemblance to what the post holder actually did – why couldn't they call him a Recruiting Sergeant, or Training Officer, because that's what he actually did. After an hour's chat with him I made the decision to apply for 'Appointment as a Constable', was handed the application form, weighed, measured, and sent on my way with the words, 'You've had a good education, you'll get in easily' echoing in my ears.

The application form was very hard work. They didn't just want my details – they wanted my life history. It had been a mere twenty and a half years, but it took me several hours daily for a few days. There followed a home visit from Sergeant Taylor for an interview with me, with my parents and with my sister, the dog slunk off to the kitchen. The Sergeant pronounced, 'He's had a good education, very promising.'

I was still in student mode, faded tee-shirt, shabby jeans, straggly beard and very thick, long hair which hadn't seen a pair of scissors for five or six years – see photo. I realised that at some stage the hair was going to have to go but please, not all at once! When a letter inviting me for an interview at Staffordshire Police Headquarters arrived, I

entered a hair salon as a stranger and left with my hair trimmed to somewhere between collar and shoulder length. A jacket and trousers which had been gathering dust saw the light of day for the first time in a year or two.

The interview was a very civilised affair with a genial Superintendent, concluding with him telling me that I'd be interviewed at a later date by the Chief Constable. He also told me that I'd have to sit the entrance examination despite having had a good education. As I left, I was quickly ushered into the neighbouring office to meet the force's 'Chief Clerk', Chief Superintendent Fred Maskery, unbeknown to me a friend of my father. A great lumbering bear of a man but exuding warmth through his grating voice, he shook me by the hand, said that given my standard of education my appointment was a mere formality, and told me that if at any time I needed help, his door would be open,
'We're one big family here.'

A few weeks later, with my hair neater and an inch shorter (but still not as short as it would have to be), I arrived at Police Headquarters for a day which would involve entrance examination, full medical and interviews. At the end of it I would know whether I'd been accepted. I was shown into a classroom with about twenty-five other candidates. At this point I discovered for the first time that police officers tend to move about a bit as the 'Liaison Sergeant' was now on Headquarters staff as a proper 'Recruiting Officer.' The entrance exam, for me at least, was ridiculously easy; several papers, basic English and basic arithmetic. One of the papers was made up of a series of phrases where two words had changed places and had to be underlined, e.g. 'Mr Jones caught the work to train.'
As I looked up, I saw some head scratching.
The medical followed then, after a substantial lunch, my final interview with the Chief Constable, Arthur Morgan

Rees CBE, QPM, DL, an imposing Welshman who had been an international rugby flanker in his younger days. Even seated at his desk he seemed to fill the room, dwarfing the two senior officers on either side of him. He looked at my entrance exam results, astonished, proclaiming the marks to be the highest he had ever seen. The interview passed in a blur, but at the end of it he said to me,

'You've had a good education and been to university. You're now in the University of Life boyo and will soon be one of my Constables in Staffordshire Police. Welcome to the force.'

He stood and shook hands with me.

Next stop was the stores building to be measured for uniform, my first encounter of many with the storekeeper, Mick Ryan. He deftly twirled his tape measure around me in a cloud of smoke and flying ash, shouting off dimensions to his assistant.

'What size hat are you?'

'Seven and five eighths', I replied, knowing that had been inside my school cap many years ago.

'Bollocks, nobody's got a head that big, put him down for seven and a quarter.'

This was September 1975. The Liaison/Recruiting Sergeant told me it could be December or January before I started. The force had a big recruitment drive on the go but could only send twenty officers every five weeks to the regional training school at Ryton-on-Dunsmore, on the outskirts of Coventry.

I'd been on the dole since leaving university but now I was going to have a job, earning £2400 a year, £50 a week! As a student I'd taken on jobs which paid me 20-30p an hour, so this seemed like a fortune. My friends couldn't believe that the long haired, scruffy student they knew so well was going to don a police uniform. I could barely believe it myself, but I knew that my beloved hair's days were numbered. Some of my friends knew police officers who'd told them how tough it was at the regional training school, with military discipline, drill, inspections and the like. I did wonder how I was going to cope with it, but the thought of that £200 a month kept me focused. I'd be on probation for the two years of my training, and my services could be dispensed with if I didn't make the grade.

I had to prepare. Ten weeks of travelling to Coventry and back meant that a car would be desirable. A friend had a lovely Triumph GT6 which he was selling, I really, really wanted it, until I went around the town for insurance quotes. Instead, a good proportion of my savings, plus a bank loan made me the proud owner of a seven-year-old Mini 1000. I also had to purchase a pair of boots, a pair of black Doctor Martens which cost me £30 – a tiny percentage of my forthcoming newly acquired wealth!

Finally, a bundle of papers arrived. I was to report to Headquarters Training Wing for my residential Induction Course on Monday 29th December 1975. On the Saturday after Christmas, I went to the barber's again but still couldn't bring myself to part with what was still a sizeable amount of hair.

2 – Swearing, Bodging and Bulling

It was the Monday after Christmas, the world virtually asleep. New Year's Day would be a public holiday for the second time. It was just beginning to become customary for people to make a full ten days or so holiday from the festive season.

Having arrived at Headquarters Training Wing with nineteen other fresh-faced recruits I recognised quite a few of the faces of the people with whom I'd taken the entrance exam, minus those who'd been scratching their heads. As most of us had come to know each other on that day there was little need for introductions. We were given the keys to our rooms on the first floor above the classrooms, and quite comfortable, told to unpack and return.

First off, a 'welcome' from one of the Assistant Chief Constables, Ivor Shepherd. This was where I began to understand the word 'bullshit', I shall say no more now. I had many later encounters with Mr Shepherd, he and my father knew each other and had a mutual loathing. The sins of the father were to be visited on the son - little did I know it at the time, but the next few years would prove it so.

Our trainer for the Induction Course was a very likeable, easy-going Sergeant, Steve Lovegrove who I would get to know well over the next couple of decades or so; when I retired many years later, he was my Superintendent. He was tasked with getting us sworn in, looking smart, build us up as a team and prepare us for the rigours of Ryton. We were to visit the Magistrates' Court that morning for the swearing-in, but Sergeant Lovegrove decided that we all needed haircuts. No problem, we were loaded into two personnel carriers and driven to a local barber's shop, Ken Philips, a lovely guy who became my regular hairdresser for the next few years. The Sergeant was driving the carrier that I was in, at one point he saw two youngsters on a bike, one on the crossbar, he wound down the window and shouted 'Gerroff it you silly little barstards!', this was 1975 – twenty years later his actions may have been more closely scrutinised.

My hair finally at a suitable length (although we were told that none of our haircuts would pass muster at Ryton), we returned to Headquarters to be photographed and fingerprinted, then driven to the court. We stood en-masse in the public gallery, repeating the words in unison prompted by the court clerk:

'I, Nicholas John Tucker do solemnly and sincerely declare and affirm that I will well and truly serve Our Sovereign Lady the Queen in the office of Constable, without favour or affection, malice or ill will; and that I will to the best of my power cause the peace to be kept and preserved, and prevent all offences against the persons and properties of Her Majesty's subjects; and that while I continue to hold the said office I will to the best of my skill and knowledge discharge all the duties thereof faithfully according to law.'

It seemed to me to come over as one big, low mumble, hardly appropriate for such a momentous occasion but this was it, I was finally a sworn Police Constable.

On returning to Headquarters, our pristine maroon warrant cards had been placed on our desks, not only was I a sworn Constable, but I also had the number 1441 which would follow me to the end of my service.

I was a Police Constable but without a uniform, so over to the stores to collect it. A speedy 'try-on' showed that my helmet was too tight (thanks to Mick's earlier 'Bollocks…') but all he'd say was,

'It'll stretch with wear, and anyway, you should be pleased', adding,

'You're the first intake to be issued with the new helmet plates' (or badges).

In this respect Mick was correct, the helmet plates we saw on other officers around Headquarters were drab affairs, ours had the Stafford (not, as some believe, Staffordshire) knot mounted on a green background inside a Garter Star, surmounted by a Queen's crown, and very smart they looked too. Each of us walked out of the stores loaded with four shirts 'collar attached' and clip-on ties, two tunics, two helmets, one cap, two pairs of trousers (button fly), a tropal lining (a quilted jacket stuffed with kapok which was *supposed* to guard against the cold), a flimsy pullover, a heavy belted raincoat, white ceremonial gloves, black leather gloves, truncheon and handcuffs, enough chrome numerals to attach to our tunics and coats, and a pocket notebook and cover. Also included was a jewellery identification chart (which never found its way out of my pocket-book cover in my entire service), a book marked 'Restricted' about what to do in the event of a nuclear attack (either stand right under it or resign were the best options), a copy of the Highway Code and finally, a whistle.

'Right lads', said Sergeant Lovegrove, 'Up to your rooms, into uniform and back here in half an hour.' This was bizarre, we changed, and all laughed as we stepped out into the corridor to inspect each other. There was much bending of the knees, thumbs in top pockets and exclamations of *'Ello, 'ello, what's going on here then?* As well as funny-ha-ha, it was funny-peculiar to be seeing each other in our uniforms for the first time.

Back to the classroom, but we weren't quite properly dressed yet, as our epaulettes were devoid of numbers. We were provided with half a dozen screwdrivers and bradawls (between twenty of us) with which to bodge holes in the heavy serge and mount the numbers. Competition for the 'bodgers' was quite intense, and it speaks little of my problem-solving skills that I didn't go out to my car and bring back a screwdriver from the toolkit. The bodging operation occupied the spare time between the various lectures we had from the force's departments over the next few days. Sergeant Lovegrove would regularly say, 'Okay lads, take it easy, have a chat, have a smoke.' It felt like a bit of a waste of time, but the real intention was for us to know each other well and build a team – we'd all be training together for the next two years.

One of our talks was from the salaries officer, Andy Wynter who I already knew, as we were both in a group that met for drinks on Thursday evenings. The longer he talked, the more my vast fortune of £2400 a year slipped away from me. We were to be paid every fourth Wednesday, the gross amount on our salary slip would be £184. After deductions for pension (who thinks about pensions at the age of 20?), tax, National Insurance and a few voluntary organisational deductions I worked out I would be getting £118 every four weeks, or £29.50 a week – disappointing, but did the tax man ever make anyone happy?

We were encouraged to take out endowment insurance policies with the Police Mutual Assurance Society or PMAS as it was better known. The rates on offer were very attractive, and PMAS could even assist with house purchase by way of endowment policies, very popular at the time but since widely discredited.

Another talk came from an officer nearing the end of his probation. He regaled us with tales of people he had arrested, motorists he had dealt with for traffic offences, the camaraderie and the practical jokes which were a daily feature. It sounded great, I couldn't wait to get into it myself.

Sergeant Lovegrove gave a series of talks on the structure of the organisation, dos and don'ts, including a session on the rank structure and insignia, or in his words,

'Who you salute, who you say 'Hello' to and who you say, 'Piss off' to.'

Very senior officers could be recognised by the quantity of scrambled egg on their hats, it was best to swerve if you saw them approaching from a distance.

There were inspections. We were expected to press our uniforms to a knife-edge crease, and 'bull' our boots to a mirror shine. As I'd never held an iron in my life this presented a challenge. No matter how hard we tried, none of us seemed to reach the standard required by the training department's Chief Inspector Ken Ratcliffe, a very stern, but sincere man with a mischievous twinkle in his eye. His mantra was *A smart copper is a good copper, a scruffy copper is a bad copper* – sounded like bullshit but experience over the years taught me that with very few notable exceptions he was absolutely correct.

Marching and standing to attention or at ease were a mystery to me, as to many of my colleagues, but we muddled through, Mr Ratcliffe telling us that far higher standards would be needed at Ryton. The pressure which my helmet put on my cranium was quite unbearable, but I foolishly believed in Mr Ryan's earlier promise.

We were taught how to wear our helmets properly – with the first knuckle of the thumb on the tip of the nose, the tip of the thumb should touch the peak of the helmet. This only served to increase the pressure.

All the time we were told how strict and unyielding the regime at Ryton was, and I wondered whether I would even last the first day. I found it hard to take to Mr Ratcliffe, but this changed significantly over time, realising that his severe manner at the time was for our benefit. He became one of the very best bosses I ever had.

Evenings were leisure time, there was a well-stocked, reasonably priced bar at the end of the residential corridor, bliss! No need to go out, we just drank all evening and off to bed at closing time. Amongst us were twins, Martyn and John. They had us believing that they could read each other's thoughts, but it was a well-practised routine which fooled us in the alcoholic haze. Another guy, Graham, was built like the metaphorical outhouse; I'd never seen anyone consume so much beer so quickly, while remaining apparently sober. He was drinking three pints to my every one, and I thought I could put it away.

On Wednesday evening we were all sent home for the New Year's Day holiday, instructed to make good use of the time with irons and shoe polish, and to return on Friday morning. At final inspection that morning, the Chief Inspector pronounced us to be *just* about satisfactory. We then met in the conference room with the Chief Constable who made it clear, in the friendliest way possible what he expected of us at Ryton for the next ten weeks.

In the afternoon Mr Shepherd made a return visit to our classroom to tell us where we would be posted to on our return. This was an anxious moment for all of us, the force seemed to post people as far away from their present homes as possible.

He came to my name, 'PC Tucker....' fixing me with a wicked gleam in his eye '......Newcastle.' Fifteen miles away from home, I didn't know the place at all apart from the many roundabouts on its bypass which had been part of my frequent journeys to and from Manchester over the last couple of years. As well as not knowing Newcastle (more correctly Newcastle-under-Lyme), I'd no knowledge whatsoever of the city of Stoke on Trent, Newcastle's linked neighbour. Apart from the short length of the A34 through Trentham, Hanford and Trent Vale, I'd set neither foot nor wheel in the city in my life. The lack of local knowledge would prove to be a frustrating handicap.

Sergeant Lovegrove then dispensed the 'Joining Instructions' for our course at Ryton, gave us directions and arranged car sharing for those who needed it. Being single it wasn't obvious to me that the married officers had, if at all, one car in their household which their wives would need while they were away. I arranged with one guy, Ken who lived near Cannock to provide him with transport. It was a bit of a diversion off my route, but the already well-developed team spirit between us all meant it didn't warrant a second thought.

We returned home, Saturday was free, but we were to report to Ryton by 9pm on Sunday.

3 - Marching to March

It was a very anxious Saturday. Aware that my hair was still too long for Ryton and having heard horror stories of the centre ~~butche~~ barber I paid my second visit in five days to Ken Philips. He made a big fuss of me, sat me in the chair and said, 'Let's make you grand!' He did, I had very little hair left now, somewhere in the region of five percent of what I'd had just a week ago.

I'd heard, 'Whatever you can get under your hat is yours, the rest belongs to the drill Sergeant', but I just wanted as little fuss as possible. This was a new beginning; my scruffy student days were over for good.

The usual Saturday night at the pub, with mates still trying to weaken my resolve with stories they'd heard of the Ryton regime, then Sunday was packing – everything I'd been issued with, plus 'suitable civilian clothing' for off duty times. 'Suitable' meant a jacket, trousers, shirt and tie; denim was completely proscribed. I also had to take a pair of white plimsolls and swimwear; the rest of my PE kit would be provided.

I set off on a very cold Sunday evening, drove to Cannock to collect Ken, then headed for Ryton. Every mile felt like a step from the condemned cell to the scaffold; I'd never felt so apprehensive before but there was no turning back now.

I arrived at the centre with my heart in my mouth. The total darkness meant I couldn't see anything of its architectural mediocrity. Having been directed to park my car and report to the main hall, I walked into a large, draughty utilitarian barn lined with tables, a uniformed Sergeant behind each.

Several bewildered young men and women like me were standing at the tables. At the door I was directed to a table behind which sat a well-built, bespectacled and bearded Sergeant. He neither introduced himself nor invited me to be seated, but reeled off some instructions in a manner which didn't invite discussion. I signed several documents, was issued with some more and was directed to a classroom where we would be given further details at 9pm.

The classroom was a freezing cold room in a barracks style building. Name cards were on each of the wooden desks in the room, I sat at the one bearing my name. Although several of us were in the room, conversation was muted; all of us stunned into silence by our experience so far. Three of my Staffordshire colleagues, John, Tony and Roger were in the same class.

On the stroke of nine, we stood as the bearded Sergeant strode in, his body language still suggesting that conversation with him was inadvisable. His very first words, delivered very severely were,

'If anyone thinks they can't handle the next ten weeks, then leave - NOW!'

I vaguely remember one young man who quickly walked through the room; the icy blast as he went through the door was all I remember of him.

Time for introduction, he was Sergeant Gibson of Leicestershire Police and was to be one of our two instructors in 'E' class for the next ten weeks, the other was a Staffordshire officer, Sergeant Dyer, who we'd meet later.

He laid down some ground rules.

No talking in class.

You stood when an instructor entered the room.

If your name was called you were to stand up.

If you put up your hand to speak, once invited to you were then to stand to attention to deliver your words.

We were told where our rooms were, to unpack and make ourselves 'at home' and report to the classroom in full uniform at 8.15am after breakfast in the canteen. We were not allowed to leave the centre at any time or to be out of our rooms after 11pm. On no account were the ladies' accommodation blocks to be visited by the men, or vice-versa.

*Jeez, ten weeks of **this**?*

He asked for anyone with military service to remain behind after the rest of us had gone, I briefly wondered why.

I took my case from my car and trudged around a maze of utilitarian blocks to the one which would be my week time home for the next ten weeks. **What a bloody dump!** A corridor ran the length of the building g with rooms off to either side. My ~~cell~~ room was about ten by six feet, with a well-worn lino floor, a very uncomfortable looking bed and a wardrobe, both of which had seen better days, a washbasin with crazed glazing and a desk and chair. The only

concession to heating was a six-inch diameter pipe running along the outer wall of the room which fought in vain against the room's very low temperature. There was no lock on the door. Most of the men I shared the block with were from the West Midlands Police with matching accents, they all seemed to be called Terry, at least that was my impression from the way they bellowed at each other along the corridor.

Having unpacked, I introduced myself to my across-the-corridor neighbour, a Leicestershire guy from my own class not called Terry, but Steve Sealey, a former squaddie, and very easy to get on with. Eventually, utterly miserable I settled in my lumpy, uncomfortable bed for a night of erratic sleep, wondering during the many waking moments what on earth I'd let myself in for. However, I focused on the £29.50 a week riches and realised that to finish now would be back to the dole office, no money for six weeks, and a waste of the substantial effort I'd put in so far. It had gone very quiet in the block, apart from the occasional sound of taps running for about five seconds, I wondered why, but I'd soon find out.

Monday 5th January dawned freezing cold, grey and misty. Having had a rather unpleasant breakfast in the canteen, I returned to my room to smarten up, then down to the classroom. No sign of Sergeant Gibson, but my neighbour Steve asked us all to go outside. It turned out that after our introduction from the Sergeant the previous night, Steve's army service had won him the job of our 'drill pig', responsible for teaching us basic drill and barking orders. Having managed to arrange us into two ranks he said,
'There are a lot of people in this place; we have to march, or we'd be running into each other all the time.'
Bullshit again. I'd previously been on a campus of over ten thousand randomly moving students without hearing of any life-threatening collisions. Nevertheless, Steve gave us a ten-minute introduction to the basics, enough to just about get us on to the parade square where we were due to be at 8.30. For the first time in my life I marched, arms swinging, but not how they should, I just could not get my right arm to go forward when I stuck out my left leg, and vice-versa; instead, right arm moved forward with right leg, left with left, known as 'tick-tocking.' It would take several days for me to get this right, it felt like I was the only one doing it.

We managed, somewhat awkwardly to arrive at the parade square at the front of the centre, in full view of the busy main road. Ryton took in recruits every five weeks for a ten-week course, so courses overlapped. For the first five weeks, we were to be the 'Junior Course', as opposed to the 'Senior Course' who were now lined up on the parade ground facing the most terrifying looking man I'd ever seen in my life, the drill Sergeant, Tom Trickett, actually a West Midlands Constable who'd served in the Grenadier Guards and given stripes as a 'protective rank' during his tenure at Ryton. He was well over six feet tall, stood ramrod straight, boots polished beyond a mirror shine, with the peak of his cap 'slashed' so that it fell straight over his forehead. He barked out commands at a volume which didn't seem humanly possible.

Soon we were commanded to move from our spectating position to behind the assembled senior course. 'By the left, quick MARCH!', drum rolls came over a tinny PA system and then - I couldn't believe it – 'The Liberty Bell', the Monty Python theme music, to which we had to march. As an ardent Python fan, I found it surreal, stifling my laughter as we marched onto the square, in full view of the rush hour traffic. Great entertainment for the passing motorists in the long queue for a nearby roundabout.

A bit of left turning, right turning, quick marches and halts followed; eventually we marched off the parade ground, to the same tune with Steve barking out 'left-right-left-right...', me tick-tocking my way along and feeling very embarrassed; eventually we halted outside our classroom and were commanded to 'Fall out!.'

My helmet had been crushing my skull for the best part of half an hour, so it came as a welcome relief to finally take it off, Mick Ryan's promise wasn't coming through yet. A quick huddle for a fag and a chat and back into the classroom.

Sergeant Gibson came in, and we all stood, a practiced pause on his part and we were told to sit down. We listened to more of the standing orders we were to comply with, upon pain of a 'meeting without coffee' with the Deputy Commandant, (Commandant? I hadn't noticed the Stalag Luft number on the gate last night) or worse. Instructors could be distinguished from students by the fact that they wore flat caps. Instructors of the rank of Inspector or above were always to be saluted. They were easy to spot, the Sergeant hinted, as their shirts were white. There was one female Inspector on the staff though, as female PCs wore white shirts you had to look out for the 'pips' every time you saw a female officer coming towards you. Much to my embarrassment and theirs, I saluted female recruits quite a few times over the coming weeks. You were to always wear your helmet when outdoors in uniform. You were not allowed to return to your room after morning classes had begun. If two or more of you were walking together then you were to march.

As it went on and on, I became steadily less inspired by my career choice – wondering whether banking may have been the better option.

Lunchtime at 12.30 was a 'parade' at which attendance was compulsory; fortunately, eating the food on offer wasn't. There was a bar on the centre, you were expected to be there every evening, - 'You WILL enjoy yourselves!' - centre staff would be watching your interaction with your fellow students. Private functions could be organised on request.

There were 'Duty Squads', each class having to do this every eighth day. They were responsible for the menial tasks around the complex, gate security, patrols of the centre and, to my delight, bar work. Once it was known I had lots of previous experience of this, I'd be working behind the bar instead of spending freezing cold nights walking around the centre or stopping cars at the gate.

We were issued with a ring-file of 'Student Lesson Notes' and a folder of stationery, including a pocket notebook which, once we'd been trained in its use, would be maintained just like an operational officer. The week's lessons were organised into distinct sections, most of the lesson notes had to be learned parrot-fashion. First thing every Monday an exam on the previous week's work would be held in the main hall. This was an objective exam of fifty multiple choice (or multiple guess) questions. The pass-mark, as I recall was 76%. If you failed you would be sent to the 'Woodentops class', more accurately the 'Supplementary Training Unit, or STU – I quickly learned that if anything in this job could be reduced to initials it was done as a matter of course. This would be for the next two lunchtimes and evenings, more parrot-fashion learning then another test. Failing to make the grade this time would result in a decaffeinated meeting with the Deputy Commandant, and possible dismissal.

However, to obtain marks of over 90% in all Monday tests and the more challenging final examination in the tenth week would reserve a place on the centre's Honours Board in the main reception area.

Formalities dealt with, we were allowed a break outside the classroom, where a large urn of tea, allegedly laced with bromide had been delivered, we could talk with each other, mix with the class from the next room and have a smoke, most of us at the time having acquired the habit.

Break concluded, the lessons started; what they call didactic style teaching these days, with the use of blackboard and the latest innovation - the overhead projector. Appointments were made of blackboard and OHP monitors, both of whom would have to spring into action at the Sergeant's command. We were taught the rank structure (again) and the organisation of police forces. One of the very first things we learned was what a Constable's role in society was, i.e.

S/he is a citizen.
Is locally appointed.
Having authority under the Crown for:
The protection of life and property,
The maintenance of order,
The prevention and detection of crime, and
The prosecution of offenders against the Queen's Peace.

Yes, I learned it parrot-fashion, and still remember it half a century later!
Locally appointed – fifteen miles from home though.

We were introduced to the Unit Beat Policing system; the 'innovative' basis of uniform policing since 1967, when the public had been introduced to the Panda Car. The true intention was to spread less police officers over more ground. Each urban Sub-division of a police force was split into areas, usually about three miles or so square. Each of these would have two Constables, living on the patch and each responsible for foot patrol on their half of it. They would be supplemented by one twenty-four-hour Panda patrol.

All patrols were equipped with radios, co-ordinated at the Sub-divisional station by a 'Collator' who took telephone calls and controlled the radio. It was their responsibility to allocate incoming calls from the public to the patrolling officers; additionally, they 'collated' information forthcoming from the uniform patrols and the public.

This had been heralded as a huge advance in policing. What we weren't taught was that it was an absolute failure but never acknowledged. For one thing, eight-hour shifts, leave, courses, rest-days and abstractions for other pressing matters combined to result in the times that three Constables would patrol an area would be almost never; the majority of the time it would be just one officer in a panda car.

Throughout the first morning, we cowered under Sergeant Gibson's rigid discipline. It was something of a relief to go for lunch, less impressive than breakfast – if such a thing were possible. After we'd eaten, Sergeant Trickett barked out a list of orders, my ears pricking up when I heard an instruction for those from our accommodation block to meet with Sergeant Wilcox in the nearby crush lounge after lunch.

I'd seen pictures of Sergeant Wilcox in a copy of Police Review that I'd borrowed from someone and had spotted him at the top table dining and laughing with his colleagues. He seemed a decent sort of fellow, an impression quickly vaporised by his apoplectic rage as he berated us for the 'appalling, disgusting' state in which we had left our eel rooms. It would not be tolerated. For the next three weeks, we were all to 'block' our beds, military fashion, each and every morning. I never saw the point of this, and I still don't, but we had no option.

It seemed we'd fallen foul of an unwritten order that personal items must not be left on display in our rooms as this could inflict untold distress and anxiety on the cleaners. It's likely that this torment was caused by just one of us leaving a toothbrush by the basin. Banking entered my helmet-crushed head again as I tick-tocked back to our classroom in a group of three.

I felt ready to get into my car and leave this ring of hell forever.

Afternoon classes started. We stood as our other instructor Sergeant Dyer strode into the room and casually waved us to sit down. A tall, slim man, he had a commanding presence but with a more casual, less rigid manner than his colleague. Firstly, he asked the Staffordshire officers to introduce ourselves and said that he expected great things of us. As the afternoon passed we became slightly more relaxed but were still on our guard.

I felt a little less downcast as we marched over to tea, which like the two other meals we had eaten, didn't fail to disappoint; then it was back to our rooms. We were exasperated by the earlier order of Sergeant Wilcox, but with a team spirit already developing, our former military colleagues demonstrated the pointless, time-consuming chore of bed blocking to us. It mattered not at all who had caused such an ordeal for the cleaners.

Whatever we could stuff in our wardrobes wasn't subject to scrutiny, so each morning *everything* went into the wardrobe. Before the weekend we realised that we could bring back our own sleeping bag and pillows to use each night. Our bed-blocks could go on the floor for the night, and we could pile our sleeping bags and pillows into the wardrobe during the day. Problem solved, time saved, team spirit building by the minute.

The early evening was taken up with revising what we had learned during the day and preparing our uniforms for next morning's parade. Each morning, a class would be picked at random from each of the junior and senior courses for inspection after the others had marched off the square. It could be our turn tomorrow, or any day at all, so we had to be prepared. If anyone's appearance was not up to scratch, then they would be re-inspected at the on-site Police Station on 'Defaulters' Parade' at 9pm. If still found wanting they would miss their morning coffee the following day whilst standing to attention in the Deputy Commandant's office.

I couldn't, however hard I tried, 'bull' my boots, Steve kindly offered to show me how. This was where I learned the meaning of the term 'spit and polish': bulling involved the use of Kiwi (or at a push Cherry Blossom) shoe polish, a yellow duster, the index finger and - finally – spit. Typical of the team spirit that quickly built up, Steve devoted over half an hour of his own time to sorting me out, expecting nothing but a pint in return.

There were alternatives to bulling, Johnson's 'Kleer' floor polish was one, and spray on ignition sealer from Halfords too, but these both cracked very easily and weren't worth the possible wrath of Sergeant Trickett; so strictly for emergency use, whilst putting one's feet down as gently as possible when marching.

There was industrial scale pressing of uniforms in the ironing room in a nearby block, the ex-military guys were always ready to lend a hand and give advice. Tony, one of the Staffordshire officers in our class had been a hairdresser in a previous life and would give us trims on the promise of a couple of drinks later.

We gave our time freely to help each other, yet more team spirit, none of us having anything better to do anyway.

By 9pm we had all had enough of studying, pressing and bulling and exited our block en-masse, not marching for the first time since lessons began and made our way to the bar, where we arrived relieved to have had no collisions, and uninjured. Several pints and talking shop later (making sure that we all appeared to be obeying the command *You Will Enjoy Yourselves*) the bar closed on the dot of 10.30pm. We were ejected at the end of the statutory 10-minute drinking up time and staggered back to our blocks - maybe a few minor collisions now - mindful of the 11pm curfew.

It was after the curfew I understood the reason for taps running periodically through the previous night. We were not allowed out of our rooms and after several pints of beer, well, you've guessed. Over the years those plugholes had seen probably as much urine (and maybe worse) as they had soapy water. The single heating pipe in our rooms was wholly inadequate, and through the depths of January and February we shivered in our beds. On more than one occasion the surface of the tumbler of water at my bedside froze.

As the week continued, we hadn't had to stay behind for the dreaded inspection, but always had to be immaculate on parade, just in case. Through the working day the uniform which had been so painstakingly prepared for inspection lost its creases or became encrusted with toxic lunch; the bulled boots lost their shine, or the solidified spit and polish cracked. There was usually ten minutes between the 'fall out' command after morning parade and the start of lessons, giving just enough time to dash to our rooms, change into our other uniform, and (once purchased in the centre shop) a pair of shoes, carefully leaving the bulled boots in the wardrobe. This worked well on most days, except those where Sergeant Trickett's drill lesson was on the timetable - when we had to stay in our 'best' uniforms all day.

Finally, the end of the first week arrived. Beginning to understand how a paroled prisoner must feel, I'll never forget the sense of freedom as Ken and I drove out of those gates into the Coventry rush-hour and as fast as my Mini would go, home. Lots of questions from my parents, despite a phone call home every evening. They couldn't believe that their son (bear in mind they still had the 'student' me in mind) was yielding to such rigid discipline and were probably very pleased.

Down to my local in the evening. I digress here but this was unforgettable. We had a folk club there on Fridays, with guest singers, mostly obscure but some well-known, including an up-and-coming guy by the name of Mike Harding. In between visits to the bar, people got up to sing in a free-for-all session, often in stereotypical folksinger pose, seated and half-doubled-up with a hand cupped over one ear, I haven't a clue what this achieved.

A guy in his sixties would step onto the stage every week. He suffered from the dual afflictions of impaired speech and tone-deafness, aware of the first, but not the latter. He sang the same song every week, it was dreadful to the point of being embarrassing. Being a friendly crowd, we'd tolerate it and politely applaud, probably out of relief that it was over for another week.

This time, as he still had a couple of verses to go, I suddenly felt a substantial build-up of gas in my lower intestine signalling that it urgently needed to leave my body. During the pause at the end of a verse, not being able to wait a split second longer I let it go, believing that the escape would be silent.

The resulting thunderclap echoed around the room. I was clearly identifiable as the culprit but made a show of looking around in disgust. Feeling that my fart was a comment on his artistic merit, the poor guy shambled off, mid-song, never to perform again. Although I was subjected to menacing stares, I sensed some gratitude that the weekly ordeal was over once and for all. My attempted apology to him went unacknowledged.

Back to the subject. I'd noticed how much my hair had grown in one week, another couple of days could mean missing my first pint at 9pm. So, on the Saturday morning, as with the previous and every coming Saturday morning I visited Ken Philips.

'Come in, let's make you grand!'

I really enjoyed my weekly chats with Ken, 'barber by appointment' to many police officers. He had many entertaining, probably highly embellished stories from them to tell, and was genuinely interested in what I'd been up to in the last few days. The rest of the weekend was given over to studying in preparation for Monday morning's exam, but not without the Saturday night visit to the pub.

Sunday evening came around all too quickly and after packing my bags I headed off to Heath Hayes to collect Ken, driving along the A446 and A45 noticeably more slowly than Friday's journey in the opposite direction. There was an air of gloom in my tiny car, my pulse and breathing quickening as we neared the outskirts of Coventry. I knew then what it must feel like to be a prisoner returning from home leave; once the entrance barrier at Ryton closed behind me, I was 'confined to barracks' until Friday - an eternity away. Why on earth was I doing this?

Knowing what to expect, the second week was a little easier. As well as classroom sessions, we had lessons in first aid, run by a formidable man. Sergeant Alan Martin of West Mercia. Then there was lifesaving, PE and self-defence (aikido) with a very cocky, vertically challenged civilian instructor, to whom, like most other people, I took an instant dislike.

I considered myself a strong swimmer, I'd swum for the county in regional competitions in my youth and had worked my way up to ASA Gold in survival. However, I couldn't do lifesaving to save my life, simply not having enough stamina to make the distance with a 'casualty' colleague in tow, I usually ended up being 'life-saved' by the same colleague – I failed. I did get some badge or other, but my failure never made the slightest difference to my career.

PE was very challenging, and I certainly came to know the meaning of 'no pain, no gain.' I felt my strength and fitness building week by week, even though like most in the gym I was a twenty-a-day man. We all had the same PE kit, and our white plimsolls always had to be spotless, not an easy task.

Self-defence was enlightening, although in all my service I can't recall using any of the many holds that I learned, you simply couldn't get the bad guys to come at you in the same way as the controlled environment of the gym. I think the 'arm-up the back' hold was the only one I ever used; it saw me through.

Wednesday afternoons were reserved for sport. Sports involving hitting the ball, kicking the ball, or fighting for the ball had never been of any interest to me. However, I was a willing participant in the cross-country run, a demanding route of around ten miles, including at one point leaping over moving conveyor belts from a nearby quarry – health and safety?

I enjoyed the run, it was an escape from the rigours of the centre but was very muddy in places. We ran in our standard issue PE kit, rendering our mandatory spotless plimsolls not so spotless. At two points during the course, in the fifth week and the final week all students had to take part in the run. In the fifth week I managed to finish in a lowly one-hundred-and-eighteenth place, but my increased fitness saw me finish an easy seventh on my final run. Our time was free after the run until evening mealtime, so I would enjoy a long hot soak in the bath, heaven! Then there was the thankless task of washing the mud out of my plimsolls, putting them on the pipe to (maybe) dry out overnight and a hurried application of white in the morning before that day's PE.

Once, we started our cross country run later than usual and were sent over a longer course. I returned to the centre covered in mud, after tea had started. After a rapid bath I ran across to the canteen to find that there was not a single scrap of food left. That was it until the bar opened – and then only crisps. I was starving, the long-awaited breakfast the next morning was almost enjoyable.

I found drill sessions with Sergeant Trickett to be quite enjoyable, despite his eye for every single flaw in our turnout. One evening's drinking time was reduced by him sending me to the defaulters' parade as my boots weren't shiny enough. Staffordshire officers had the advantage of wearing brand new uniforms, whereas our West Midlands colleagues, outnumbering us greatly, were part of a massive recruitment drive. They were often issued second-hand uniform and regularly had to miss their first pint of the evening.

I found Tom to be a very likeable man with a great sense of humour, but this was years before political correctness. His opinion was that there were only three types of people, starting with 'Brummies' – his own tribe. The other two were those from north of Birmingham (Jocks), and from the south (a four letter word rhyming with 'bogs'). Red hair gained you the name of a 'Poisoned dwarf' and so it went on. It was a different era, completely inappropriate by today's standards but taken in good spirit by everyone.

If a recruit couldn't handle the abuse handed out by the drill sergeant, they certainly wouldn't cope with their later experiences on patrol. Resilience is a vital part of a police officer's character.

At the end of the fifth week, we were treated to a long weekend and headed home on the Thursday evening, because of the following day's passing out parade for the senior course. When we returned on the Monday we would take their place. I took a sideways glance on the following Monday morning's parade at the terrified faces of the new intake - I knew just how they felt.

As the course progressed, discipline relaxed fractionally each week, lessons were interesting and enjoyable, with a lot of laughter involved. I was gaining over 90% in every Monday morning's 'slip' test, to the point where it felt like I was walking a tightrope. The others in the class were egging me on by the time week five arrived, and it would have been bitterly disappointing for me to have dropped below the line. My lowest score so far was 92%, but in the same week my colleague Bob managed 100% and didn't let me forget about it.

We were all thoroughly enjoying ourselves, as instructed a few weeks ago; we worked hard and played even harder. Every night in the bar, and every week a disco in the assembly hall, the social life was fantastic, we didn't really feel the need to venture outside the centre, despite rumours that several made their way through the fence undetected. The sense of comradeship between us grew incredibly strong, we worked together as a team all the time, gradually realising that the rigid discipline had been aimed at forging team spirit and raising personal standards.

We had regular individual tutorial sessions with our instructors. Mine were with Sergeant Gibson who was very pleased with my progress but unsurprised as I'd had a good education. I realised how far I'd come in a very short period of time. I was taking pride in my appearance, both on and off duty, I had far more self-reliance and discipline, and above all my confidence had increased massively.

As well as the classes, we had practical situations to deal with. Instructors would dress up as offenders and we would have to take the proper action with them. One or two officers would handle the scenario while the rest looked on. The 'offenders' would give ridiculous names or occupations (such as 'saggar maker's bottom knocker', in fact a true occupation as any native of Stoke-on-Trent will tell you). However, they were always 'no-win' situations which ended with the 'offender' running off into the distance, and the rest of the class in helpless laughter at the misfortune of the officer/s dealing. These practicals bore little resemblance to what we would have to encounter a few weeks later; I think they were of greater value to the instructors, who could have some fun at our expense.

Being taught traffic control involved an officer standing on a crossroads in the centre while their colleagues lined up at the end of each road, representing cars waiting to get through. It was an early insight into the fact that the best way to keep traffic moving at a busy junction is to make sure there isn't a police officer within a million miles of it.

Road accidents (Road Traffic Accidents – abbreviated to RTAs of course) happen every hour of the day. We were shown how to deal with these, there being a national reporting 'accident book' known as an HORT7 (Home Office Road Traffic form 7) to be filled in. This was pretty straightforward, although I discovered in the following months that each small book (like everything in the police force) ended up with a bulk of other paperwork attached, something never mentioned at the time. The crashes at Ryton were represented by one or two of the 'bangers' used for training purposes positioned about half an inch apart and we had to imagine that they were seriously damaged.

One practical involved a sudden death. We were shown into a darkened room where there was a 'body' in the bed, and we had to deal with it. One of our class was a well-bred, immaculately coiffured young lady from deepest Shropshire, clearly having had a sheltered upbringing. Whilst not the sharpest knife in the drawer, she was just as keen as the rest of us. Her reaction to this contrived situation was to break down in floods of tears. She was absolutely lovely, but I can't imagine that she lasted more than a few weeks on the streets. I still wonder what inspired her to join.

We were schooled in interview techniques, public order and explosives, the latter consisting of Tom Trickett having a great time detonating plastic explosive on the sports field, demonstrating how a huge explosion could come from a tiny amount of it. We learned what constituted 'obscene language', there being just two words in the English language which fitted the title, both having the second letter 'u', one beginning with 'f' and the other with 'c.'

Part way through the course the parade square changed places with the car park at the rear of the centre. Rumour had it that the former car park had been a little too secluded and there was night-time 'wild life' going on there, one allegedly involving a student and the wife of one of the senior officers. Coventry's commuters lost their morning entertainment. The change of parade venue however didn't relieve the pain inflicted by my helmet, still resolutely unstretched.

Sergeants Gibson and Dyer noted that it was my twenty-first birthday on the final weekend, and encouraged me (well, told me actually) to ask permission of the Commandant to hold a private party in the Instructors' Lounge on the final Monday of the course.

On the last weekend at home, probably like the rest of the people on the course I had my head in my lesson notes in preparation for Monday's final exam; despite my birthday on the Saturday for which my parents laid on a family celebration. For most of the family and close friends this was their first glimpse of Nick the policeman, the striking change in my appearance being much remarked on. My Mum baked me a special birthday cake with a figure of PC Plod at its centre. My birthday included a visit to Ken Philips and collecting a dinner suit from the town for the coming Thursday's 'Dining In Night' at Ryton. This, and the passing out parade were held to mark the end of each course.

Back to Ryton for the final time the next evening, the feeling of surrendering to custody replaced by a sense of relief that it was nearly over. Monday dawned, everyone dreading the final exam after parade. I had managed to score over 90% in all the previous slip tests, so a place on the Honours Board was within sight. The questions presented me with no problems, we returned to the classroom and a cup of coffee, all feeling quietly confident that we had passed.

Our relief was short-lived. Bizarrely we were told that we would all have to re-sit the exam before lunchtime.

It later came to light that another class instructor had laid their hands on the final, top secret question paper and had coached their class to pass. This undoubtedly ended their secondment to the centre, and probably their career prospects.

So, with a feeling of deja-vu we went through it again. I felt reasonably confident that I'd done well. Our appetite for lunch, normally close to non-existent, was even less as we wouldn't know the results until the afternoon.

Back to the classroom and after we had all settled, a Sergeant from the STU, also responsible for setting and marking exam papers strode in.

Very sternly he asked, 'Which one of you lot is PC Tucker?'

Rising quickly and standing to attention, 'I am, Sarge.'

'Can you write?'

Puzzled, I replied, 'Course I can, Sarge.'

'You've got a speech to write then, you're top student, just one wrong answer on your exam, so you're on the Honours Board too.'

I couldn't believe it, what a moment! Before the Sergeant stopped speaking, the class went crazy, cheering and applauding me. Both Sergeants Gibson and Dyer came and shook hands with me. It was the proudest moment of my life to date, and they were all proud of me too. I was completely overwhelmed.

As top student, I had the honour of presiding over the dining in night at the top table seated next to the Commandant. As the STU Sergeant had said, I also had to write a speech with which to close the course. Although it was to come entirely from my own hand, it would be vetted by the Commandant, but my enjoyment of the course ensured that nothing controversial would be said.

It was a double celebration on the Monday night, for my twenty-first and for my achievement. A great time was had by all, much beer was drunk and the taps in our block seemed to run all night long. As we left the bar, I saw that my name had already been added in gold-leaf lettering to those on the Honours Board in the reception area, as well as the 'Top Student' board.

Over the next few days preparations were in full swing for our passing-out parade. Sergeant Trickett drilled and rehearsed us incessantly. Inspections were made but no defaulters' parades now, the Sergeant instead giving us well-intentioned advice on how to add the final touches, making it clear all the time that it was *our* passing-out parade, for *us* to enjoy. A feature of each parade was traffic signals performed to military music, and sometimes even to the 'Wombles' signature tune. This had featured in the TV programme *The Generation Game* a few months previously. Classroom discipline relaxed to the point that Sergeants Gibson and Dyer told us that they were now to be known as Geoff and Glyn, the latter actually had the middle name of Oswyn, his initials causing great amusement.

I was hard at work on my speech, there was a Wednesday evening deadline so that it could be typed and vetted by the Commandant. A tradition with the speech was that the students' nicknames for their instructors were to be read out on the night, I had to research this, but it wasn't too difficult chatting to the other students in the bar. Geoff had been named 'Chummy Boy' by our class, and Glyn 'On yer bike youth.' A great time was being had by all every evening now that studying was at an end, more beer flowed over the bar and taps ran constantly through the night. However, I felt a distinct tinge of sadness; we were all to part company at the end of the week, the team broken up forever.

Dining-in night came, and we ambled – not marched - together to the canteen in our dinner suits, meeting up en-route with the dazzlingly dressed ladies. As we congregated in the crush lounge for photographs to be taken, we were introduced to Geoff and Glyn's wives who'd joined us for the evening, I don't know what the sleeping arrangements were as most instructors slept in single rooms like us (although Glyn and his family lived in a police house on the centre).

There was a real sense of occasion, everyone walked into a completely transformed canteen, resplendent with tablecloths and table decorations. I had to remain behind though as I was to enter with the Commandant and senior centre staff as everyone stood for us. I suddenly realised that although I had the honour of being on the top table, and the one and only time in my entire life that over a hundred and twenty people would stand for me, I was separated from the class with whom I'd enjoyed so many moments over the last ten weeks - I really wanted to share this time with them. The food, for once, was pretty good.

Despite the separation from my comrades, I did enjoy the company of the Commandant, Chief Superintendent Dick Murby of Northamptonshire, a most gracious and engaging man. He was very interested to know my views on the centre and the way in which the course had been run. I complained about bed-blocking and other disciplines, his response was illuminating,

'You're all miles away from home, a lot of you for the first time. In the first few weeks we want to have you hating us lot so much that you don't have time to get homesick.'

I saw his point, commenting that it had also created a strong team spirit; this was intentional too, he said. He and his staff had succeeded on both counts.

Although I say so myself, my speech went down very well indeed, and I received many compliments. I made one hugely embarrassing mistake though, renaming Geoff as 'Sergeant Wilson', maybe my love of Dad's Army combining with my nerves, although the living and fictitious Sergeants could not have been more different. Geoff was very forgiving, but I was absolutely mortified at this snub to one of the two men who'd inspired me so much throughout the course, for both of whom I had the highest respect.

A disco in the main hall followed together with entertainment, some of which had been put together by members of the course. Tom Trickett got on the stage at one point in his dinner suit and performed the traffic signal routine to thunderous applause. A night to remember, particularly as the 11pm curfew had been extended to midnight for the one and only time. The curfew was neither as strictly observed, nor enforced as usual.

The next morning, heads throbbing, we paraded for the final time, followed by a rehearsal for the passing-out parade. A few bits in the classroom and then on to our lunch. Both lunch and breakfast seemed better than usual, maybe because of only half the usual number needing to be fed today. The sky blackened ominously though as we returned to the classroom. As we had done over the previous ten weeks, we brushed each other down and marched out to the parade ground, this time to a real brass band with our invited families there to watch. Rain began to fall, and we were denied the full parade as it turned to a torrential downpour. After a (very) brief inspection by Richard Matthews, the visiting Chief Constable of Warwickshire, the traffic signal routine was abandoned. The 'slow march' off the parade ground was a poignant moment, the last thing we would ever do together. Despite cursing the rain, I was to learn in coming years that rain was a very good friend to police officers, dispersing many a weekend night's mêlée.

Over to the assembly hall, out of the rain for presentations. I was first up to the stage, receiving the PMAS Book Prize (a big dictionary, well used over the years and which I still have, dogeared and held together with stickytape) for Top Student from Mr Matthews. Other presentations followed and curled-up sandwiches and drinks were served as families posed for photographs.

The ten weeks which I thought I'd never survive were over. I wouldn't miss the cold room, rigid discipline, marching everywhere, pressing my uniform and bulling my boots every evening but I still felt an overwhelming sadness. I'd enjoyed every minute after the first few days, I was as fit as a butcher's dog, far more confident and disciplined, but I'd made good friends, many of whom I would never see again.

I'm sorry to say I can't remember farewells, but there must have been some. I returned to my room, changed into 'civvies' and loaded up the car, leaving for the very last time - alone, as Ken's wife had driven down for the afternoon.

The rain was becoming heavier by the minute as I headed along the A45 into Coventry's manic traffic for the tenth time – I wouldn't miss this!

As a newcomer to the foibles of the Austin Mini I wasn't aware of one of its greatest design flaws - having the distributor directly behind the radiator grille. Aftermarket shields could be purchased; a sheet of plastic in the boot was (much) later identified as one and duly fitted. Water and electrics do not mix, and the driving rain saturated the distributor. Five miles west of Coventry my pride and joy began to run very roughly indeed. I willed it into a layby, just making it before the engine spluttered to a stop, refusing to start again as colleagues passed – they'd be home a long time before me. I didn't have any waterproofs readily available, so I had to remove the epaulettes from my gabardine uniform coat to venture out of the car, hardly fashionable and I must have looked very unusual to the proprietor of a nearby café as I walked in and asked for help. He kindly arranged for a local garage in Meriden to come and dry the electrics out for me, the cost of which made me decide to join the AA at the earliest opportunity. An ignominious finale to a memorable day.

Half a century later, I remember those ten weeks with immense fondness, they marked a significant turning point in my life. If it was possible to do it all again, I'd relish every minute. The formidable Tom Trickett had taught me self-discipline, smartness and resilience. This PC wearing stripes must have developed the confidence, discipline and conduct of thousands of young police officers with his firm, vigilant authority over the years. I still see photos of him leading Remembrance Day parades in his hometown of Dudley, even in his eighth decade he is as imposing as ever. Geoff Gibson reached the rank of Superintendent in his home force but had a very untimely death while still serving. I have now known Glyn Dyer for almost fifty years, he has been both my Sergeant and Inspector at various times. We're still in contact and see each other occasionally. We've had our moments, as does anyone in such a demanding job but his influence, and that of Geoff on my life and career during those short ten weeks were invaluable.

It was now March, spring had sprung, and I was ready for anything - *or so I thought*!

4 - An Inside Job

A weekend off, a proper one with no travelling on the Sunday. It was back to Headquarters on Monday for our Local Procedure Course, to learn about the multitude of forms and books which we'd be using each day. Every form had a number and was always referred to as such; a miscellaneous report was referred to as a '65', a sudden death form as a '12', a crime report was a '34', a telephone message was a '27' and so it went on. The most revered book of all was the 'Book One', a thick heavily bound book into which any incidents of note and all crime and RTAs were recorded in best handwriting.

For this course we were not cossetted in the well-appointed rooms in the training wing, but in stark dormitories in Baswich House. This was an ancient, crumbling but very attractive building which formed part of the Headquarters complex, since outrageously demolished in furtherance of the profits of greedy property developers. The dormitories had seen far better days and after one night in a lumpy bed, enduring the snores of others I decided to sleep at home and return to Headquarters for my breakfast. I only ever spent one more night at Headquarters, many years later.

In one of our 'Have a chat, have a smoke' breaks I decided to see Mick Ryan about my helmets - neither of which had stretched even a millimetre. He stubbornly refused to acknowledge my head size but put one helmet on a 'stretcher' and sent me off wearing the other. The following day I collected my 'stretched' helmet and left the other one with him for 24 hours, it made not the slightest difference. Much later I was to discover that Mick could become far more helpful and obliging if you offered him a fag when you went to see him, even if he was already smoking one, which he invariably was.

Some amusement was provided by a visit to Stafford Crown Court, which at the time was housed in Stafford's imposing, historic Shire Hall. We sat in the public gallery of Court One, a typical traditional courtroom, imagine Rumpole of the Bailey. On trial were several Irish travellers charged with conspiracy to rob an electrical store on the outskirts of Wolverhampton. The prosecuting counsel was delivering his opening speech, informing the court that these men had made detailed plans. They had acquired firearms from an illicit source, stolen a large getaway van and changed its number plates. They had 'cased the joint', and drawn plans had been recovered; all in all, a thoroughly calculated operation. A flaw in their scheme emerged though. They arrived at the store in their stolen van, pulled balaclavas over their faces and charged out of the van waving their guns, only to discover that it was half-day closing. The solemn atmosphere of the court gave way to laughter.

On Wednesday, I was summoned to the telephone to speak to Newcastle's Liaison Sergeant (this time his responsibility covered training as well as recruitment), Sergeant Dodd.
'Hello PC Tucker. You're coming to join us on Monday, aren't you?'
'Yes Sarge'
'We've put you on C Shift at Newcastle, you'll be starting on earlies, that's 6am to 2pm'
'OK Sarge.'
'You've asked for accommodation...'
'...have I?' (I hadn't, despite being a distance away, Newcastle was an easy fifteen minutes' drive from home)

'...so we've given you a room in the single men's quarters here...'

'...okay, so where is it?'

'...tell you what, why don't you come to the station on Sunday afternoon, I'll tell the shift on duty to expect you, and they'll take you there with your kit.'

I didn't dare ask where the police station was.

We'd met with the Chief Constable before setting off for Ryton, and he saw us again that week in the conference room. He read each of our final reports from Ryton in turn, announcing that he was very proud of us all, particularly that I'd been top student, 'I'd have expected as much with your education boyo.'

Initial Training - over. The next step was to begin work at a real police station, but it would be some time yet before I saw anything other than the inside of one.

On the Sunday, having researched where it was, I arrived at Newcastle police station. I was greeted enthusiastically by the station officer, PC Jim Bickerton. He called for a panda car to escort me to the single men's quarters and in fact two arrived. Everyone was eager to meet new colleagues and to get to know them, in this job where you needed to know on whom you could depend. I followed the two panda cars at breakneck speed to Water Street, about a quarter of a mile away. Here was the former County police station from the days when Staffordshire had a multitude of separate police forces. Newcastle had both a Borough and a County police force with stations just a few hundred yards apart; I would be working at one and sleeping at the other.

I was shown to my room which was part of a former Superintendent's house, separate from the main building. It was very large, befitting the rank of its former occupants and the bedrooms had been sub-divided into (much) smaller rooms. To even call my accommodation a room was a stretch of the English language, it was smaller than my Ryton cell and there was just enough space for a bed and a wardrobe. Had I fallen out of bed in the night there was every possibility that I could have fallen down the stairs too. Just like at Ryton, there was no lock on the door. After unpacking I made my way across to the main building which housed a sizeable (closed) canteen, a (ditto) bar and more rooms upstairs. There was a common room into which I wandered to be greeted by a group of lethargic police officers either just having awakened after working nights or returned from an early shift. We all introduced ourselves, as well as Newcastle officers, Water Street (as it was always referred to) housed single officers from the nearby Stoke on Trent city stations. By now it was about 4pm and I asked what it was like to work early shifts, someone remarked that if I was on 'earlies' I may as well go to bed now.

I don't think I slept that night, but I rose at 5am, bulled my boots and checked my uniform for fluff. It was only about five minutes' walk to the police station, so I left my car behind. I donned my uniform, buckled up my raincoat and clamped on my helmet. Without a second thought I walked out in full uniform onto the darkened streets of Newcastle. It never occurred to me that it would be some time yet before I was allowed out on my own; had I encountered anybody I wouldn't have had the first idea what to do. A meeting with any of the Newcastle night shift on patrol would have been very embarrassing. Fortunately I arrived at my destination without event. I discovered that it was normal, in those days at least, to travel to work with a civilian coat over one's uniform.

Arriving at 5.40am I was directed to the Parade Room, a large room lined with desks, filing cabinets and a multitude of stationery drawers. In the centre of the room was a very large table around which officers reporting for duty would stand while being given their duties and briefing for the day by the Sergeant and Inspector. The windows of the room, and in fact the whole station had the arched tops typical of police dramas, everything had a rather faded and old-fashioned air about it. As well as feeling as if I was on a film set, it seemed as if I'd stepped back twenty-five years in time. The room was empty, and I stood nervously awaiting the arrival of the people with whom I would be working for the foreseeable future.

This was Monday 22nd March 1976. Until today, I'd been surrounded by and working with my own generation, whether it be at school, university or Ryton. Today, for the first time my peer group would include people who were much older than me, some the same age as my parents – a culture shock everyone entering the world of work for the first time must encounter, probably just as unprepared for it as I was.

At Ryton and Headquarters I'd been used to everyone around me being immaculately turned out. The room began to fill with my new colleagues, around fifteen of them. Tom Trickett would have been apoplectic at their appearance, even though they could be considered reasonably smart. Boots were unbulled, trouser creases were blunted, corners of tunic pockets were turned up from constant use, diced hatbands were grubby, and hair was of variable length. All of them looked even more weary than the guys I'd met yesterday. While being warmly greeted, I was a little concerned at being referred to as the 'new tea-boy.' A few minutes after the last of the shift entered, the Sergeant followed. Sergeant Barry Rotchell was in his mid-forties, short and of well-rounded build, possibly the least well turned-out of all in the room. He had a permanent smile, a casual air and his bespectacled eyes constantly twinkled, certainly not the rigidity I'd been used to seeing from a man of his rank. He told me to watch and wait while he briefed the rest of the shift and said he'd see me afterwards.

Once he had sent the shift on their way Sergeant Rotchell sat me down for a chat. I took an instant liking to him as he told me that I could now grow my hair a bit, I didn't need to bull my boots for day-to-day duty. As long as my uniform was clean and had visible creases it would be fine by him and everyone else. He said I would be attached for the next five weeks to the 'Reserve Office.' Funny, I thought, I believed I would be working in the front office of the station, but once again, it was the police way of calling one thing something else.

The Reserve Office *was* the front office, consisting of the control facilities and enquiry desk, staffed by the Station Sergeant and the Reserve Officer, who was actually the controller and responsible for the enquiry counter. The reason that he/she was called the 'Reserve Officer' was that they could be called on to turn out in the event of any major incident, not that I thought one person could make a huge difference to any situation, and anyway, who would staff the front office while they weren't there?

Sergeant Rotchell took me into the Reserve Office and introduced me to the Station Sergeant. Bill Norman was younger, in his mid- thirties but with a greater air of authority than his partner. He had a cast in one eye which gave him a permanent bemused, quizzical appearance and pronounced his 'r's as 'w's. I couldn't help but be reminded of Warden Hodges from Dad's Army by his appearance and demeanour.

He greeted me enthusiastically and made me feel really welcome, little did I know at the time just how much I would depend on him during the next two years, and the huge influence he would have upon me. Significantly, for the very first time since I'd joined, I was being addressed by a Sergeant as 'Nick' rather than the 'PC Tucker' which I'd been used to at Ryton.

One thing he seemed to be saying regularly was, 'If you can't stand a joke, you shouldn't have joined.'

The Sergeant asked the Reserve Officer to show me around. PC Mick Geraghty was a couple of years away from retirement, around the same age as Sergeant Rotchell, with a constant flustered, but very genial air about him. He went around the station showing me, first and most importantly, where the toilets were. He confused me by telling me that the office with the 'Inspector' plate on the door was 'Mr Bills' office' and a few moments later he referred to the office with the 'Sub-divisional Commander' plate as 'Mr Bills' office' again. Later in the morning I discovered the first Mr Bills was Mick, our shift Inspector who was off that day; the second Mr Bills was his older brother Syd, our Superintendent. Another office that I was shown was that of the Collator. Recalling Unit Beat Policing I was confused to see that it contained neither a radio nor, for that matter, a Collator.

At 6.50am our tour ended in the mess room, a small canteen on the top floor. This is where the 'new tea-boy' label became clear. I was to make a large pot of tea for the shift who, after a quick turn around the patch came into the station for a seven o'clock brew before any bosses turned up - their presence would render the station a virtual no-go area for the uniform patrols. Tea making would be my responsibility until the next new probationer joined the shift. In my mercifully short stint as the shift's tea-boy I never mastered the art of making tea for a large group, being the butt of constant complaints about 'floaters' - floating tea leaves in the cups.

After the semi-formality of the morning parade, the tea break gave an opportunity for me to get to know the shift better. They were a good crowd, conversation rippled with laughter, and I instinctively knew I was going to enjoy working with them. However, as junior member of the shift I was going to be the subject of relentless piss-taking and practical jokes in the next few months. The next most junior member of the shift, very pleased to have lost his responsibility for tea making duties to me was PC John Jeffries. John had a twin brother in the job who worked at Burslem, it was absolutely impossible to tell them apart and it was rumoured that they occasionally swapped places. I also met PC John Clowes, the shift's most senior and experienced officer, who would be my Tutor Constable for five weeks when I was *finally* allowed outside, a distant prospect at the moment.

Once the shift had left, I tidied up the mess in the mess room, washed the cups and went back downstairs to re-join Mick.

'Time to get the prisoners up', he said.

Prisoners? Blimey! The reality of being in a proper working police station, with cells, prisoners, interview rooms and police cars hadn't yet completely dawned on me. Mick took me through a locked gate into the cell block. This had a smell of its own, one with which I would become very familiar over the coming decades, a mixture of BO, vomit, urine, faeces, stale alcohol fumes and despair, as well as disinfectant which was fighting a hopeless battle.

We were joined by a PC with a fearsome looking German Shepherd dog as Mick unlocked the cell passage, while another of the guys on the shift brought through two tin plates with fried breakfasts floating on grease. I was puzzled why it took four Constables and a dog to serve breakfast.

Mick prepared two tin mugs of tea using sterilised milk, sugaring both liberally – two dessert spoonfuls in each.

'Give 'em plenty of sugar, keep 'em sweet.'

'What if they don't take sugar?'

'They're bloody prisoners, not hotel guests!'

Mick put a spoon on each plate, he told me that knives and forks could be used as weapons, so all prisoners' meals had to be eaten with spoons. In later years plastic cutlery would be used, but even this could be weaponised.

We went into the first cell, one PC stayed outside the gate as the dog and his handler joined us in the corridor. Mick opened the first cell, a heavy steel door with a peephole in it. I'd never seen the inside of a cell before, a high room with a domed light, lined with white glazed bricks, about 8 feet square. It had a brick built low bed, topped with a thin mattress, and rough grey blankets wrapped around a man who'd been brought in drunk in the early hours.

'Breakfast' announced Mick loudly as he shook the semi-comatose body, leaving the plate and mug on the floor, slamming the door behind him.

Past an empty cell then on to another occupied cell at the end of the corridor, another bobby built like a battleship was seated outside the cell door. On opening the door to a much larger cell, our guest sprang to his feet facing us disdainfully but stiffened on seeing the dog. He was a few inches shorter than any of us but very powerfully built, standing to attention, jaws firmly clenched together in a gesture of defiance. He never took his eyes off me as Mick carried the plate and drink over to the bed and put them down. The prisoner's dark eyes bored into me making me feel as if he was looking straight into me, I felt really uncomfortable.

Mick said to him,

'Okay with your breakfast?'

The man nodded perfunctorily, neither blinking nor taking his piercing eyes off me. I'd never in my life felt so intimidated as I was by this small, mysterious man, nor would I ever be.

We went back into the Charge Room and Mick began to make entries on the charge sheets (Form 90) confirming the feeding of our prisoners.

'You know who that was on the bottom cell?'

'No, gave me the bloody creeps though. Why's he getting so much attention?'

Mick showed me the name on the sheet, *Donald Neilson*, lodged overnight pending a remand hearing at the

Magistrates Court that morning. Orders had been given that he was to be watched constantly from the cell passage, never to be approached by an unaccompanied officer, and that a dog and handler should be present when the cell was open. He was constantly looking for opportunities to escape, but despite his violent disposition he was terrified of dogs, hence the instruction.

In my first two hours at Newcastle Police station, I'd served tea to my new shift, and helped serve breakfast to the Black Panther.

Back to the office where Mick started going through the multitude of books with me,
- Book One.
- Desk Diary - not a diary at all in keeping with the force's tendency to give everything a confusing name, but a book detailing miscellaneous visits to the station by members of the public.
- Lost Property book.
- Found Property book (Book 33).
- Lost Dog book. (Book K9 - only joking, can't remember)
- Official Register of Dogs Seized (Found Dog book).
- Telephone Message Book (Book 27, already knew that one) - not intended for messages but an official log of incoming incidents and action taken.

and so many others.

Mick told me that the greatest bugbear of all was book HORT2. We'd been taught at Ryton how to issue HORT1s (better known as 'producers') for drivers electing to produce their driving documents at a police station, but not what happened when the documents were actually produced. Everything had to be recorded longhand, if documents were not in order the person had to be reported there and then for summons; many drivers came in to plead that they could not locate their documents and asking for more time, which was granted even though this wasn't legal – this could be for weeks or months at a time in some cases. Even a straightforward production involved at least five minutes' work. Mick told me,

'You'll get a dozen a day of these.'

He was right, I did, he didn't. Every time someone arrived at the counter brandishing an HORT1, Mick disappeared or busied himself on the phone. The amount of police time wasted nationally by this burdensome procedure was colossal. Thankfully, later in my service the system within the force was streamlined, including outlawing the already illicit extensions. Given today's instant access to driver and vehicle records by computer this massive waste of time, which could have been far more usefully spent, has been rightly consigned to the dustbin of history.

8.30am: Mick suddenly whispered conspiratorially,

'Fags out, stand up', as a tall white-haired man in a suit walked into the office and sat in the chair previously occupied by Mick.

'Morning sir', said Mick and the Sergeant in unison.

'As you were, sit down everyone', came the reply even though there was only one chair remaining.

This was Superintendent Syd Bills, his shock of hair had long-since earned him the nickname of the *White Wonder*, he took no notice of me at all. Mick brought him the Book One and the book 27; our Sub-divisional Commander perused them, asking the odd question of my colleagues.

Ten minutes later he vanished to his office, and we lit up again. Over the next half hour, an assortment of other senior officers appeared, asked various questions and went on their way.

Sergeant Norman asked me what I was doing about my breakfast; I was due my refreshment break. I told him I hadn't given it any thought, engrossed as I was in what was going on. Many officers brought bacon, sausages and eggs to cook themselves in the mess room. He kindly loaned me his civilian anorak and suggested I either go into the town for a sandwich or go to the canteen for a cooked breakfast.

I returned to Water Street where I had a full English. The past twenty-four hours had been such a whirlwind, and I realised that this was the first time I'd eaten since Sunday lunchtime, twenty hours ago. I noticed an oddity on some plates, melted cheese, new to me but a part of the Potteries staple breakfast. I was yet to discover another creation, not today though, as it was Monday, read on.

I downed my breakfast, still keen as mustard I walked back to the police station and was back in the office after just half an hour. Sergeant Norman looked at me disapprovingly; the refreshment break was forty-five minutes, and I must take all of it. I headed off to the mess room on the top floor for another quarter of an hour, chatting with some of my new colleagues. When I returned, the Sergeant seemed more satisfied.

A member of the public came to the counter asking for directions to the fire station, anyone would expect a local policeman to know this without a second's thought, but not me. I had to excuse myself and ask Mick, who was just as incredulous as the man who'd asked me in the first place; acutely embarrassing. So much for the ACC's policy of posting his officers miles away from home, very efficient.

As well as the HORT2 book, another incredibly time-consuming task was generated by the town's army of Traffic Wardens. By daytime there could be as many as half a dozen of them patrolling the town; whatever malice they inspired in the motoring public, they actually did valuable work. Anyone aggrieved at receiving a parking ticket (or more accurately a Fixed Penalty Notice) could ask for payment to be excused, which resulted in a stream of irate people calling in at the police station. Most of them should have been sent on their way as their excuses were risible, but force policy dictated that everyone could ask for an official excusal. For the officer at the counter (Mick reacted similarly to the sight of a parking ticket as he did to an HORT1) this was another unnecessarily cumbersome form filling exercise which could take ten to fifteen minutes, with an impatient queue building behind the indignant illegal parker. One of the forms - headed 'Form of Certificate by Constable of Statement as to Motor Vehicle' (Uh?), (CTO13) had to be completed in triplicate, it was rare for any serviceable carbon paper to be available, so it could need writing out three times.

Mick gave me sound advice that the most troublesome aspect of a police officer's work was property, whether it be found, seized as evidence or taken from prisoners. It absolutely had to be accounted for. During my five weeks in the Reserve Office, it was the first of these that occupied me most; any handed in by the public was entered in a register, in triplicate, another ten to fifteen minutes' work, Mick became suddenly absent or busy on sighting these type of visitors too.

In the rear yard of the station was a block of kennels for found dogs. People would drag in a motley (or muttley?) assortment of them; an entry would be made in the register, and they would be put in the kennels. It was the responsibility of the Reserve Officer to feed them, although on a busy day this could be easily overlooked. People who lived in the town would complain about the barking; a vet had given us a huge supply of sedatives which would be mixed in with their food. The most demanding dogs were known to 'escape', either whilst being fed or taken to the kennels. The way we treated these poor animals was quite appalling.

Those that did not make a break for freedom would be kept for 24 hours before being collected by the PDSA, where they faced an uncertain future.

All but a very few strays and lost dogs were the result of irresponsible ownership. People would call in to report their dogs lost but invariably stated that their dog didn't have the required collar with their details on.

Those claiming their found dog from the kennels had to produce their Dog Licence (a legal requirement at the time costing 37½ pence) which had always been issued a few minutes earlier at the nearby Post Office. There was a charge payable on claiming a dog, so cash and receipts become involved. More time consumed.

Sergeant Norman was well known for hating dogs with a passion, his view being that stray dogs should be shot on sight. Every time they were mentioned, or even if he saw one, he launched into a tirade about them.

Office hours began in earnest, the station was full of its army of civilian workers. One of these introduced herself as Joan from Divisional Office, and she took me upstairs. A lot of paperwork followed, with consent to 'Divisional deductions' to further erode my salary. She said that the Divisional Commander wished to see me, and after a quick trip downstairs for a session with the clothes brush, she showed me into his office.

Chief Superintendent Harry Willett was a tall man with a stiff, unmistakeable military bearing and a commanding presence; until recently he'd been Dick Murby's predecessor at Ryton. After I'd saluted, he came from behind his desk and shook hands. Despite his high rank and air of authority I found him to be very approachable, pleasant and welcoming. He referred to my success at Ryton, and to my standard of education, saying that he expected to hear great things of me. I only had sight of him once between then and his retirement presentation less than six months later.

The pecking order within the station became clearer, as the building was both the Newcastle Divisional Headquarters, and Newcastle Sub-divisional Headquarters, the other Sub-division within the Division being Kidsgrove Sub-division - with me so far? Housed in the building was the Divisional Commander, the Deputy Divisional Commander, Superintendent Alf Mann, the Divisional head of CID, Det.Ch/Insp. Arthur Poynton, the Sub-divisional Commander, Syd Bills, and the Deputy Sub-divisional Commander, Chief Inspector Tom Hall. At Kidsgrove the latter two posts were taken by Chief Inspector Frank Alison, and Inspector Louis Stackhouse. Simple!

I'd yet to meet the most important person in the building though. Joan took me downstairs to meet Sergeant Ray Adey, in charge of Sub-divisional Office, to whom I was introduced in the Parade Room, probably fortunate as the adjoining office where he was assisted by a retired Sergeant, Cyril Buxton seemed barely large enough to contain him. He was a gigantic man, both in height, girth and general build; even at six feet tall I felt as though I was craning my neck to look him in the eye. His forearms were giant knots of muscle, complete with tattoos, and I was put very much in mind of Popeye after a helping of spinach. He was a very easy going, friendly man though, with the relaxed air of one whose number of working days to retirement after thirty years could be measured in mere double figures. He took one look at me and his grating, deep sounding words have stayed with me for ever,

'Dunna mither yowth, the fost twenty-nine years are the wost.'

Roughly translated from the local dialect he was telling this young man not to worry, the first twenty-nine years in the job, prior to retirement after thirty years were the most difficult.

The reason that Sergeant Adey was the most important man in the station was that he organised duties and courses, processed leave applications, and allocated overtime; a guy it was handy to stay on the right side of!

Back to the Reserve Office. As well as the public enquiry counter, this was where telephone calls from the public were received, and 999 calls relayed from Headquarters. Patrols were directed to reported incidents by radio. I found myself yet again wondering where the Collator fitted in with this.

Incidents were recorded in the Book 27, the nearest available patrol dispatched, and the *Result of Action Taken* recorded in a small space at the bottom of the page. It would have been sensible for this 'marking-off' to be done by the Reserve Officer when the result was relayed over the air, but no - most pages would have a slip of paper pinned to them with the relevant officer's name on it for them to finalise the entry. The closing five minutes or so of a shift were frantic, with ten or more officers clamouring for access to the book before going off-duty. Those same officers also competed for possession of the Book One, for the required incidents to be written up. These few minutes were quite needlessly chaotic.

The Police National Computer (PNC) was a new development at the time, only limited vehicle details were available, its main use was for recording stolen vehicles, of which there were many each day. Morris Minors, Minis and 1100s, Ford Cortinas, Escorts, Anglias and Vauxhall Vivas were ridiculously easy to steal. The form-filling involved was considerable, as usual: a witness statement (Form 95D) from the owner, a crime report (Form 34) pro-forma and a form PNC150 containing a minutely detailed description of the vehicle. The form 95D was only ever needed for court proceedings – of which more later, the Form 34 proforma, *may* have been transferred to a full crime report form by a Detective Sergeant. It was however possible that it never made it that far (if detection figures for the month were on the low side, the proforma had every chance of ending its short life in a waste bin). The PNC150 only came into play if the vehicle was still missing after 48 hours, which it usually wasn't as the vast majority of stolen vehicles were found abandoned within a few hours – but it *still* had to be filled in. A lot of time spent and wasted, again!

A few hours into my first proper working day it was clearly obvious that the organisation was inundated almost to the point of paralysis by paperwork. There was a form for everything, and everything had to be recorded, in duplicate, triplicate, quadruplicate, whatever; but only a tiny proportion of it would ever be of any use to anyone.

The clock made its way past noon, and I began to feel really tired. How would I cope with all these shifts? A man presented himself at the counter to report he'd been involved in a road accident, Mick suggested I sit in with the officer who dealt with him. The man had exchanged details with the other driver at the time, so there was no need for him to have reported it at all. This took the best part of an hour, the other driver would later be interviewed, and a sketch plan made of the scene. Nobody had been injured, insurance would take care of the damage, and nobody would be prosecuted. Many sheets of paper would be attached to the completed HORT7 to which we had been introduced at Ryton. It would then be filed, never to see the light of day again until destroyed a few years later – absolutely pointless!

It hadn't occurred to me at all to enquire about the shift system in detail, so it was a surprise to learn that after today, we would be on rest-days for two days, this after I'd just had a weekend off. A pint or two with the shift in the Borough Arms at two o'clock was followed by me returning to Water Street, packing my bags and heading home to Stafford.

I was back at 1.45pm on the Thursday for my first noon (2pm-10pm) shift. There were one or two new faces on the shift who hadn't been there on the previous Monday, including my shift Inspector, Mick Bills. He was a short, powerfully built man with a handlebar moustache which gave him quite a fierce appearance, but he was one of the kindest, most approachable and thoughtful people I've ever known. Intelligent and well-read, he was very fond of randomly quoting literature, one of his favourites being an adaptation of Kipling:

If you can keep your head when all around you are losing theirs and blaming you, then you've completely failed to understand the gravity of the situation.

He was a keen motorcyclist, despising cars and everything they stood for. Welcoming me to the team, he noted that I seemed well-educated, and reiterated what Sergeant Rotchell had told me on the Monday. Having him as my Inspector for the first few months of my service, and later as my Chief Inspector was the best thing I could have hoped for, a truly inspiring and supportive man.

Returning to the front office I noticed some sniggering going on, realising that it concerned me. They'd taken a collective decision on what my nickname was to be as just about everyone in the job had one. Mine was to be *Tommy* for an obvious reason, it stuck to me like glue, and there are still people nearly fifty years later who still believe that it's indeed my name.

I was given the alternative of *silly,* but the rhyming slang didn't appeal.

On Saturday, Inspector Bills asked me back into his office. *What have I done?,* but it turned out that he wanted to sort out my annual leave situation, something to which I'd never given a single thought. I'd accrued four days' leave which needed to be taken by 1st April, the same number of days away. So, as of 10pm I was on leave until 5th April including rest days; my first two weeks at my new place of work had consisted of just four working days. Many would be elated by this, but I was as so keen at the time that I'd have worked twenty-four hours a day if I could.

My leave was unplanned, so I didn't have any particular use for it. It was a welcome break though, as it had been non-stop since my first day at Headquarters, three months ago. When I returned for my next shift I was as eager as ever. Inspector Bills solicitously asked me if I'd enjoyed my leave,

I said that I had but would rather have been at work. How that outlook would change over the years...

Later that day, Mick Geraghty came to me, saying excitedly,

'I've got you your first offence!'

*Fan-**tas**-tic!*

One of the Traffic Wardens had placed a notice on a parked car requesting the driver to report to the police station as the street in which it was parked was governed by 'No entry except for access' signs – the ones that look like a low-flying motorcycle which nobody seems to understand. This was not something that a Traffic Warden could deal with as the offender had to be reported ('knocked-off') by a police officer. I issued him with the required caution, took his details, noted his driving documents and told him that he would be reported for the offence.

At last, I'd dealt with a real 'offender'! A detailed account of this then had to be written into my pocket-book, and a Traffic Offence Report book (HO/RT6) had to be completed after which I heard nothing more about it. The Superintendent would probably have marked it for no further action or a written, pointless caution letter, and then, as usual it would be filed, forgotten and destroyed. Mick's proud announcement that he had 'got' me my first offence was yet again him avoiding paperwork. That being said, I learned a great deal during my first few weeks with Mick, he was a lovely bloke who gave me a huge amount of help in my early days in the job.

A couple of days later I was going to experience my first ever 'quick changeover', this meant finishing my noon shift at 10pm and returning less than eight hours later at 5.45am; I was dreading it but then the day before, Sergeant Norman told me that I would be on 'float shift', which would be 10am to 6pm. This was an improvement, but I'd be working with comparative strangers for the final four hours.. In Mick's absence, I was reluctant to ask questions but realised that I was gaining confidence and actually didn't need a constant guiding hand.

The following morning, I was back with Mick and Sergeant Norman on early turn. They asked me to go and fetch newspapers from a nearby shop so at the same time I bought myself a Daily Mirror and put it on the windowsill by my desk, intending to read it with my breakfast. As the daytime office staff started to file in, a very large PC walked into the office. He looked around, looked through the books, and while I was taking a phone call reached over my shoulder, picked up my Daily Mirror from the windowsill and walked out of the office. I was flabbergasted and asked Mick who it was who'd taken my paper, but he said he hadn't noticed. I walked out of the office and looked along the corridor, sighting my paper thief in the Collator's office, munching on a bacon sandwich, reading *my* newspaper,

'Can I have my paper back please?'

'What paper?'

'The one you're reading; you had it from the windowsill.'

'Fuck off youth, I bought this on the way in.'

His body language and expression suggested further discussion was unwise; I quietly withdrew, learning the important lesson that there are a lot thieves in police stations - not all of them in the cells.

Talking of the Collator's office, it was becoming increasingly clear that the role of the Collator in the Unit Beat Policing system was fictional, just like the system itself.

After breakfast, Inspector Bills came into the office.

'Get your tunic and flat-hat Tommy, we're going for a ride.'

My first time out in a police car! In those days, we were required to wear our hats at all times, including when inside a car, my flat-cap was just as tight as my helmet, and hadn't even begun to stretch, but I was thrilled to don the chequered band for the very first time. The Inspector said that as I wasn't familiar with the area he'd try to give me some idea of the layout of the Division, apart from Newcastle and Kidsgrove it was mainly country farmland. The rural areas were policed from smaller police stations in the villages of Madeley and Audley, known as Rural Patrol Units, or RPUs. Heading out into the countryside the conversation flowed. During training we'd been conditioned into regarding Inspectors or higher ranks as infallible, godlike lifeforms. Here I was, alone with one of them and he was actually behaving and chatting with me like a human being.

We made our first stop at Madeley police station. I was introduced to the WPC in the station, a very large lady in both personality and size and very experienced. The Inspector examined the books, just as his brother had done earlier at Newcastle. After a drink we carried on our way, my hat clamped on my head as we headed towards Audley. The countryside was beautiful, half-timbered cottages were scattered along our route, the roadside bursting with multi-coloured blossoms in the spring sunshine, the foliage on the trees coming to life. We stopped at a bridge over the M6, got out and leaned over the rail of the bridge, silently watching the motorway traffic as the Inspector puffed on his pipe. It was amusing to see so many cars braking suddenly at the sight of a police car and two officers, something with which I'd become very familiar.

As I stood contentedly a sudden gust of wind blew. Despite my brand-new hat being firmly clamped to my head, it flipped off, fluttered down onto the busy carriageway and was instantly crushed by the wheels of a lorry and broken up by the vehicles behind it. My companion spluttered and doubled up with laughter; I was mortified, outside, in uniform *but no hat!* I felt naked.

'Never mind Tommy, it happens, just ask someone to help you fill in a form C5 when we get back and I'll sign it for you.'

I saw an opportunity here, so when we returned to Newcastle Mick Geraghty helped me with the Uniform Replacement form (C5), under 'size' I entered 7⅝, thinking that finally I'd have at least one hat that fitted me., The replacement which arrived the following week was 7¼ - Mick Ryan was obviously trying his hardest to annoy me.

Another early turn, as I came down into the office bearing the 7am tea tray the shift was coming in from their first patrol. John Clowes came over to me,
'Got something for you Tom, you've got the tray, I'll stick it in your pocket.'
He unbuttoned my right-hand shirt pocket and slipped something inside. I thought little of it as I put the tea tray down, then I felt movement, developing into jerks. Peering down into my pocket I saw the eyes of a frog staring back at me - the assembled shift laughed uproariously. I can't remember what followed, I can only hope that I found the frog a suitable place to continue its day.

This was the first of many occasions when I would be 'set up' by my colleagues. These days people can easily become offended on behalf of others who aren't, and such initiation rites can lead to dismissal. Times were very different, there was no malice, it was all in good spirit and as the target I found myself joining in with my colleagues' laughter. These now proscribed events were important for team-building. In particular, my colleagues could gauge my reactions, knowing whether I could be relied upon to deal calmly with incidents in future. Many may disagree, but as the target of quite a few such set-ups in my early months I never had a problem.

Think back for a moment to that first breakfast on a couple of Mondays ago. During the tea break today, I overheard someone saying, 'Who's getting the oatcakes?' To me, oatcakes were a hard, dry Scottish delicacy but I thought little more of it until breakfast time. Here, I saw for the very first time, a Staffordshire Oatcake, a pancake made from oatmeal. In the years that have followed I have eaten thousands of them, either rolled up as an accompaniment to my grilled breakfast, or on their own with fillings of melted cheese, cheese and bacon, mushrooms, eggs, tomatoes, just about anything. Never mind the bone-china and pottery, they truly are North Staffordshire's greatest invention. They were only available in the mornings from Thursday to Sunday though; queues stretched outside the many oatcake bakeries in the area.

As the days went by, Sergeant Norman occasionally allowed me to go out for an hour or so with the panda patrols. It was a real thrill to be out in those early days in my uniform; I spotted some extremely unroadworthy cars in some of the less reputable areas; I couldn't wait for the day when I'd be let loose upon their owners. It would be a long wait, after my attachment to the Reserve Office I still had to spend time with other departments in the station.

One morning I had to escort a prisoner to Kidsgrove Magistrates Court while another PC drove. He'd been found drunk and semi-conscious by a patrol during the night and had been arrested for being drunk and incapable, as well as for his own safety. We sat in the back of the car handcuffed together, me feeling as if I was with a master criminal. This contrasted with the driver Phil, chatting to him amiably. After the miscreant had been fined £5 by the magistrates and sent on his way Phil sensed my unease with the casual treatment and simply said,

'Treat 'em right mate unless they don't treat *you* right. Far easier and it might do you a favour one day.'

Valuable lesson from a routine job, as I was to learn next year.

Eventually, the shift I'd been dreading came around – nights. More of the pros (not many) and cons (very many) of shift working I'll explain later but in 1976, nights began at 10pm on Tuesday, with seven straight eight-hour shifts ending the following Tuesday morning. There was a completely different atmosphere, with no bosses or anybody other than the shift present in the building the team spirit was stronger than ever. I'd only ever gone twice without a full night's sleep before; once was as a student when I'd helped in the organisation of an overnight sponsored walk, and the other at school when we had an all-night fund-raising event. This was different, nights would be a third of all the hours I worked. I don't remember much about that first night, apart from the feeling of being completely drained by the time Wednesday morning came around and I was able to head off to bed. I do remember being confused on the first night to answer the telephone to hear a heavily accented male voice,

'Nine five ooo kee'

'Pardon?'

'Nine five ooo kee'

'Sorry, I don't underst...'

Mick took the receiver from me, 'OK Pete, cheers.' Pete was the night watchman at Tiffany's ballroom checking in with the code phrase 'Nine five, okay', what it meant goodness knows. We'd receive calls from him every hour throughout the night.

Senior officers laboured under a misapprehension that the night shift didn't have enough to do. So, the Reserve Officer had to type the 'Night Report', a compilation of everything that had been written into the Book One over the past twenty-four hours, distributed to the Divisional and Sub-divisional Commanders, their deputies, and the Detective Chief Inspector and Detective Inspector. It was quite ridiculous that each of these recipients would read through the Book One at the start of the day, then go into their offices where a typewritten copy of the same awaited them.

The station photocopier was in a locked office, and carbon paper, as I've already said was quite difficult to come by; a hunt around the station usually had to be made to obtain sufficient supplies. Carbon paper would only make three decent copies so, the Night Report had to be typed at least twice, more if carbon paper was unobtainable.

As usual, with Sergeant Norman's approval Mick sub-contracted this task to me. I could type at a reasonable speed. This worked to my advantage in future months as I was frequently ordered back into the station to type this superfluous report - guaranteeing me an hour or so of warmth. Cold or wet nights had a strange effect of slowing my typing speed and it could be as late as 5.55am when I hurriedly handed over the finished reports to Sergeant Norman.

My other important task on nights was to make tea for the shift at 4am. My tea-making skills hadn't improved, my colleagues continuing to complain of 'floaters' in their tea. I hadn't known to warm the pot. Night-time brews were made with sterilised milk, disgusting stuff.

Our breaks took place in the mess room as Water Street canteen only operated in the daytime during the week. There was always a game of dominoes on the go, I wasn't familiar but learned quickly. Once, I was surprised to find that the exact domino I was about to play was already on the table, then noticed a few more duplicates.

'We're playing with duff dommies!', I exclaimed, to howls of laughter. Yet another test, someone had put a few dominoes from another set in with the ones with which we were playing. Someone said,

'Looks like you've learned to play then Tom!'

I'd yet to be given a locker; a major inconvenience as I had to bring my uniform and kit with me in a holdall every day. One night I went into the locker room to collect my sandwiches and saw a black cat lying on top of my bag, glaring at me. I've always despised cats; no amount of verbal coaxing or handclapping would make it move, it just carried on watching me, unblinking. As a last resort, I steeled myself and lifted it off my bag. It didn't move, so I let it go, thinking it would land and run off. Instead, it fell to the floor with a sickening crunch. It had been dead - another test! As usual, to the inevitable laughter I realised my colleagues had been watching. This wasn't my first corpse of the week.

A black-suited gentleman, smelling quite strongly of drink came to the counter.
'Can I help you?'
'We're taking one to the mortuary mate.'
'Errrrr.......M-i-i-i-i-ck?' Mick came across and recognised him as one of the local undertakers, delivering a recently and suddenly deceased person to the mortuary at Hartshill, a mile or so up the road to Stoke. Newcastle and Stoke police stations held keys for these night-time 'deliveries', of which there were more than a few.
'This'll be good experience for you ', said Mick, 'take these keys and go with these men up to the mortuary and I'll get one of the pandas to meet you there.'
'This'll be good experience for you' was a phrase that I would come to know well. It usually meant that either I wouldn't like it, or that the person saying it hadn't the slightest intention of doing it.
So, I donned my uniform and went out to the hearse parked outside. Getting in I inhaled for the very first time the scent of death, with which I would become very familiar, from the departed passenger in the rear; laced with the spirited breath of both the driver and his colleague. The driver really should have been breathalysed.
Arriving at the mortuary there were already two unattended panda cars parked outside, and we were shortly joined by the one sent there to assist us. My colleague got out, took the keys from me and opened up. I asked him why

the two other cars were there, and he said that maybe it was a couple of Stoke patrols on a job in the area.

Walking into the main area of the mortuary the smell of death was far stronger. Lined up around a tiled floor were banks of floor-to-ceiling high fridges, each with four slots in their doors for labels bearing the name of the occupant of their temporary resting place. I'd never seen a dead person before, now I was surrounded by them. The first one I'd see was being wheeled in by the undertakers in a plastic coffin. One of them looked for a door without a name on it, opened it, and loaded a seven feet long tray from it onto a trolley. Opening the coffin, they took the body out and laid it on the tray, lifting the head up onto a wooden block. It was a very elderly gentleman in his pyjamas who looked just as if he was asleep. One of the undertakers went over to a table, wrote the name of the unfortunate man on a label and tied it to the now lifeless big toe, before wheeling it over and pumping it up the level of the empty space in the fridge, rolling the tray in, closing the door and putting another label in the slot.

To me it was surreal, and I was quite spooked by being surrounded by so much death. The undertakers, task completed, went on their way.

'Hang on a minute Tom', my colleague said, 'I'll show you around.' He showed me into the next room which was the post-mortem area. Very much like a hospital operating theatre, he showed me some of the post-mortem instruments, gleefully telling me that I would be seeing a post-mortem at first hand in the next few weeks – for which I'd be quite happy to be on a long waiting-list. Returning to the fridge area he encouraged me to look in one or two of them,

'It'll be good experience for you' - the second time in half an hour.

'Have look in here Tom', he said.

I opened the door and looked in, there was a single body in there, covered by a white sheet, but I could see other covered bodies in the surrounding compartments. I heard a barely perceptible low moan. My heart leapt into my mouth as suddenly, the white sheet moved and the body sat bolt upright, still covered with the sheet - I was terrified.

The white sheet peeled away to reveal one of my colleagues. From behind me came the helpless laughter of three other members of the shift (hence the other panda cars outside) who'd crept in unnoticed. Still shocked, it took me some moments to laugh with them, but I did – another initiation test passed.

The seven nights finished at 6am the next Tuesday, in the end I thought I'd coped quite well. I had Tuesday and Wednesday off, so I drove home to Stafford and had a couple of evenings in the pub with my friends, before returning at 10am on the Thursday. This was a 'float' week where I could be ordered to work any eight-hour daytime shift for the next seven days.

Suddenly, my body-clock broke its mainspring. Over the previous week my system had become nocturnal. Now, I had to get up at 8am, just the time when for the past few days I'd been sound asleep. The effect of this drastic change on my body was shattering.

During float week, the Black Panther was to appear before the magistrates at Kidsgrove town hall for committal proceedings, I was to be one of those present to maintain order. My only previous experience of Kidsgrove had been regularly passing through on the train between Stafford and Manchester; looking out at its canal, the water stained a solid orange colour by oxide from nearby iron ore seams, a down-at-heel rail station surrounded by forlorn, shabby buildings. I thought it was not somewhere I would like to live; it later became my home for over twenty years, where my children grew up.

The committal was a major event, Neilson's murder of Lesley Whittle and his other brutal crimes had made national headline news for months. The town hall was surrounded by a mass of outside broadcast TV units, cameras and reporters from local and national newspapers.

This was the first time I saw Newcastle's Detective Inspector, Malcolm Bevington who'd been instrumental in the murder hunt. Immaculately coiffured, the former guardsman's chin was shaved to a reflective shine, his suit threatening to cut to shreds anyone coming within three feet of it. Strutting around in a cloud of after-shave and looking very pleased with himself he made sure that he was seen by - and looked into - every single camera lens. Barrington Black, who'd gained near-celebrity status as Neilson's solicitor parted the crowd as he parked his gleaming, trademark Jensen Interceptor. As he got out, his suit closely competed for sharpness with that of the Detective Inspector.

I took my position in the crowded public gallery. There was silence, then a collective, hushed gasp as the Black Panther was led into the dock, handcuffed to two prison officers. Standing there he looked quite pathetic, noticeably diminished from the menacing figure I'd seen at close quarters a few weeks ago. The event was concluded in less than five minutes, the presiding magistrate telling Neilson that he was committed for trial at Stafford Crown Court and remanded in custody. I didn't see Neilson again but came face-to-face with his waxwork in Madame Tussaud's five years later – it was chillingly accurate.

At the end of float week, we had a four-day break, our 'long weekend', the guys on the shift told me that we'd be on early turn on the following Monday. I arrived at the station at 5.45am to find myself surrounded by unfamiliar faces - I'd been set up again. I was supposed to be on noons. The station Sergeant took pity on me, instead of sending me away he allowed me to work the full shift in the Reserve

Office. My own shift colleagues laughed at me as they came in at the end of my shift, but I retaliated by saying I was going off duty in a few minutes and they had eight hours still to do.

A very important lesson learned – believe nobody, check everything!

I was allowed the next weekend off. My Reserve Office attachment had ended, but I was still confined indoors. For the next two weeks I was to be attached to the Divisional Traffic Office, followed by a week in Courts Office. Apart from introducing me to more people who worked in the building, these administrative attachments were pointless. I was so eager to get outside to do the job I'd been trained to do.

The Courts Office attachment included a couple of days at the Magistrates Court, actually in the same building as the single men's quarters at Water Street. People expect a visit to court to be interesting and exciting; it's actually mind-numbingly tedious. Very little happens and when it does, it happens very slowly.

Among the defendants appearing before the bench was a pathetic young man with obvious learning difficulties (a phrase not in use at the time), charged with indecent exposure. His equally pitiful, but obviously very loving mother spoke up for him in court and he was fined £5.

There was a reason for these frustrating indoor attachments. You could be appointed Constable at the age of eighteen-and-a-half, but our Chief Constable didn't want anyone under the age of nineteen working alone on the streets. One week at Headquarters, ten weeks at Ryton, another week at Headquarters, five weeks in the Reserve Office, plus another four weeks on office attachments meant that after five weeks with a Tutor Constable, exactly six months' service would have been accrued, meaning that an eighteen-year-old recruit would be nineteen before being allowed out on their own. The fact that I was twenty-one counted for nothing due to the one-size-fits-all system of Staffordshire Police, and of the service in general. Talking of sizes and fitting, in nine weeks I'd only had to wear my helmet twice, and it still didn't.

One of these helmet-on occasions was an inspection of the station by Her Majesty's Inspector of Constabulary (HMI), Mr. R.G. Fenwick. All uniform staff working in the station's offices would be inspected on a formal parade, including me. On that morning the station was abuzz with activity and bosses were tripping over each other. I was unfamiliar with some faces that I was seeing; one was heading up the stairs towards me, I saw all the metalwork on his shoulders and scrambled egg on his hat, so I stood to attention and barked out,
'Morning sir!'
He returned the greeting, but I saw that he was Commandant of the Special Constabulary, with no seniority over me - better safe than sorry though.

With Ryton still fresh in my mind this parade was going to be a doddle. I took my place in the station yard, boots bulled, sharp creases and haircut, but mine were the only bulled boots, the only sharp creases and the only haircut. Everybody else was dressed in everyday working uniform. A couple of dozen members of the public witnessed the parade from the street.

The HMI and his entourage came into the yard, and we were brought to attention - feet stamping in cascade rather than unison. As Mr Fenwick walked along the assembled ranks, his face darkened, the Chief Constable behind him began to seethe with anger, joined by my nemesis ACC Ivor Shepherd following him, then Chief Superintendent Willett, who seemed to be visibly shrinking in height. Superintendents Mann and Bills, and Chief Inspector Hall followed, all looking as if they wished they'd taken the day off. When the gaggle of brass hats reached me the HMI spoke to me, asked how much service I had, congratulated me on my turnout and continued along the line. Reaching a Ford Escort panda car which had been cleaned and dazzlingly polished for the occasion, he took a cursory glance at it and turned to Mr Willett.

'Bring a car in off patrol, now. I want to see it...'

As we waited, the HMI addressed us, observed by the public watching from the other side of the station gates. It was by no means a congratulatory speech, exacerbated by the arrival some minutes later of the car from panda patrol. Caked with mud, the inside full of detritus, the ashtray overflowing with cigarette butts and sweet papers and an incomplete jumble of kit in the boot, it added further to Mr Fenwick's displeasure, as well as the acute embarrassment of our senior officers.

After concluding his furious dressing-down he went back into the station with the rest of the party, but the Chief Constable remained in the yard. The wrath we'd already experienced was nothing compared to the formidable silence, slowly building to an incandescent rage that Mr. Rees poured upon us. He referred pointedly to me, saying that there was only one officer who had taken the trouble to dress properly for the parade and that he was utterly ashamed. Even the spectating public began to shrink away.

Then he came over to me.

'Not you boyo, well done. These men have let you down.'

I didn't know whether to feel proud or embarrassed.

I can't begin to imagine the conversation that followed between Messrs Rees and Willett, but the latter, together with our Sub-divisional Commander and his deputy retired just a few weeks later.

The end of my pointless office attachments had finally arrived. Time to go out!

5 - Shifting About

Now that I was to finally go out onto the 'patch' I'd be spend most of my on and off duty time ruled by the shift system. Policing is a twenty-four hour, seven days a week job. Apart from the float week, our working days were 6am-2pm (earlies), 2pm-10pm (noons) or 10pm-6am (nights). Most working weeks were of seven days' duration, with two, three or four days between, there seemed to be a long-standing belief that *there are seven days in a week, therefore you will work seven days.* Perversely, this mantra came from Headquarters where a five-day working week was the norm.

Although our masters believed that we hadn't enough to do during our night shifts, it was absurd that an outright ban was imposed on taking leave or any other time off on nights. This made it difficult for officers with families to book leave as the week of nights beginning on Tuesday impacted upon two Monday to Friday working weeks. As the shifts rotated every five weeks this only left three weeks out every five available for a fortnight's holiday. This resulted in intense competition for leave, particularly during the summer. As a single man this wasn't an issue for me, but it led to a lot of discontent amongst older colleagues. During 1976, the shift system was adjusted, with nights beginning on Monday, easing matters slightly.

In 1980 the system had a major overhaul, the previous five shifts of officers were condensed into four, with the rotation changing to four weeks instead of five. There were now more officers on each shift. Long weekend came around every four weeks instead of five, but so did nights, as a compromise leave on nights was no longer embargoed.

So, from 1980, for the next twenty years, the shifts rotated as follows:
- Starting with seven nights on a Monday, half the shift working 6pm to 2am on the Sunday.
- Three rest days, then three noons, followed by early shift or 10am-6pm on the Sunday, then three earlies.
- A long weekend, Thursday to Sunday, then three noons, three earlies, one Sunday rest day and repeat the above.

It had the flaw in that only two shifts of officers were available on Sundays, instead of the usual three, but at the time this was our quietest day by far. One of the shifts covered 6am-6pm, half the shift coming on duty at 10am. The other shift covered 6pm-6am, half the shift working 6pm-2am.

It worked, that is until the Sunday trading laws were changed. Over the next few years Sunday slowly became the busiest day of the whole week. By the late 1980s it became obvious that the shift system was not fit for purpose, for any day of the week.

Our leaders opted for tinkering around the edges, rather than a desperately needed ground-up reform. An extremely unpopular system of 'flexible rostering', superimposed on the existing system was dumped on us. Particularly despised was a change to the definition of an 'early' shift to beginning at any time between 6am and 10am, finishing correspondingly later. Although 6am starts were very tiring, the plus side of early-turn was finishing at 2pm and having the rest of the day free. The later starts and ends to the early shift impacted heavily on longstanding childcare arrangements and other domestic routines. Despite many representations from the Police Federation, the Chief Constable flatly refused to countenance any further change.

Then it became even worse. For many, many years football matches had been played simultaneously at 3pm every Saturday across the whole country. In the 1990s they began to have staggered starting times, eventually with league football being played on Sundays as well. This maximised revenue for the football clubs and broadcasters, but the effect on us was extremely unwelcome. Matches had for many years been policed by use of overtime, partly funded by the football clubs themselves as they were obliged to pay for the police presence inside the ground. Those on overtime would be supplemented by a greater number of officers extracted from the normal working shifts around the county. Because of the antiquated shift system it wasn't possible to take officers from on-duty shifts for Sunday matches, as they were already working at full stretch. Therefore it was mandated that these matches would be policed by the long weekend Sunday rest day being *re-rostered* with no overtime at all.

Under Police Regulations re-rostering meant you had to be given twenty-eight days' notice that your rest day was cancelled and could be taken on another day. While you lost a Sunday, there was no hope of it being replaced with another Sunday due to the existing pressure on that day. This wholly detested development became the norm for any special events that took place on increasingly busier Sundays. It became usual to have just one Sunday off every four weeks, this being the one and only rest-day in a fortnight.

Late notifications of shift changes were commonplace, as well as being called into duty at a moment's notice. There were regulations to cover this, being recalled to duty entitled one to at least four hours' overtime payment, regardless of the time worked; however, those trying to make such a claim faced significant barriers. These changes and the disruption they caused to family life were unwelcome, but our senior officers used the Police Regulations phrase of 'exigencies of duty' (i.e. unforeseen circumstances) as an excuse. More often than not these *exigencies* were solely a result of poor management and planning of matters that were easily foreseen.

Once in the mid-1980s, it was just two weeks until Christmas and our duties for the period hadn't been published, even though Regulations required twenty-eight days' notice to work public holidays. We were all up in arms as we couldn't make our own plans for the festive season. In frustration, I applied for leave for the entire period and was called in to see the Chief Inspector.
'You've applied for leave at Christmas.'
'That's right, you've not published the duties, and people like me need to plan, and know what they're doing, for the sake of our families.'
'Well, we don't know what our commitments are going to be yet.'
'Rubbish, of course we do, Christmas isn't exactly unexpected is it? We know what it was like last year, and the year before, and the year before that. Nobody else has applied.'
'That's not the point…'
'I'm the only one on the shift that's applied for leave, in normal circumstances it would be approved…'
He spluttered, 'O-o kay, I'll sign it off, on this occasion, now get out.'
'Get out' seemed to be a feature of many of my conversations with my bosses in the 1980s. The style of management at the time gave an overwhelming feeling that the senior ranks actually wanted us to have no certainty in our lives as you will see in my later chapter on 'Donkeys.'

Working rotating shifts plays havoc with the body-clock and can be extremely debilitating. Once or twice every four weeks there was the dreaded 'quick changeover', from noons to earlies, with a gap of only eight hours between; less if you finished you noon shift late, which was often. It was impossible to wind down enough to sleep properly after a busy day and the added fear of oversleeping the next morning - with possible disciplinary implications – meant three or four-hours' sleep was the best anyone could manage.

The most drastic quick changeover, outside of Regulations and only ever voluntary was from nights on Saturday to noons on Sunday. It sounds pretty extreme but had a hidden bonus, so I'd readily volunteer for it. Over the week of nights, your body clock adjusted to the different hours; after working seven nights, it was quite possible to sleep until 2pm on the Monday rest day, then be wide awake on Monday night and sleep all Tuesday morning – the best part of two rest days lost. It was possible to repeat this on Wednesday too, all the rest days gone. A Sunday quick changeover was a shock to the system but forced a reset of the body clock - by the end of a Sunday noon shift I'd be more than ready for bed and wide awake early on the Monday morning ready to enjoy my three days off properly.

I loved working nights in the summer, I could see the sun come up before my shift ended, go home, have a few hours' sleep, then spend the afternoon and early evening enjoying a fine day before heading for work. The winter months were the polar opposite though, it was possible to go for seven whole days without seeing daylight at all, which was depressing and draining.

Shift work impacts on the digestive system as well as other health issues. I was having quite awful stomach cramps and indigestion after my first few months and was making frequent visits to my doctor, pleading for ever more powerful antacids - Gaviscon was then a prescription-only item. The symptoms became so severe that it was suspected I may have an ulcer, so had to undergo tests, including the wonderful everlasting bog-stopping white-shit barium meal X-ray.

Eventually my system settled down; this seems to have been something most of us experienced in our early service. What didn't go away though was wind; my colleagues suffered the worst of mine on early turn parades - I just couldn't control my loud, noxious farts, (at least nobody was trying to sing though).

Tommy's a good bloke, but his shit stinks

Officially, our salary included a shift allowance, but those who didn't work shifts were paid the same as those who did, which caused some friction at times. They could enjoy far more flexibility with their annual leave. A 'normal' fortnight off for anyone working Monday-Friday is sixteen actual days including three weekends, using ten days or less of leave entitlement. On our shift system you'd have to use at least two more days of leave allowance to have a 'real' fortnight off.

The officers who didn't work shifts became known as 'Esso workers' (Every Saturday and Sunday Off) or 'Bongos' (Books/Boots On, Never Goes Out).

It was really only in the few days following a long weekend, or annual leave that you could feel fully rested and refreshed. For the fifteen or so other days of the shift pattern, particularly when working for thirteen days with just one day off in the middle, everyone would be debilitated to some degree. So, as the system made us not fully fit for duty, most of the time, it's hardly surprising that mistakes were made, jobs weren't done properly, and sickness was so prevalent. This was the result of obdurate leadership that refused to change in the face of compelling evidence. The public deserved better from us, and we deserved better from our senior management.

The Working Time Directive rendered our archaic shift system unlawful in 1999, so wholesale changes had to be made. It should have happened twenty years or more previously, but it came too late for me.

6 – Going Out

Monday, 1.45pm and I was parading with the shift eager to go out for the first time with my tutor, John Clowes. We were to be on panda patrol of Clayton, Westlands and Town Centre, call sign Mike-Four-Zero. It seems incredible now, but at the time it wasn't considered necessary, in fact a little frowned upon to carry either truncheon or handcuffs during the daytime. We carried just one radio between the two of us. Radio communication, as I'd discovered in the office, was extremely unreliable. The whole of Newcastle town and its suburbs, as well as most of the southern part of Stoke-on-Trent were served by one radio mast on a hill at Penkhull, which wasn't even on our Division. Another hill between Penkhull and the suburbs of Bradwell and Chesterton made radio coverage very patchy indeed. We made repeated complaints but Headquarter dismissed our concerns by responding that we weren't charging our batteries properly.

Our panda cars at the time were base model Ford Escort 1100s. They were equipped with hazard flashers, not a standard fit in those days, a manually operated reversing light (often left on accidentally for miles), a rather feeble blue light and an equally feebly illuminated 'POLICE' sign. They were not fitted with sirens despite sometimes needing to get somewhere very quickly – well, as quickly as such a humble car would allow. The seats were sagged from repeated jumping in and out, and there was a variety of obnoxious smells from prisoners who'd voided bowels, bladder, stomach or a medley of all three en-route to the station.. One panda car even had urinal blocks in the footwell - a vain attempt to dispel the smell.

It was a glorious, sunny day early in May. I was looking forward to an afternoon packed with stopping cars, domestic disputes and arresting people - I was to be disappointed. First stop was a back-street garage on the outskirts of the town, a one-man business run by one of John's friends. After half an hour or so of chatting we drove to the back of my tutor's police house in Clayton where he assisted an off-duty colleague with a car problem. I heard Mick Geraghty's voice crackle on the radio,

'Four-zero, four-zero over'

Wow, here we go!

'Four-zero' John replied, dropping a spanner and wiping his hands on a rag.

'Four-zero, can you go to Kingsbridge Avenue, a lady wants to hand a purse in.'

Anti-climax or what? It was a few yards away, next to the local library.

'The library, book him Danno', John quipped as we passed.

An elderly lady excitedly flagged us down and handed me a purse she'd found containing some cash but no details of the owner. Having recorded details in my pocket book and asking her to sign it, I'd dealt with my first incident. There would follow the inevitable triplicate entry in the Found Property Book at the station; conveniently timed for a mid-afternoon cup of tea in the mess-room. In those days the noon shift was the quietest shift of all, this was the only 'incident' we were sent to all day.

The next day, after parade we went for another half hour at the back-street garage, then ventured a little further. John spotted a Yamaha moped coming the other way, buzzing away very loudly.

'Bring your steel tape out tomorrow, Tom, he's taken his baffles out, we'll have him.'

The Yamaha FS1E (or Fizzy as it became known) was a popular introduction to motorised transport for teenagers in the 1970s. It was classed as a moped so could be ridden on L plates by a sixteen-year-old without needing to take a driving test. At the time, mopeds had to have physical pedals, but the pedals on the Fizzy both pointed the same way and were impossible to use – if anyone ever did master it, it would have been hilarious to watch. A few years later the definition of a moped was changed, with no need for pedals.

The exhaust note was like a swarm of wasps in a paper bag. Youngsters would remove the baffles from the exhaust in a laughable attempt to make their moped sound more powerful. All that this achieved was to make the swarm of wasps sound slightly angrier.

The next afternoon, armed with my tape we spotted the same moped. John overtook, switched on the blue light and police sign, and slowed to a halt in front of it.

'Right Tom, stick your tape up his exhaust (Ooer!) and see if it's got any baffles, if it hasn't then knock him off'

As I approached the moped the rider took off his crash helmet, I recognised him as the pathetic young man I'd seen at the Magistrates' Court just the week before. He admitted that a friend had taken the baffles out (as time passed it always seemed to be 'friends' who modified vehicles to render them illegal), so I told him that he'd be reported, issued him with an HORT1 and sent him on his way.

He seemed destined to lead a troubled life. He was my first 'knock-off' on patrol, and I can still remember his name.

Back in the car John dictated my pocket-book entry to me.

There was a junction in the town with a prohibition on making right-hand turns, but there were many drivers who did, despite ample signage. It was an ideal place to generate the traffic offence reports that our bosses wanted to see from probationers. John and I would spend hours at this junction, my confidence building as the knock-offs came thick and fast.

However, after one session I realised that I'd made a big mistake.

'John, one of these I knocked off, I didn't take any details of the car. What am I going to do?'

'Leave a line blank, we'll go and have a look up his drive later.'

'I can't, I've already written after it.'

'Is it on the HORT1?'

'Didn't issue one, he produced his docs to me.'

'Best forget it then.'

We did, and we never heard any more of it. I can just imagine the man, vocal at the indignity of being reported, anxiously watching his letterbox for weeks, awaiting the summons that would never arrive, but not daring to question why it hadn't.

We were on a quick changeover to earlies. Whether my alarm clock went off or not I don't know but I was woken by an Alsatian's wet nose in my face. It was 6.05am and Jim Finn, the shift's dog handler had been sent to Water Street to rouse me.

'Best get going Tommy, you're in the shit!'

I dressed rapidly. A little time was saved as I'd shaved the previous night, something I'd already made a habit for earlies. No walking to work this time - I leapt into my Mini, drove furiously down the road, screeching to a halt across the road from the station at 6.15am, just as everyone was turning out on patrol. They came over to me, John Jeffries, panic in his voice said,

'Bloody hell Tommy, you're in deep shit mate. Mr Willett's in the front office and asking where you are. We've covered for you, we'd best get you in through the back door.'

Shi-i-i-i-t! Regretting the attention my noisy arrival may have attracted, I made my way round to the cell block entrance. The front office stood between me and the locker room, but somebody made sure the coast was clear. I put the rest of my uniform on and went into the empty parade room. The phone was ringing as I entered, I nervously picked it up,

'Parade room. PC Tucker.'

A loud voice boomed back at me. 'PC Tucker. See me later!'

'Yes, sir, sorry sir.'

The line clicked off.

Oh shit!

Five minutes later I was in the panda car with John taking great delight in telling me how terrifying a bollocking our Chief Superintendent could deliver. This exacerbated my early-turn wind, so we spent the next half-hour or so with the car's windows wound down.

Back in the mess room at 7am, I'd made the shift's tea. Everyone else joined in the torment, confirming John's view that this meeting in the first-floor office would be far less enjoyable than last time. They were having great fun at my expense while I broke wind at a phenomenal rate.

As I washed up, the phone rang.

'Get that Tommy', someone said, even though everyone was closer to the phone than me.

'Mess room, PC Tucker.'

'PC **Tucker**', a voice boomed, 'see me **now**!'

'Yes sir, yes sir, right away sir', more wind escaped, slowly enveloping everyone in the room.

'Come on Tom', said John sympathetically, 'let's get you smartened up, I'll go in with you.'

The team ushered me down to the front office, Sergeant Norman looked at me disapprovingly while the shift, as one man, brushed me down and straightened out my uniform.

Trembling, a bag of nerves by now, I followed John up to the first-floor office. He knocked on the door, after an agonising few seconds the *Enter* light came on. Indicating to me to wait, John marched into the office, turned on his heel, stood to attention and saluted.

'PC Tucker to see you sir.'

'SEND! HIM! IN!' an unseen voice barked, as John beckoned me to stand beside him.

Petrified, but using my best Ryton-learned drill, I marched into the office, right-turned, and just as I was raising my arm to salute saw that PC John Gimbert was sitting behind the Chief Superintendent's desk, a wicked smirk on his face as he slapped our boss's brown leather gloves together. I turned to the right and saw the rest of the shift gathered in the corridor.

'You BASTARDS!' I yelled - they laughed riotously, I slowly joined in.

As we made our way downstairs we passed through the front office. Sergeant Norman was joining in with the laughter, he winked,

'You'll never be late again will you Nick.'

Dead right Sarge.

Notably, Bill Norman was the only member of the shift who never used my nickname, he always used my name.

A directive came from Headquarters that vehicle mileage had to be strictly controlled, due to a substantial rise in fuel prices. At Newcastle it was ordered that no vehicle was to exceed seventeen miles per shift without extenuating circumstances. This was completely unworkable in practice, excess mileage recorded in a vehicle's logbook drew the attention of an Inspector, but one look at the officer's pocketbook showing what had been dealt with that day showed clear justification. Some spent a quiet hour at night reversing in circles around a deserted car park to turn the clock back, but it quickly became common knowledge that the speedometer cable of a Ford Escort could be very easily disconnected, it was illegal but...

Mileage went down, but the fuel consumption figures correspondingly rocketed. Folk buying these cars at auction thought they had 70,000 miles on the clock, but it's quite possible that the real mileage was a good deal more than twice that. Testament to the durability of the Ford Escort perhaps.

I didn't like living at Water Street, I had no privacy and there was little to do in my spare time, Stafford was where my friends and established social life were. My leisure time in Newcastle revolved entirely around the job, from which there was no escape. The nearby 'Bombay' restaurant acted as our evening canteen, and although I enjoyed Indian food, the spices were compounding my digestive system issues, as well as the bills impacting heavily on the £118 that was landing in my bank account every four weeks.

One of my colleagues, Ivan, also lived in Stafford and said that he travelled every day; he suggested that we could share transport when necessary if I applied to live back at home. I applied and permission was duly granted, provided that I *reported for duty promptly*' and *travelled at my own expense.*

Local council elections took place while I was being tutored. Police had always provided a presence in polling stations. I was scheduled to cover four of these, three miles away in the Chesterton area, despite still not being allowed out on my own. John had shown me where my stations were.

Coming on duty that day, I was given further instructions by Sergeant Norman. I should move around between my allocated polling stations, remaining at each for about half an hour before moving on to the next.

There was one vital detail missing.

'How do I get there Sarge?'

'You walk or get a lift in one of the pandas.'

'How do I get from station to station.'

'You walk', squinting at me as if I was an imbecile.

'But I'm not allowed out on my own yet.'

'Ah….er...you'd best use your car then.'

'Can I claim expenses Sarge?'

'What do you think? Now get your arse up to Chesterton.'

It was quite a leisurely day. The polling station staff were very hospitable, I was awash with tea and full of biscuits. Sergeant Norman, maybe aware that I was unofficially out on my own for the first time made very regular visits to keep an eye on me. A supervisory officer would sign your pocket-book at any meeting, primarily to confirm it was up to date. I ended the day with seventeen of the Sergeant's signatures.

My first arrest came in the small hours of a night shift. We came across a Morris Marina embedded in a roundabout with no sign of the driver. Fortunately, it was one of the very few cars that then had the owner's details on the PNC, so we made our way to his home in Knutton, a couple of miles away. Having woken his bleary-eyed wife and ascertained that he'd not yet arrived home we parked in the darkness of a nearby side street to lie in wait. After only a few minutes a dishevelled, clearly drunk man came staggering past us and we stopped him by his front gate. He freely admitted to being the driver.

With excited anticipation I assembled the breathalyser, but he made only a half-hearted attempt to blow into it. Having told him he was under arrest for failing to provide a specimen we took him to the police station for the necessary procedure, which in those days involved a blood test taken by a doctor.

While our prisoner waited at the station, we went to the police surgeon's home on the Westlands, a nearby well-to-do area, and brought him to the station; routinely done because he was frequently more unfit to drive through drink than our detainees. The would be the first of many times that I'd have him as a passenger.

After the blood analysis my first arrest was charged and handed a disqualification at court after pleading guilty.

Following the 4am night-time tea break, we'd all turn out; ostensibly for a final look around the patch before the end of the shift, but the reality was rather different. We'd all reconvene at Tiffany's ballroom on the edge of the town centre, joining the night watchman Pete – of the 'Nine-five-okay' code phrase. Glad of the company, Pete would make tea and frothy coffee for us, while some would kick a ball about on the dance floor.

One Saturday morning the ballroom looked like a bomb had hit it. There was broken glass everywhere, chairs were scattered haphazardly while half consumed glasses of souring beer stood on the tables. Close to the bar area I could not believe my eyes – there was a gigantic turd on the carpet, as I gaped John commented,

'Somebody's thrown their hot dog away.'

How could someone have done this in a crowded ballroom? I was astounded. I didn't envy the cleaners who'd arrive a few hours later, not just for the ballroom bowel movement but all the mess.

I couldn't help feeling that we were abusing both Pete, a small, gentle, inoffensive man, and our supervisors who'd allowed us the unofficial 4am break, and then we were doing this afterwards.

Each day, around 5.15am, Inspector Bills would walk into the town to meet the foot patrols. As he left the police station, he'd come onto the air asking for everyone's positions. Except for one of us, all the town centre patrols in Tiffany's were 'off their patch'; a disciplinary matter although usually enforced by a swift, sharp word. The town centre patrols would 'scramble' from the ballroom, and there was an ongoing competition between them for whoever could come up with the furthest possible location from Tiffany's and still be there in time for the meeting. He must have known this, it was probably just as much a game for him to enjoy – he'd meet up with each of us in turn, as we'd try not to show that we were out of breath from running a mile or more.

In the very quiet early hours of a Tuesday morning, just before our rest days, four of us parked in a line in front of Newcastle's Guild Hall, listening to some sporting event on the radio. Unexpectedly, the Inspector came onto the air requesting meetings with the panda patrols. Apart from me and John, everyone was off their patch so there was a similar scenario to Tiffany's, this time involving the panda cars being driven as quickly as possible to some far-flung corner of their patch. John and I stayed put as engines started and revved furiously, tyres squealed and suddenly from a few feet away there was a massive crash. John Gimbert had been parked with his front bumper close to a lamp post. Instead of reversing away, he had gone straight forward. Needless to say, my tutor and I made a swift exit as we listened to the aftermath on the radio. A crash usually involved the suspension of one's driving authority; after 'Gimbo' had radioed in, the response from Sergeant Norman, with a hint of glee in his voice was,

'I'm coming out, get your big hat on.'

The loss of his driving permit was of little consequence though. After our rest days, two further days at Newcastle and a weekend off, both Gimbo and I would be attending driving courses at Headquarters.

One evening during those two days we were sent to the home of an elderly lady at Porthill. I can't remember why we went, but what I do remember is the smell of the house. It was extremely strong and absolutely vile, although neither of us could identify what it was, it wasn't body fluids. The house, although not exactly clean wasn't particularly dirty either, but the odour was absolutely disgusting. The lady was completely unaware of it. That was the day I learned to carry a small jar of Vick wherever I went. It was maybe twenty years or more afterwards that I returned to the same house on a routine enquiry. It was now occupied by a young couple who'd gutted and renovated it to a high standard. Maybe I imagined it, but I could still catch a hint of the revolting smell.

By now, the shift had well and truly accepted me as one of the team, I'd passed all the 'tests' they set up for me – so far, and I'd joined in with the fun. We all got on really well together, we watched each other's backs and willingly helped each other out wherever we could. I began to feel very settled and contented in my new career.

In five weeks, I'd learned a great deal from John, although we hadn't stopped many cars, and we had only made one arrest. I hadn't issued any fixed penalty tickets and more importantly hadn't spent a single minute on foot patrol - the most essential element of police work to a new Constable. This was down to Sergeant Rotchell who should have been allocating foot patrol to us as well as panda patrols. John would now leave the shift to join the Scenes of Crime department, so wouldn't be on hand to guide me through the first few challenging months on my own.

The next five weeks would be quite different though.

7 – Driving Force

About a year before I joined Staffordshire Police a decision had been taken to give driver training to probationary Constables, and in some cases, cadets. This had the unintended, unforeseen consequence of missing out those who were towards the end of their probation, so it was commonplace for many with two or more years' service not to have had driver training, while many with just a few months' service were already qualified drivers. This was manifestly unfair and extremely unpopular. My being sent on a driving course with only six months' service didn't go down at all well with the other members of the shift, some of whom were well out of their probation and still not authorised to drive. However, they accepted that I wasn't personally to blame for this; I resolved to do my very best to pass the course, as failure would be letting them down.

Staffordshire Police's Motor Training Centre didn't just train Staffordshire officers but offered advanced driver training to other forces in the country, as well as internationally. An Advanced Driving Certificate from Staffordshire's MTC meant its holder was amongst the most skilled drivers in the world; sadly, the service frowns on such 'elitism' today. The instructors were very experienced police drivers, with years of motor patrol work behind them.

John Gimbert was here for such a course. If successful, he'd be authorised to drive Crime Cars and high-powered patrol cars. I was here for a Standard driving course which would allow me to drive panda cars and various other small vehicles. The basis for the training was the same, whatever course you were on. The 'bible' of police driving was a blue HMSO book entitled 'Manual of Police Driving Instruction', better known as 'Roadcraft.' The first three days of the course were classroom based, we had Roadcraft stuffed into us in large doses and were also given instruction in elementary mechanics. Whole passages of Roadcraft had to be learned by heart. Instructors would randomly ask us to quote them, and woe betide anyone who wasn't up to speed. It was the beginning of June; on the Wednesday I looked out of the window and saw driving snow across the nearby dog training field. This was the day before the long, scorching summer of 1976 began.

The basis of all driving in Roadcraft is the *System of Car Control*; a sequential method of what to consider on approaching any situation which may need a change of speed or direction. Whilst driving, it should be thought through continuously. We were told the majority of police vehicle accidents happened when the System wasn't properly applied. If properly used the likelihood of a collision, whether the driver is at fault or not is very low. The ratio of police vehicle crashes relative to the mileage covered bore this out – at the time anyway, as for today, read on.

Naturally, aged twenty-one and four years after passing my driving test, I thought I knew everything there was to know about driving. By the end of the second day in the classroom I seriously wondered how I'd survived on the road for so long. A simple example – most drivers when turning left out of a junction don't look left before they do; take a look at a few drivers at junctions and you'll see they're only looking to their right. An admittedly nonsensical maxim was that *driving is 99% concentration and 99% observation;* however, most drivers day-to-day don't give even 50% to either.

As well as Roadcraft, we were also expected to know the Highway Code virtually word-for-word. Although most don't look at the Code after they've passed their test, if they have a crash, and haven't complied with the rules in the Code then they're deemed at fault. Similarly, driving that doesn't conform to the Code can be used as evidence of dangerous, careless or inconsiderate driving.

Sadly, financial constraints of recent years have bitten hard on the quality of police driving. Staffordshire Police's driver training, like many other forces, is now run on a shoestring. Civilian instructors are used whenever possible, without the police driving experience which was once considered essential. The bean-counters cynically consider it cheaper to pay the excess on insurance claims than to invest in high quality driver training. The resulting drop in police driving standards is there for all to see, these people should be setting an impeccable example to the public. It provokes much discussion amongst my retired Traffic Division colleagues. Furthermore, Roadcraft has become so diluted and dumbed-down over the years that it bears little relationship to what we learned.

Anyway, back to 1976; several guys who'd joined with me were on the course. Others had their driving course immediately after the Local Procedure course and arrived at their stations as trained drivers. On the Thursday we were finally set free from the classroom into sweltering sunshine. I was one of three pupils in the car, my companions were both out of their probation; one from Cannock who was a provisional licence holder, and the other from Leek. Our civilian instructor was Bill Jones, who'd been a traffic patrol officer with Wolverhampton Borough Police. He had a happy-go-lucky nature, a great sense of humour and constantly spoke in spoonerisms, such as 'cycermotle' (motor-cycle). Above all, he was an absolutely amazing driver and very capable of passing on his skill, As he took us for a demonstration drive across Cannock Chase in a Morris Marina (1.8TC no less), he amazed me with his calmness and the details he was observing in his commentary. His gear changes were silky smooth, so much so that one could have believed the gearbox was automatic. Never before had I seen someone so in control of a car, and it looked absolutely effortless.

Progress always happened slowly in the police force. Despite synchromesh gearboxes having been commonplace for over twenty years we were still required to double-declutch for every gear change. Slowing-down arm signals were compulsory before braking for a hazard under the System, except on the motorway. To this end, the driver's window on all MTC cars had a wind deflector, and was always down, come rain or shine. It had to be wound up on the entry slip-road to a motorway but wound down again on the exit slip. All very old fashioned, but it did sharply focus the concentration, as was the intention.

At the end of Bill's demonstration drive we turned into Cannock police station for a coffee break, then it was our turn to drive. He told us to drive as we would normally so that he could see what he had to build on. After a brief spell each at the wheel we returned to Headquarters for lunch.

Back in the car after lunch, Bill said that the first thing we needed to concentrate on was steering, as we were all crossing our hands on the wheel, an absolute no-no! The push-pull steering technique is difficult to acquire, but once properly learned becomes second-nature. To this end, we spent the whole afternoon on a manoeuvring area at the MoT goods vehicle testing station near Swynnerton practicing this skill. It was hard work in the rapidly increasing summer temperature, and without power steering as well as being pretty boring. After this gruelling session it was on to the Central Traffic Group base in Stafford for fuel and back to Headquarters where all the cars had to be washed and leathered off before we were allowed off duty.

I'm top right
Note the undersized hat!

The blistering summer was the worst possible time to be on a driving course, sitting on the vinyl seats of a car for the whole day, wearing our caps too – mine still crushing my cranium; there was no air-conditioning in those days either. We hit on the idea of taking towels out with us to put on the seats, which eased things somewhat. As temperatures rose the Chief Constable gave his permission, unprecedented, for the whole force to remove their ties and wear their shirts open-necked.

We clocked up the miles in a variety of cars, the Marina, a Triumph 2000, a Vauxhall Viva, but most commonly an Austin 2200, a smooth, comfortable and pretty quick motor, the trunk road patrol car of choice at the time. It had recently been superseded in production by the notorious wedge-shaped 18/22 series. Although the force had already put a number of these into use, including one at MTC, it had already been decided that no more of these inferior replacements would be purchased and a fleet of 3-litre Ford Granadas was already on order. As well as on-the-road training, we had regular sessions on the force's skid-pan - nothing at all teaches you how to handle a car better than this. The knowledge and skill gained on the skid pan, both on this and later courses has kept me away from insurance claim forms on more than a few occasions. If you ever have the opportunity for a session on a skid pan I can't recommend it enough.

One day I was walking back from lunch in the canteen to the MTC; it was wise to take the longer route around the back of the main Headquarters building, thus avoiding coming into contact with any bosses. However, being a little tight for time I walked along the front of the building and came face-to-face with the Chief Constable, to whom I threw a salute up. His Welsh lilt boomed out,
'Good afternoon PC…..er….'
'Tucker, sir.'
'Of course, PC Tucker, I've been hearing good things about you, you're stationed at….er…'
'Newcastle sir.'
'Of course, PC Tucker, at Newcastle, you're here for….'
'My Standard Driving Course sir.'
'Yes, well best of luck with it boy, I'll see you again soon.'

After throwing another one up to him I set off at a very quick march to the MTC, realising that Mr Rees hadn't remembered my name at all, or where I was stationed, but that he had 'extracted' the information from me. I arrived back in the classroom with seconds to spare, and to cheers and jeers from those who'd been gleefully watching my ordeal through the window.

The course ended with written exams on Roadcraft and the Highway Code, a skid-pan test and a nerve-wracking, very demanding driving test on the final Thursday. We wouldn't know until the next day whether we'd passed. An end of course 'do' followed in the evening but the weather had been so hot that for the duration of the course that I'd barely touched any alcohol, combined with the heat it just didn't agree with me; how I've changed! Someone thought it would be amusing to spike my soft drinks with vodka, so I ended up roaring drunk.

I had a very bad head indeed the following morning, which was taken up with car cleaning and polishing. A drought had been declared several weeks earlier. A nationwide hosepipe ban had been declared, and all vehicle washing had been prohibited by the government; this made little difference at MTC, every car was washed, every day, often with hosepipe assistance.

We waited nervously in the classroom after lunch as we were called in one by one, in alphabetical order to see the Divisional Commander of Traffic Division, Chief Superintendent 'Bungalow' Jack Buxton for our results. Being a 'T' I was one of the last to go in, everyone else was coming out waving their new driving permit in their hand, making me even more nervous. I'd no need though, and left MTC that Friday afternoon as an authorised police driver.

(Bungalows don't have anything upstairs).

8 - Flying Solo

'You're still a walker!'...

...proclaimed Sergeant Norman as I walked into the station the following Monday afternoon, but then he congratulated me on passing the course. I paraded with the shift for my first time out on my own. As well as the six panda areas, there were four town beats, Town One through to Four. As the junior probationer I'd be Town Four, call sign Mike-Five-Five for the foreseeable future; elevation to Town One or *Top Town Man* would come with seniority, and after at least three more probationers had joined the shift. You had to remain on your 'patch' as I've already mentioned and Town Four was something of a backwater away from the main shopping streets. If you were very senior, and all the town beats were filled, you were given the coveted 'Town General' beat and could wander wherever you liked with impunity.

Walking the beat was a skill which nobody had taught me. Having spent the last ten weeks as either the passenger or driver of a car, going out on foot was something of a comedown despite the beautiful weather. I knew that walking the beat was an essential part of my training, but I was still itching to get behind the wheel of a panda car for the first time – several I'd joined with already had. Nonetheless I was very excited at the prospect of going out on my own for the very first time, although I had a pressing and very difficult matter to deal with first.

The weekend had brought unwelcome news. A long-standing close friend lodging in London had become embroiled in an extremely serious criminal matter, and I was desperately worried about him. I wanted to do all I could for him and his family who lived in the same road as mine, but there was a strong possibility of career damage if I didn't handle the situation properly. I found myself sitting in Inspector Bills' office, telling him of my dilemma, he listened carefully and sympathetically, making notes and assured me that I'd done the right thing by coming to him.

Concluding, he simply said,

'Don't worry too much Tommy, leave this with me and I'll see what I can do. Don't talk to anyone else about it, just get out there and enjoy your first day on your own, I'll see you later.'

I left him, feeling somewhat relieved, booked out a radio, checked out my pockets for pocket-book, HORT1 book and fixed penalty tickets, clamped my helmet (unused since the HMI debacle) onto my head and headed out into the town; apprehensiveness at my friend's situation still at the back of my mind.

The earlier part of the shift brought no incidents for me to deal with. Just after 5pm, when Mick Geraghty came on the radio.

'Mike-five-five, over

'Mike-five-five, in the High Street over.'

'Yes five-five, ten-twenty, Dorolyn's dress shop over.'

'Five-five, will attend.'

My first incident, on my own! Ten-twenty was the code for a burglar alarm activation. At the time, naively believing that this equalled burglars to be caught, I strode rapidly through the town to the shop, a couple of minutes' walk away. On arrival, it was locked up and secure.

Experience quickly taught me that the huge majority, as much as 99%, of intruder alarm activations were false, caused by carelessness when opening or closing the premises. Having arrived and checked the premises, the poor attending Constable then had to wait for the keyholder, who at this time of day was probably homeward bound in rush-hour traffic, so a long wait was in prospect. These false alarms wasted an incredible amount of police time, and nobody seemed to have a mind to tackle the problem.

As I waited, Inspector Bills joined me.

'About your friend, Tommy. I've spent a lot of the afternoon on the phone to the Met about him. It's sorted.'

I could have kissed him, handlebar moustache and all!

After going into detail about what had gone on he continued,

'He'll be home tomorrow, but he's got to stay well away from London for now, I'm sure you'll do your bit won't you?'

I couldn't thank him enough, he just said,

'Hopefully we'll never have to talk about this again, and our conversations this afternoon never happened.'

I'd already developed a huge amount of respect for this man and now had a whole lot more.

My friend was extricated from his problems and the matter was never spoken of again or even hinted at by the Inspector.

My feet were aching by the time I trudged back to the police station and the mess room for my meal break. My responsibility as tea-boy didn't extend to mealtimes as quite bizarrely, everyone brewed their own pot of tea; amongst the dominoes spread out on the table, there were six or more small teapots. Even years later, this was something which drew comments in other stations such as,

'Have you ever noticed at 'Castle? Everyone brews their own little pot of tea, it's daft.'

I'd just left the station after my break when Mick Geraghty came on the air.

'Mike-five-five, can you return to the station, got a little driving job for you.'

Yes-s-s! Here we go!

It was a 'little' driving job. The occupant of an ancient box-van had been arrested by another patrol in Chesterton. I was taken to it and had to drive it to the compound at Water Street. I can't remember the make or model, but what I do remember was the pattern of the gearshift. It was upside down and back to front so first gear was down and to the right, with fourth gear where one would normally find first, synchromesh was also either absent or broken. The double-declutching of my driving course actually became useful but the drive from Chesterton to Newcastle was far from smooth and I was glad to have no passengers.

Later, Sergeant Rotchell picked me up and we rode around together for an hour or so. Asking how my first day was going, he remarked that I'd already acquired a new nickname, 'Speedy.' This was my colleagues remarking that I was walking around my beat very quickly. I told him that nobody had taught me even the basics of foot patrol. He said it needed a slow, steady pace, looking carefully around at all times and missing absolutely nothing. It also meant that members of the public could easily approach you; this was how you gained information about what was going on, the 'ear-to-the-ground' that was so important to day-to-day policing, fundamentally lacking these days.

Being approachable also meant dealing with a multitude of 'FSQ's. The SQ stands for Stupid Question, as for the F… Such questions could be to ask the time, even if you were standing under the clocktower of the Guild Hall, or where a particular shop was, even if you were standing outside it. Then there was, 'Is it alright to park here?', despite the obvious double yellow lines. During the course of the day, the sheer volume of these questions could be quite exasperating; the stupidity of Joe public having no limits. To respond other than with stoical patience could invite a complaint, so handling FSQs was another of the arts of foot patrol to be mastered. Experience led to recognising incoming FSQs from a fair distance, giving an opportunity to dodge out of sight. A surprisingly common FSQ, believe it or not, would be from the cab of a lorry,

'Which way to the docks mate?'

'Er, this is Newcastle-under-Lyme, I think you want the other one, it's about two-hundred and fifty miles away, turn right off the A1.'

Tea-stops were a vital part of foot patrol, not just for the chance to rest one's feet for a few minutes, light up and quench your thirst, but to get to know the people working and living on your 'patch.' They often had useful information to pass on about what was happening in the area. It was expected that you would find the back doors of shops, talk to the people who ran them and cultivate relationships with them. You kept your tea-stops to yourself as far as you could, sharing them meant that a place could become overrun by other colleagues who may find out something before you. In a job littered with contradictions, you were expected to cultivate your tea-stops, but woe betide you if you were ever discovered, cup in hand, by the Sergeant or Inspector.

Two tea-stops were shared though and used as places for impromptu 'shift meetings' out of the public eye. Firstly, the Wimpy bar, where a cup of coffee was always thrust into your hand with the offer of a snack as you walked in through the back door; the staff were often too busy to talk to you, so you usually drank and ate alone or with other colleagues. The other popular tea-stop (although refreshment was never on offer) was 'Ernie's', the public conveniences in Pepper Street. Ernie Brownsword was the attendant, he had a large 'office' in the Gents, with comfortable seating and a varied selection of reading material, some of it 'top shelf.' He was a friendly, but grumpy and very unhappily married character, easy to wind up but he always welcomed us, taking a genuine fatherly interest in the young bobbies around the town. He took enormous pride in the cleanliness of his establishment, the copper and brass fittings were polished to a mirror shine; the place had the air not of a public lavatory but a hospital ward, fresh and clean as it was. The conveniences fell victim to spending cuts and became, of all things a wine bar, which is probably a good deal less clean. Ernie is now polishing copper pipes in the sky, having arguments with his wife and the bobbies who have gone before me.

Foot patrol around the town on nights was completely different. You were expected above all else to 'check your property' or to be cynical, 'shake door handles.' You had to check that every building on your patch was secured properly and that there were no signs of intruders having visited. This had to be done twice, before and after your meal break. If, heaven forbid, a burglary was reported the following morning at one of *your* properties then you could expect to be summoned from your bed, to complete a statement and account for your implied failure to make the proper checks. I was once woken up and asked to account for a small broken pane of glass, no more than four inches square, ten feet above the ground in a dark alley.

This diligent checking was pretty pointless but the visible police presence in the town was probably a strong deterrent to would-be burglars; break-ins were very rare indeed. Town One beat had the advantage that a courageous top town man could climb to the rooftops of a whole section of the High Street and walk its entire length, with only an intervening six-feet wide gap to jump. From this vantage point they could survey almost the whole of their patch all night long. One PC on another shift failed on two occasions to jump the gap and fell about six feet, becoming slightly injured. On the second occasion that he missed his footing, Superintendent Mann suggested on the injury report that the hapless PC be *issued with a parachute.* After this, climbing was officially forbidden but still happened.

Walking out into the town after my break one night I tried to switch on my torch and found that it wasn't working. This wasn't unusual; we were issued with standard 'Ever-Ready' rubber torches which took two D type batteries. They were absolutely bloody useless and often needed a shake, a sharp tap or a fiddle with the batteries to encourage them to work. 'Shake and tap' having failed I unscrewed the battery compartment and found a small piece of paper between the battery and the spring on the cap. I thought it was odd but in my night shift jaded exhaustion didn't think any more of it.

At about 3.30am, once everyone was back out from their meal breaks, Mick Geraghty called me on the radio.

'Mike-Five-five, Five-two's seen someone going into the alley from the Midway to Henry White's. Can you go in from the High Street side and stop them from coming through? We need to see what they're up to.'

Without realising that I hadn't heard Five-two's recent call over the air, it was time for action, maybe my first solo arrest. I was just a few yards away and was in the alley entrance in seconds. I paused to check my torch, it was working this time.

Then, Mick called,

'Mike Five-five, Five-two can hear someone moaning.'

Once again, I hadn't heard anyone call in, but it didn't register.

Adrenalin flooded my blood stream as I cautiously made my way along the pitch-dark alley, probing the blackness with my torch. Suddenly, the beam caught upon something moving above and ahead of me.

I made out the form of a blood-soaked human body, hanging from the railings of a fire escape, legs twitching in the last throes of life. Time stood still as I loudly exclaimed, with a perfectly natural but not very professional,

'Fucking hell.'

I reached for my radio transmitter and was just about to press the button when from behind me came a series of explosions and the sound of breaking glass. I couldn't make sense of the situation and stood, frozen in time for what seemed like hours, although probably only a couple of seconds passed until I heard the by now familiar roars of laughter from the whole shift descending a fire escape from the rooftops into the alley. I'd been set up again, and how!

The piece of paper in my torch suddenly made sense, someone had doctored it during our meal break, intending that it wouldn't work. The elaborate setup had involved someone finding a mannequin and some old clothes at the council tip, which in those days was never secured so was always accessible. After dressing it and applying some red colour to the head they'd hung it from the fire escape. Pieces of string had been tied to the legs, and John *Noddy* Noden was pulling them from the shadows, making the legs appear to twitch. The explosions had come from some scrap strip lights which had been found in bins and were being thrown from on high, exploding as they hit the ground.

I couldn't help but join in with the laughter even though I was still shaking, my colleagues were slapping me on the back and proclaiming,

'Tommy, you were bloody brilliant, you're really one of us now.'

I'm sure they all enjoyed this elaborate practical joke, the real test for me was whether I'd stand my ground or run away, I'd passed. The glass was swept up and the 'body' taken back to the tip where its presence may or may not have alarmed one of Ernie's council colleagues the next morning.

Back on noons I was summoned to Chief Inspector Hall's office. Wondering what I'd done wrong I anxiously knocked on his door. He roared an invitation to enter, and as I opened the door, I could hear tinny, excited speech from a transistor radio on his desk. Putting his finger to his lips he waved me to sit down and listened very attentively to a horse racing commentary. He started to jump up and down in his chair, bellowing,

'Come on, come on my beauty, come on.' The commentary slowed as the horses passed the post.

'Ah, bollocks!' exclaimed the Deputy Sub Divisional Commander, screwing up a betting slip from the top of a pile on his desk and tossing into the bin, continuing,

'Right son, next race in ten minutes, six-month staff appraisal, let's have a look what Mr Bills has to say.... oh yes, very pleased with you...bit impetuous but keen and hard-working, get on well with your colleagues, that's what I like to see, do you play any sport?'

'No sir, never been interested.'

'You need something to keep you fit son, like me, superfit, that's what I am, superfit! Right, what shall I put on this form? I know, 'a very hard-working smart, polite officer', will that do?'

'Yes sir.'

'Okay, sign here and then you can get back out on the town.'

Superfit he certainly was, and it was also his nickname. Tommy Hall was an immensely likeable and very funny man. When not in uniform he'd appear in an immaculate silver-grey tracksuit in which he went running; he positively radiated health. Retiring some weeks later, he died very suddenly after a similar number of weeks. Maybe *superfit* wasn't the best way to be after all.

I made my way back into the town. Allocation of staff and shifts didn't really take account of demand. Four designated pandas were put onto the road, and if there were sufficient vehicles and drivers available a patrol was designated 'panda general'; every other available officer was directed to patrol the town centre. Returning from nights to float shifts, (usually noons) on a Thursday could mean two whole shifts on duty at the same time. So, a dozen PCs could be patrolling the town centre, supervised by three or more Sergeants and two Inspectors. Highly visible policing and plenty of officers to deal with anything that may arise.

But it was half-day closing. The dozen bobbies were just about the only people in the town, constantly bumping into each other, and all their tea stops were closed. With a little imagination they could have been better deployed elsewhere; unfortunately imagination was in very short supply.

Having plenty of officers visible in the town centre wasn't a bad thing. We were still in an age when people didn't regularly venture far from the town they lived in, using their local town centre for all their shopping needs. Regular visits to the town-centre would almost certainly include sighting at least one PC while they were there, giving the impression - perhaps illusion would be a better word - that the police were omnipresent. You still hear the clamour for a return to the *Dixon of Dock Green* days with *bobbies on every street corner*, but the truth is that they never truly existed in the first place.

One day I was met in the town centre by Superintendent Bills, impressive in his uniform, complete with stick. He walked and talked with me for half an hour or so. Normally a very mild-mannered man he appeared to be quite furious about something, eventually asking me,

'Why are you the only PC walking the town at the moment?'

'I didn't know I was sir.'

'Well, you are, why?'

Over the years I came to know a tendency for senior officers to ask questions of someone least able to answer them, then blame them for not being able to, as well as for the situation that had arisen. This for me was an early example of exactly that.

'I don't know sir, you'd have to ask Sergeant Rotchell, he's the patrol Sergeant.'

He was not at all happy and stormed off back to the station.

It was August by now, and I still hadn't arrested anyone on my own, but this was to change. Mid-morning one day, I was directed to Woolworth's where the store detective had detained a shoplifter, an elderly man. He had advanced cirrhosis of the liver, with a yellow complexion and a hugely swollen waistline, he didn't appear long for this world. I was joined by one of the panda patrols who prompted me through the procedure – now I was in the position of my first solo arrest I'd completely forgotten what to do. Anyway, with my prisoner on board we returned to the police station where we went through the process. In later years it could easily take the entire length of a shift (and more) to process even the most straightforward of arrests, but within an hour the shoplifter was interviewed, charged and bailed to appear at court. The file of evidence took even less time than that. I have a good memory for dates, names and places, but I can't remember the name of this, my first ever arrest or even what he stole. I do remember the name of my second arrest, for the same offence, also at Woolworths, the next day.

A couple of weeks later, while on noons I was sent to a flat on the edge of the town centre where the sole occupant hadn't been seen for a few days, the address seemed vaguely familiar. There was the tell-tale sign of several bottles of milk on the doorstep. It could well be that the tenant had gone away and forgotten to tell the milkman, but the near certain probability was that there was a corpse in the flat.

Having checked on the radio with Sergeant Norman that it was the correct course of action, I broke a pane of glass in the door with a nearby broom handle, reached through and let myself in. Throughout my service, going into any building where there may be a body to find was one of my least favourite experiences; I've done it many times, often alone and I've never been able to dispel the dread of what I may find. More often than not there'd be a dead body, in bed, in a chair, on the toilet or simply collapsed on the floor; but the occasions when the person had taken their own life, or - worse still - had it taken from them by someone else always shocked me to the core. Until I found a body, each opening of a door in a building brought with it a new sense of trepidation.

The man was dead in bed, apparently having died in his sleep, the sunken features of his discoloured face were vaguely familiar. I did as I'd been taught, checking the body for injuries, which involved turning the body over. This is when the human body produces its final, sometimes extremely loud and always stench-ridden fart; sometimes accompanied by the escape of trapped gas through the mouth producing a moan as it passes the vocal cords. First time on my own, and thoroughly unpleasant.

Next, I needed to identify the man in the bed, the concerned neighbour who had called us only knew his first name.

A check of letters on the sideboard revealed the truth. The first person I'd ever arrested on my own was lying in the bed a few feet away, dead, so he would also be my first solo sudden death. My earlier prognosis of him had been quite correct.

And I still can't remember his name!

It was a Saturday morning in float week, and I was working early turn. Someone had made a mistake with duties and apart from me, there were only three drivers available. Jim Bickerton, the first PC I'd met at Newcastle, was Acting Sergeant for the day.

'Have we only got three drivers?'

'I'm a driver...' I piped up quietly.

'Thank Christ for that', said Jim, 'Panda Four then.'

At last, I was to get behind the wheel of a police car, on my own. I excitedly took the keys from the board and set out to patrol the slumbering streets of Clayton. I returned for the usual seven o'clock brew, prepared by a probationer on the non-float shift; it made a refreshing, pun intended, change. Turning out again at 7.20am I realised ten minutes later that I'd already used twelve of my allocated seventeen miles, five miles left and six and a half hours to go. I parked the car and set out on foot patrol around Clayton for half an hour, without seeing another soul. At 8am I had a radio message to return to the station; a more experienced officer from my shift had booked on at 8am and was to take over my car. So, it was back to the big, misfitting hat for me. I was disappointed, but I'd driven a panda car at last, even if it was only for an hour.

Annual leave through the summer left the shift constantly short of panda drivers, so I was occasionally allocated panda patrol duties, becoming more often as the weeks passed. This naturally, and quite understandably wasn't welcomed by my more senior colleagues who'd yet to attend driving courses. Inspector Bills, and the two shift Sergeants were somewhat reluctant to allow me to patrol alone, so whenever possible I'd have one of the more experienced non-drivers partner me. However, as the weeks passed, they became more and more willing to allow me out on my own. I was attending a lot of incidents, gaining experience, and generating a more than acceptable quantity and standard of paperwork. I was busy, the shifts passed quickly, and the occasional day on foot with my undersized big hat on gave a welcome change of pace despite the discomfort.

On panda patrol one Saturday afternoon I was sent to an alarm call, by now I'd become accustomed to false alarms, so didn't make any particular effort to get there quickly. It was the wooden pavilion to a bowling green; a section of the outer wall had been crudely smashed in, and I could hear voices inside – it was a genuine alarm. I couldn't do much on my own to tackle the offenders and called for assistance, reply came there none. I called for urgent assistance – a *10-9* call, which should have had every patrol in the area come blue-lighting to me, still no reply. It would appear that Sergeant Norman was in the cell block and Mick Geraghty was dealing with someone at the counter, so my call went unanswered. The offenders got away from the other side of the building.

It was the *only* genuine alarm call that I ever attended.

Mick had always said that if I yelled *'priority'* into my radio he'd drop everything to respond. I can only assume his hearing was failing as he didn't.

Another time, I came across a crash involving several cars at a busy junction. I desperately needed help to manage the scene, even a more experienced officer would, and called for assistance. No response. After several more unsuccessful attempts over the radio, I called 999 from a nearby phone box. Five minutes later Mick radioed me, directing me to the crash that I was already at and had reported.

It was an unacceptable situation and really unsafe. The need for a dedicated controller, undistracted by the enquiry desk was patently obvious, but it would be more than another two years before this actually happened. The number of times that calls for help went unanswered were far too many.

In the neighbouring city, someone had been setting fires at night in some of the many pottery factories in Longton. Initially, the problem had been tackled by CID officers on overtime doing observations in the area. This became fruitless, and the incidents of arson stopped, probably because the offender noticed the area was swamped with people who were obviously detectives. However, the local bosses were unhappy about stopping the operation altogether, for fear of another incident. The upshot was that PCs from neighbouring Divisions were taken from their usual night shifts, told to dress in warm plain clothes and loaned to Longton to carry out the same work which had previously attracted overtime. I was one of them and spent seven nights huddled under a lorry trailer in Anchor Road, overlooking a pottery factory from 10.15pm until 5.45am. No meal break and I had to be inventive regarding toilet facilities. Many of us were suffering the same ordeal all around Longton's many 'pot bonks' with not even the consolation of overtime. I did start to contemplate my career choice again, I had plenty of time as I sat in the cold. The arsonist was never caught, but rumours circulated years later that it was actually a rogue police officer.

Walking around Newcastle town centre the following week, even with an extremely uncomfortable hat was heavenly compared to the previous week of night shifts!

My first time in court inevitably came. I'd dealt with a minor collision reported at the police station enquiry counter. I'd interviewed both drivers and drawn a sketch plan of the scene. The driver at fault was summonsed for driving without due care and attention. These days there would never have been any police involvement from the outset.

I was very nervous.

I stood in the witness box, took the oath and the prosecting solicitor said,

'Thank you, officer, please give your evidence.'

'I have no evidence to give, your worships.'

Very embarrassing but it was the truth. After he'd asked one or two questions to establish the facts, the defence solicitor questioned me.

'What were weather conditions at the time officer?'

'As far as I know it was fine and dry your worships.'

'But that's not true is it Constable? My client says that the road was icy and that he skidded on the ice.'

'That's not what the defendant said to me when I interviewed him, your worships.'

The defence solicitor, famed for posturing in court asked for the case to be adjourned until after lunch, so that an expert from Keele weather station could come to give evidence in support of his client.

The solicitor would have been best advised to ask questions of the weather man *before* putting him in the witness box as it went like this,

'What was the weather like in this area on *[such and such a date]*'

The man checked the paperwork that he'd brought to court.

'Fine and dry, temperature around 10 degrees Centigrade.'

'Had there been an overnight frost?'

'No, temperatures remained well above freezing.'

Then, in desperation,

'When was the last snowfall?'

'I don't know for certain, [checked paperwork] but it was several weeks previously.'

The magistrates weren't impressed.

Having arrived at the court shaking with nerves, I left shaking with suppressed laughter.

A National Front activist, Robert Relf had advertised his house in Leamington Spa, with a board outside – '*For sale to an English family only.*' Relf had refused to comply with a court order to remover the racist advertisement, so was held in contempt of court and committed to Stafford prison. Taking exception to this, the National Front planned a huge march and demonstration in the county town. What would nowadays be termed 'anti-fascists' intended to stage a counter demonstration.

Plans were drawn up on a mammoth scale, officers were brought in from surrounding forces to support us. The demonstration and counter-demonstration were going to be policed by over two-thousand police officers, of which I was one. It was probably Staffordshire Police's largest ever planned operation.

Although rowdy, it passed off quite peacefully, in no small part due to perfect planning keeping the two demonstrations well apart. The National Front marched from Stafford railway station to the prison, carrying placards bearing the legend *Free Robert Relf.* More than a few bore the slogan *Free Robert Ralph*, testament to just how ill-informed these knuckle-draggers were, and demonstrating their depth of knowledge of the actual cause.

I was close to the front escorting the march. As we neared the prison, the road had been completely blocked at the main gate by a line of mounted police, in front of which were around a hundred-and-fifty officers standing in three tiered rows. Front and centre stood the Chief Constable, resplendent in his uniform, arms folded in defiance at the approaching mob. It was an impressive, awe-inspiring sight which almost completely silenced the demonstrators. I doubt whether Mr Relf/Ralph even heard what was going on outside. Following the somewhat muted demonstration, the horde turned around and we escorted them back to the station.

After they'd dispersed and become the responsibility of British Transport Police, Mr Rees came and chatted to us all, 'Light up your fags boys, find somewhere to rest your legs. You've done a great job today, I'm proud of every one of you.'

He was a great, inspiring leader.

9 – Always Look on the Bright Side of ….
Death

Death features prominently in police work, it comes in many forms; police officers have many tales to tell, from tragic to darkly hilarious. All members of Leek, Newcastle and the city Divisions were appointed as 'Coroner's Officers' by Her Majesty's Coroner, with responsibility for investigating all sudden and unusual deaths. We'd probably have at least one of these during a shift.

For many years, the Coroner for North Staffordshire was Frederic George Hails, a stern, irascible man with a natural air of great authority. A well-read intellectual, he wore a monocle, chain smoked St Moritz cigarettes and carried a small, very hairy dog which looked just like him under his arm wherever he went. His insistence on investigations being thoroughly carried out, and protocol being rigidly observed led to many officers fearing getting on the wrong side of him. However, he fought tirelessly for road safety improvements, as well as people bereaved by industrial diseases in the area, which were many in the pottery and mining industries. As such, he was responsible for many changes in the law. Despite his fearsome reputation I found him to be a very sharp-witted, caring man and I developed an enjoyable working relationship with him.

The first, tragic sudden death I attended was while being tutored, a cot death on a Saturday morning. A girl had been born at home in the presence of a midwife the previous day, the couple's second child. She'd been born quite normally and there were no concerns at all. The little girl had been bedded down in a carrycot overnight in her parents' bedroom. She'd woken for a feed twice in the night and quickly settled afterwards. In the morning her parents had found her unresponsive and called for an ambulance, but the little mite had already been dead for an hour or two. As a twenty-one-year-old single man I had no understanding of the situation or of its devastating effect on the stunned parents. John was visibly shaken by what we were having to deal with, telling me to make drinks and stay quiet while he did what he needed to.

Tragic events like this were not handled with appropriate sensitivity at the time, but John knew what he was doing. A particularly callous aspect was that Mr Hails required the bodies of cot deaths to be taken by the reporting officer to the North Staffordshire Royal Infirmary, for a full skeletal X-ray. It would have been far more sympathetic and sensitive for the body to be taken from the home by an undertaker and the X-ray done during the post-mortem.

The rationale behind the Coroner's mandate was to rule out any initial suspicion of foul play, an unfortunate, but necessary part of any investigation of sudden death. However, to my mind this took things too far and should have only been done if the officer dealing had well-founded suspicions.

Paperwork completed, John carefully wrapped the child's body in a blanket and carried her outside; the effect on the bereaved parents of their beloved, precious new-born being taken from the house and placed on the back seat of a police car must have been utterly devastating. At the hospital John carried her through the permanently crowded A&E department to X—ray. There we were, at least, given priority over the others in the queue but still had to wait for a few minutes. Two uniformed policemen with a dead baby waiting in a queue with you – can you even begin to imagine it? The abhorrent process concluded, it was back to Newcastle for keys and from there to the mortuary to put the tragic little one on a tray in the fridge.

John, despite remaining calm and professional throughout, was clearly extremely upset; once I had family of my own I understood perfectly. Thankfully, cot deaths are now very rare, the smaller number of bereaved parents are treated with far more compassion and proper support is available to them. The cold-hearted treatment to which they were subjected in the 1970s was barbaric.

My second sudden death came the next morning. A far more routine matter, the not unexpected, peaceful death of an elderly gentleman in his sleep. The only reason for our involvement was that his own doctor was not available on the Sunday morning to issue a death certificate; circumstances common to the majority of sudden deaths that we attended. The deceased's doctor would phone the Coroner on the next working day, issue a death certificate and that would be the end of the matter. However, even in these circumstances Mr Hails insisted on all the paperwork being completed properly, with fully typed Form 12s and statements. This needless work for the police would take at least two hours, and often a whole shift to deal with (particularly if it was cold or raining…), then the time taken in Sub-divisional Office to type it all.

Having lost a loved one, the last thing any bereaved people want is police officers invading their home and intruding on their grief. This time the family had expected the death, so with the relief that comes to many people at the end of weeks or months of suffering, they were very cooperative. John explained that he was teaching me, and with the family's understanding he was able to take me step-by-step through the whole process. I dealt with hundreds of sudden deaths over the course of my career, the lessons learned from this one (the late Mr Eric Ector of Chesterton) helped me to do it properly, often pointlessly, every time.

In a nights week, John and I were turned out from parade to deal with a sudden death. After we'd sent the clearly redundant ambulance crew on their way we joined the family in the living room, with News at Ten showing on the TV. Seated to the side of it, looking through sightless eyes was the body of an elderly gentleman who'd passed away within the last hour. We started the paperwork, during which time Inspector Bills arrived. The Coroner preferred all sudden deaths to be visited by a senior officer whenever possible. The Inspector stood, cap under his arm, hands on hips glancing briefly at the news.

He looked over to the seated corpse.

'Strikes, eh? Where will it all end?' then,

'Okay PC Clowes, where's the body? I'll take a look and be on my way.'

'You've just been discussing the woes of British Leyland with him sir.'

The family saw the funny side - fortunately.

Bodies have to be identified. This is straightforward if relatives are present at the scene, just one line in a statement, but often there's nobody there and the body has to be identified at the mortuary. The Coroner insisted on this being done as soon as possible after death, and before him being informed; at times this could be very difficult and unnecessarily distressing. Mr Hails' word, however, was absolute. It was no problem in the daytime as the mortuary staff handled it.

However, if someone died at night, in the street, alone at home or say in a car crash, next of kin had to be traced, the news broken to them and the identification done. This would be done by us at the mortuary; bearing in mind that the person identifying the body as well as being shocked and distressed, is in a state of total disbelief.

More often than not, certainly in my case many times, it was the same lone Constable who'd delivered the message who had to go through the identification process.

Having driven them to the morgue (not wishing them to drive in their state of mind), I'd sit the bewildered person in the waiting room. Then into the fridge room where I'd:

- Locate the body.
- Open the fridge.
- Wheel the hydraulic trolley over to the fridge and pump it up to the level of the tray in the fridge.
- Pull the tray and corpse out of the fridge onto the trolley.
- Wheel the trolley over to the hatch leading into the identification room.
- Pump the trolley so that the tray and corpse are at the level of the hatch.
- Leave the room.
- Open the hatch from the other side.
- Pull the tray through onto the bier (pushing from the other side can result in the tray overshooting the bier and the corpse ending on the floor, as nearly happened to me once).
- Close the hatch.
- Lift the head of the deceased corpse onto a purple velvet pillow.
- Put a purple velvet sheet over corpse, making sure the tray and head block are not visible.

Out of breath, I'd then ask the relative through, show them the body, ask them to identify it and wait for their reaction. You had to be ready for anything here, from stunned silence to hysterical distress. Having done that, I'd then show them back to the waiting room while I did all the above again, in reverse. Out of breath again, I'd wash my hands, go back to the waiting room to take a statement, then drive them home.

Sometimes there were two of you to do this, but I did this alone, many times.

An elderly lady had been cooking on her gas stove whilst wearing the type of apron that's plastic-coated fabric so that it wipes clean. They're lethal and should have been banned long ago, her apron had caught light from the hob, and it rapidly took hold. She was taken to hospital with severe burns and died within hours. I established with gas engineers that there was no fault with the stove, and that it was entirely accidental. I had to visit her daughter in Middleport to complete the Form 12 the next day. She was obviously very shaken, so I was in 'super-sensitive' mode. There was one question which I'd been dreading to ask, so I deliberately left it until the very end – this was whether the family wanted burial or cremation. It's necessary as it involves different paperwork between the coroner, undertaker and local authority. As delicately as possible, I put it to her,

'I hate having to ask you in the circumstances, but will you be wanting your mother buried, or cremated, or haven't you decided yet?'

'Well, since she's done half the job herself, we may as well have her cremated', adding with a smile,

'I don't suppose we'll get a discount?'

One hot summer's Saturday afternoon a few years later, I was on my usual patch - the Bucknall and Bentilee Incident Response Vehicle (we didn't have pandas any longer, see Chapter 11). I was already tied up on a job, but over the radio I'd heard an incoming incident on my area; a man hadn't been seen for several days, and his milk hadn't been taken in - the usual ominous sign. Sergeant Mike 'Dixie' Dean had picked up a foot patrol from the city centre to deal with it.

Later, having finished my job I drove past; Dixie was outside and flagged me down.

'I *dare* you to go in there, Nick!'

I've always loved a challenge. The man lived in an upstairs flat of a two-storey block; the gas board (as it was then) had been called to the street several times in the past week to investigate the smell of a leak but had drawn a blank. The windows of the flat appeared completely black. Dixie and my other colleague had forced their way into the flat and found the man dead. That wasn't all though - do skip the next paragraph if you're of a delicate disposition.

Vick applied, I climbed the stairs to the flat, dense squadrons of thousands of flies buzzed past me, so densely packed that they were colliding en-masse with my face and clinging to my uniform, I had to hold my hand to my face to avoid breathing them in. The man lay half clothed on the floor of the hallway, decomposing rapidly in the summer heat. There were flies everywhere, his body was writhing from myriad fat maggots hatching and feeding on the putrid flesh. His scrotum had inflated with decomposing gases to the size of a rugby ball, flies were launching into flight from every orifice, it was surreal. The blackened windows were a result of tens, if not hundreds of thousands of flies standing on every available square millimetre of glass, trying to move towards the light. As for the smell, well, it's no wonder the neighbours had suspected a gas leak – my Vick lost the battle this time. I understand that the body completely disintegrated when the undertakers tried to remove it, I do not envy them that gruesome task one tiny bit.

Early turn, 9.30am, I was looking forward to my breakfast in half an hour's time when the same type of report came in, man not seen, milk on doorstep. I knew what to expect but really hoped that a less morbid explanation would present itself. After fruitless knocking, I looked through the letterbox, nothing to see, but tendrils of the unmistakeable smell of death drifted out. Out with the Vick again, boot to the front door and in I went. Tried to open the living room door, locked. Boot to the door again, nobody in the room. Tried the kitchen door, locked again. I began to wish I'd held off on the Vick until I actually found the body, I may have been able to find him more quickly and with a lot less effort. The man must have been extremely security conscious, every single internal door in the house was locked; I had to kick every one of them in, except one. Having kicked in the front door, three downstairs doors and two upstairs I found the man; in bed where he'd died in his sleep, maybe a couple of days before. I was exhausted.

A very late breakfast for me that day.

Another time, I was sent to an elderly person's bungalow. A transport ambulance had called to take the occupant to a hospital appointment but couldn't get any answer to the door. I didn't get the usual suspicion of death though, for one thing there were no bottles of milk on the step and no familiar odour through the letterbox. I decided not to kick the door in but knocked on a few nearby ones instead. A few minutes later I updated the Control Room with the result,

'Yes Kilo-alpha, the man is deceased.'

'Roger Three-Zero, do you have any details for the Coroner's Office.'

'No need, Kilo-alpha, the funeral was yesterday.'

The man had died in hospital and been buried. The ambulance service hadn't been updated.

One very difficult part of the job was delivering death messages. You had to be sympathetic, but very direct, leaving no room for doubt in the mind of the unfortunate recipient.

Whether it's true or not but knowing the officer being talked about it's extremely likely; one of my colleagues told me about a 'deathogram' when he was being tutored. They approached the front door of a house together to deliver the awful message, and when a lady answered the door his tutor simply said, 'Are you John Smith's widow?'

I didn't deliver messages like that.

Cheshire Police asked us to deliver one, a motorcyclist had been killed, and the bike was registered to an address in Chesterton. Cheshire provided us with a description of the rider, but the body was badly mangled, so the description was not particularly good.

I asked if I could come in and sat down with them.

'Does [whoever] live here?'

'Yes, he's our son.'

'Does he have a Honda motorbike registered number [whatever...].'

'Yes, I think that's it.'

Then, as best I could I asked for a description of their son.

'I'm very sorry to tell you, that motorbike has been involved in an accident in Cheshire and the rider was killed. The description you've given me would suggest it's your son.'

The stunned silence was followed by the mother wailing hysterically while her husband tried his best but failed to comfort her.

Then I heard a motorbike pull up at the back of the house, the back door opened and slammed shut.

'M-UUU-MM? What's for tea?', as their 'dead' son walked into the room, then,

'What's that copper doing here?'

He'd swapped the bike in Cheshire that afternoon, so our neighbouring force were given details. I took my leave of two stunned, bemused, confused but ultimately relieved parents and their resurrected son.

However, a young man's parents a few miles away were about to have their lives changed forever.

I went to a report of a man collapsed in Sneyd Green, dog sitting beside him, the ambulance crew were there but the man was clearly dead. The dog was friendly, I read the details on his collar (present just for once); the address was about seventy-five yards away around the corner. I went to the house and rang the bell. An elderly, but very spritely lady came to the door, she looked at me smiling with a radiance that took my breath away. It was heartbreaking to see that beautiful smile slowly dissolve as I gave her the news.

I attended many suicides, every single one a tragedy. They always affected me, even when I'd a good few years' service under my belt; uncovering the tragic circumstances leading to someone taking their life could be very painful.

One I particularly remember was an elderly lady in Clayton who had hanged herself. The family told me that she had lost her husband of many years some months previously but was coping fairly well, with their support. Earlier that day her much loved elderly dog had been put down after a terminal prognosis from the vet; it had completely broken her. It was heart-rending, I left with tears stinging my eyes, which began to flow as I drove away.

A particularly shocking (unintended pun alert) one was a lady who'd climbed into a warm bath and pulled a live electric fire into it with her. She'd guaranteed her intention by replacing the fuse with a nail in the consumer unit. Apart from the lady, it was all still live when I arrived, and the water appeared like soup. A fair percentage of her body must have gone down the plughole. Horrible.

There were many others.

A middle-aged woman who took an overdose after her husband, ironically the MD of a drugs wholesaler had left her for a younger woman.

A man facing serious criminal proceedings, unable to deal with the pressure and shame.

Some haunted by traumatic experiences.

Others who had lost their jobs and the means to support their family.

However, I quickly came to realise that anyone *threatening* to commit suicide was wasting our time, it was just attention seeking. They were clearly in need of mental health support but they, and the barely functional services supposedly available to them would cause the loss of an incredible number of hours of police time.
It's only recently that this situation, intolerable for many years, has begun to change.

Some with whom I worked seemed completely immune to death, either that or they hid their feelings unfathomably deep. Not me, if you become conditioned not to be affected by death, I think you've lost a big part of your humanity. Every single death I attended affected me in some way, although I still managed to remain sympathetic, practical and professional.

Out of the gaze of the public it really helped to have a sense of humour though.

10 - All Change

One thing I hadn't yet realised after only eight months in the job was how quickly things changed. I'd gained a completely false impression in this short time that our bosses had been in their posts for years, whereas it was often likely to have been for a few months, or as time went on, mere weeks.

September 1976 arrived with seismic changes at Newcastle, possibly precipitated by the fallout from the HMI's inspection. Chief Superintendent Harry Willett, Superintendent Syd Bills and Chief Inspector Tom Hall all retired. Superintendent Alf Mann was promoted to Chief Superintendent and took over as Divisional Commander. He was a completely different character, a quiet, thoughtful, very approachable man, with steely determination and a wealth of practical experience.

A retirement presentation was held for Mr Willett at the police club in Water Street. Attendance at such functions in those days was more or less compulsory for anyone who was off-duty. It fell to our new Divisional Commander to make the presentation in the crowded room. For all his positive qualities, Alf Mann was not a confident public speaker.

'Mr Willetts…', he began, getting his former boss's name wrong,

'…er, has a magnificent… er… record at all levels within the police force… er… he leaves the police force… er… owing it absolutely nothing.

'Er… the police force, in turn… er… owes him absolutely nothing.'

You could have heard a mouse break wind.

The retirements brought with them other moves. Superintendent Graham 'Cuddles' Wootton, (the nickname a reference to his teddy-bear like appearance, but certainly not to his nature) moved into Mr Mann's former office. Mick Bills had a well-deserved promotion to Chief Inspector, moving into the office formerly occupied by the soon to be late Tommy Hall. Chief Inspector Elwyn Evans from another division, a universally disliked, thoroughly odious, devious Welshman, was promoted to replace the retiring Syd Bills. If Arthur Rees had one fault, it was that he showed great favour to anyone in the force from his own nation, particularly if they played rugby.

The most significant move for myself and the rest of the shift was that on a Saturday we'd worked an early shift with Sergeant Norman as Station Sergeant. The following Monday we were on nights, Sergeant Rotchell was now Station Sergeant, and our new shift Inspector was, Inspector... Norman, promoted a few hours previously. This was highly unusual, promotion usually involved a transfer to another Division; remaining at the same station, let alone the same shift was unprecedented. It wasn't a popular move with us, particularly with Barry Rotchell whose former shift partner was now his boss; they'd never got on particularly well in the first place.

Our patrol Sergeant was newly promoted from the Drugs Squad, Melvyn Cartwright, who sadly passed away a few days before I started to write this chapter; he was probably the best Sergeant I ever had. He had no airs and graces about him, insisted on being addressed as 'Mel' and had his finger on the pulse of what was going on everywhere during every minute of the shift. As far as he was concerned, I was now a regular panda patrol, and the times I had to pound the town centre streets were now quite rare.

In all fairness, Bill Norman showed himself to be a very competent Inspector, fitting quite quickly into his new role. Our new Inspector was also a Captain in the Territorial Army and seemed very fond of showing himself off in both his police and TA uniforms, with frequent changes from one to the other.

A town centre patrol came in for his meal-break one day and related a conversation they'd just had with one of the Inspector's neighbours. Apparently they had a nickname for him - *Action Man.*

More death. First job for me that night was another one, in a Ford Cortina parked in a quiet country lane on the edge of Clayton. On my arrival, there was an ambulance present but far too late to be of any use. With them was a woman, mid-forties, in a state of hysteria, and somewhat dishevelled. Lying on the reclined passenger seat of the car was the body of a man in his fifties wearing nothing but an open, unbuttoned shirt and a frozen, rictus grin.

Asking the lady what had happened was like pulling teeth. They were married, but not to each other, they were next door neighbours and had been meeting like this for some months. They had arrived here about an hour previously. After undressing he had lain down on the passenger seat and she had climbed aboard. At some point during the next five minutes there'd been a premature expiration.

CID, Scenes of Crime and a photographer attended, although foul play was quickly ruled out. While this circus was about its business, Action Man and Chief Inspector Bills arrived. I greeted Mr Bills with a salute, as required for anyone of his new rank and above, congratulating him on his promotion, he looked embarrassed,

'No need for that Tommy, thanks, but please don't salute me again, ever!'

There are some people who were changed by promotion - not him. The two senior officers moved to a quieter part of the scene, engaging in conversation for a long time, probably Mr Bills passing on some of his wisdom. Our new Chief Inspector left big shoes to be filled and although Bill Norman excelled at his job, he never quite matched his predecessor.

The ambulance crew removed the body from the car to take the man to the mortuary, I was to collect the key from the police station and supervise the arrival. Having helped them put the body in one of the fridges I then had to inform his family and arrange the identification – exactly as detailed in the previous chapter.

By now it was after midnight. An address had been found for the man's son; we thought it may be better to inform him rather than the wife, who may be alone.

This was the first time I'd delivered a death message; not something that had cropped up while being tutored, and I was completely on my own. After several knocks at the door, an upstairs window opened and a young man, a few years older than myself looked out at me. Having persuaded him to open the door and let me in, I asked him if we could sit down.

'Does your father have a Ford Cortina?'

'Yes' (this answer could have applied at the time to any of several million people)

'Do you know the registered number?', the number he gave matched the one on my pad.

I already knew that the best way to deliver these messages was in the most direct, unambiguous way possible.

'I'm sorry to say that we've found a man's body in that car earlier this evening. I believe it's your father; he's dead.'

I've done this time and time again since. Reactions range from hysteria to quiet disbelief. This time it was the latter.

'How, wh… I mean what's happened?'

'We found him in a lane in Clayton a couple of hours ago, the ambulance was called but they couldn't do anything for him.'

'If it was down a country lane, who called the ambulance?'

There was an edge to his voice which put me on my guard.

'His passenger in the car', was the best I could manage.

'Who was that?' His voice was rising steadily. I made a show of consulting my pad as I considered the next, difficult reply. I named the woman, adding,

'...I believe she lives next door?'

I was expecting a torrent of rage, but instead an uneasy calm followed. He didn't ask any more questions, but I could see that he'd worked it out for himself.

I explained the need to identify the body, offering him a lift to the mortuary which he declined, saying that he and his wife would follow in their car, and he'd visit his mother afterwards.

At the mortuary, having gone through the exhausting procedure outlined earlier, I arranged the grinning body in the identification room then, out of breath, I fetched the son through. He solemnly looked at the body and said that it was indeed his father. I noted the tension in him, suddenly he exploded with rage, pummelling his father's corpse, yelling,

'You fucking bastard, I fucking knew it! Shagging that tart! How could you do this to Mum?'

I had to drag him off.

In the days when we attended every Fire Brigade callout, I followed them to a report of a flat fire. There was smoke billowing out of the windows, firemen in breathing apparatus were in the process of rescuing the elderly lady from inside. She quickly recovered, sitting on a bench outside. She'd been making her morning toast under the grill and gone to the loo. As number one was unexpectedly joined by number two, she'd taken longer than expected. Her toast had caught fire, with added fuel from the pool of bacon fat underneath. As soon as the pan was pulled out, put in the sink and all the windows opened, the smoke cleared quickly and there was no damage. As I held open the door for her to go back inside, she turned to me and the firemen,

"'Have you all had your breakfast? Does anyone want some toast?'

I was sent to keep the peace at an eviction from a council house in Chesterton, the family having accrued serious rent arrears.

The family left the house without fuss or protest and the bailiffs stepped in to change the locks - I wasn't needed.

Councils have a statutory duty to find housing for homeless people. The evictees went to the Civic Offices in Newcastle, presenting themselves as homeless. Fortunately, a property in Chesterton had fallen vacant that very morning. The paperwork was signed, and they were handed the keys.

Within three hours of being made homeless, the family were back in the house from which they'd been evicted, with new locks, and their rent arrears written off.

It was a common occurrence. What a pointless waste of time and money.

I quickly tired of my Mini, and at the end of July splashed out on a five-year-old, very low mileage Austin Healey Sprite. I loved it and even now I still remember it as the most enjoyable car I ever owned. It was ideal for the summer of 1976; I'd spent all the time since buying it with the roof down. The summer had been stiflingly hot with drought conditions and people were having to use standpipes for their water in some areas.

By September the whole country craved the first signs of rain; one evening in Stafford it arrived in torrents. I stood in the back garden, soaked to the skin but enjoying every cool, refreshing drop of rain that fell on me. Then I remembered my car was in the drive at the front, top down. I dashed around to see the footwells filling up with water. Hastily putting the roof up I knew I had work to do the next morning. A new carpet set was sourced from a scrapyard a few weeks later when the musty smell of rotting pile became unbearable. This was probably why one of the rear springs entered the passenger compartment uninvited the following year, needing some expensive welding.

The next morning, before going on noons I had to bail out my car. Newcastle was still awaiting its share of rain, which arrived immediately on us turning out on patrol. A long spell of dry weather leaves tyre residue on the road, this had been a *very* long spell so there was a *lot* of tyre residue. When rain arrives, it mixes with the residue to form a very slippery surface - none more slippery than road leading from Brampton downhill along Queen Street to Nelson Place in the centre of Newcastle. A driver coming down the hill had braked for the roundabout; the wheels had locked, and the sliding car came to rest embedded in the roundabout. The following traffic braked with similar results, each car crashing into the rear of the one in front. Eventually around twenty cars had crashed forming a long concertina, fortunately without any injuries. The tarmac was incredibly slippery, just like ice, it was difficult to stand up, let alone walk. While a couple of us started taking details, the rest were frantically flagging down all the traffic coming downhill, until the long overdue arrival of the council two hours later to put sand on the road.

Over the next few months, we adjusted well to the new leadership of our team, although Inspector Norman faced a difficult challenge with one of our colleagues becoming derailed by his domestic situation. The first sign of this was when, normally a calm and easy-going guy, he openly and very aggressively argued with the Inspector on our afternoon shift parade. The rest of us were astounded as it went completely against the disciplined regime; it's certain that words were exchanged in the office afterwards.

The circumstances soon emerged, Mick was married to one of identical twin sisters and having an affair with the other. A few days after the incident on parade, his wife had found out, Mick had gone missing and was due on nights. A missing police officer was cause for great concern, both for their welfare and the possibility of unwanted attention from the media. By the time we arrived for the night shift, our Inspector had been in the building for several hours, trying valiantly with the Chief Inspector to resolve the crisis. In an unusual but completely understandable agitated state, he had the twins in his office, trying to gain clues as to where to begin to look.

No parade took place that night, Mick Bills told us to get out on the patch and use every means possible to find Mick, and to keep the matter strictly to ourselves. We found him a few hours later in a deserted area, safe and well, but very distraught. We didn't see him again for a couple of weeks, he'd obviously been given time to sort himself out.

Apart from ourselves, it seems only Mr Bills and our Inspector had known of this, and successfully kept a lid on something that could have spiralled out of control, true leadership.

It was all in vain though. Unbeknown to anyone Mick's escapades continued and a few months later he made it onto page three of the Daily Mail under the headline 'The Panda Romeo.' He subsequently left both the job and the twins, settling down with a young lady from the typing pool, becoming manager at the local McDonald's and later a DIY superstore. Bill Norman was acutely embarrassed by the whole thing, I think quite needlessly.

As John Gimbert was to put it, *'A standing cock has no conscience.'*

The arrival of Superintendent Evans had been very unpopular. My first face-to-face meeting was for my nine-month staff appraisal. It was not so much an appraisal as a bollocking. Those who knew him had recommended that I stand up to him firmly or he would walk all over me. As it happened, I was starting to get braver and more confident – I don't think I'd have survived the ensuing intimidation with fewer months' service.

In his mocking Welsh lilt, without any reference to why I was there he started,

'You've had a good education son, but it counts for nothing with me. You think you're so clever don't you? Well you're not as clever as me! You'll soon find that out! It's what you do out there, not passing exams that matters.'

'Excuse me sir, does it say on there that I'm not up to scratch?'

'No, it says you're doing well, but…'

'So, you don't know me, you're just trying to intimidate me. I know my Sergeant and Inspector are very positive about me.'

'Just watch it boy, I've got my eye on you, and I don't like what I see. You've not heard the last of me.'

That was my appraisal. I didn't know what he wrote, and I hadn't signed it. I didn't care. On my way out, Mick Bills was just stepping out of his office, he looked at me and quickly ushered me in. He closed the door.

'What did that bastard want Tommy?'

Taken aback, I told him.

'Take no notice, he's as thick as pig shit. Just doesn't like anyone with a brain 'cos he hasn't got one of his own. We've just got to treat him like a mushroom.'

'Sorry sir?' I hadn't heard the expression before.

'Keep him in the dark and feed him on bullshit', he guffawed, slapped me on the back and I joined in.

'It's alright for you Tommy, you only see him sometimes, I have to deal with the twat every bloody day.'

He tapped the side of his nose twice. I was stunned that a Chief Inspector would speak like this about a Superintendent to a probationer of a few months' service. He hated the man even more than the rest of us put together and had good cause.

The first anniversary of my appointment came, and in January 1977 I was at Headquarters for the second of three probationers' courses. Our instructor for the course was a newly promoted Sergeant with a very high opinion of himself, with an equally low opinion of everybody else, which matched what everybody's opinion of him was. After introductions he looked around and said to us all,

'I notice that you're all looking a lot less smart than last time you were here.'

'Last time we were here, you were driving a panda around Cannock Sarge', one of the lads quipped.

He was less cocky after that, he made his way to Chief Inspector, remaining thoroughly obnoxious throughout his entire service.

One evening I was sent to an incident in Cross Heath where the driver of a heavy breakdown truck had crashed into a wall, he was collapsed over the wheel. I climbed and opened the driver's door, having to move quickly to prevent him from falling to the road. He absolutely reeked of booze, although obviously very drunk he was very cooperative. Having somehow managed to seat him the car I tried to breathalyse him, but he was too drunk to blow at all and so I arrested him. He was agreeable and friendly throughout at the station, providing a blood sample to our somewhat less inebriated police surgeon.

As I was showing him out of the station we were met in the corridor by Inspector Norman. Wanting to display his newly promoted status of being 'in charge' he asked the man if he was happy about how he had been treated. We'd already explained what would happen next, but our leader took it upon himself to tell him again. I've previously mentioned his slight speech difficulty, this time it was side-splitting.

'*Your bwood sample will be anawysed at the West Mid wands Fowesnic Science wabowatwy in Birmingham. We will get a weport back fwom them saying whether you had more than the wegal wimit of eighty miwigwams of alcowol in a hundwed miwiwetres of bwood. You've been pwowided with a bwood sample of your own which you can have anawysed at a pubwic wabowatwy if you wish.*'

I was chewing through my tongue, and the guy just listened to this, dumbstruck. As we descended the station steps he turned to me,

'Bwoody hell, was that Elmer Fudd?'

I came across the guy frequently after that. We got on well, despite him having lost his driving licence - the *weport* having stated that his *bwood* had two-hundred-and-fifty-six *miwigwams* of *alcowol*, against the *wegal wimit* of 80.

On a freezing cold night in the winter of 1977/8 one of the panda patrols was turned out off night shift parade to an emergency. As he roared out of the police station yard, he hit a patch of ice and collided with a car parked across the road, causing extensive damage to both cars. He had to fill in two insurance claims. The first was for the police car (Form 85, a dreaded one which nobody wanted to ever have to complete), the second was for his own car - with which he had collided. A couple of weeks later he left the shift to join Traffic Division, to which I had an eagerly awaited two-week attachment in the spring

I definitely had a preference for traffic policing, I was on the lookout for traffic offences all the time and hoped to get behind the wheel of a 'jam-sandwich' one day. I've always had a great interest in cars and was looking forward to a fortnight of riding in a patrol car, dealing with dodgy looking cars and bad driving. However, I never had the opportunity to submit a single offence report, and we only stopped a handful of vehicles. Most of the time was taken up with going to various wholesalers to purchase DIY kit with the readily available discount provided by a uniform; as well as assisting a colleague on annual leave with some home decorating. As a young PC I was hardly in a position to protest.

'Never let your work get in the way of your shopping', they would say, and I ended the attachment feeling quite disappointed. I did learn where to get reasonably priced, decent quality hardware but can say quite honestly that I never indulged in the dubious practice of 'shopping in uniform.'

Of much greater benefit a few weeks later was a five-week attachment to CID. My mentor for this was DC Roy Ashley, a very capable detective, one of the most experienced in the force, and a natural teacher. Nearly all the practical policing skills that I needed during my career were learned from him; it was by far the most useful five weeks of my probation. A former guardsman, he was a giant of a man, well over six feet tall and built like the proverbial brick outbuilding.

I already knew Roy quite well; he had been with our shift a few times as the lone night CID officer and was well liked and respected by all. After you'd stitched him up in the ever-present dominoes game, he'd say in his North Staffordshire dialect,

'There's three kinds of turd. There's cus-turd, there's mus-turd and there's you, you big shit!'

We were on a 9am to 5pm day shift. After Roy had found me a desk, he answered the phone. It was the Chief Superintendent, he'd had a call from a local magistrate reporting that he'd had a stone birdbath stolen from his garden. Any other member of the public would have spoken to the front office. The Divisional Commander, quite wrongly in my view, had decided that this merited a visit from the CID rather than a patrolling Constable. There was little to no chance of catching the opportunist offender, and Roy wasn't one to waste time. A statement was required from all victims of crime in those days; had I taken it, it would probably have extended to two or three paragraphs including when last seen, description and anything else I could think of. The statement Roy quickly wrote out simply read,

'At some time between 8pm yesterday and 8am today an unknown person has taken a stone birdbath worth £50 from my front garden. Nobody had permission to take it.'

Having obtained signatures and offered platitudes we were on our way back to the station. I asked Roy why the statement was so brief.

'Tommy, perhaps nobody's told you that a 95D (statement form) is writing down what someone is going to say in court. If it doesn't go to court, then it's a waste of time, ink and paper. It's very unlikely, but if this ever goes to court we can come back and get some more details.'

He was right, nobody had told me. Nevertheless, the practice of obtaining statements from all victims of crime, regardless of the possible outcome, continued for many years afterwards. Another colossal waste of time and paper.

The area for which Roy had particular responsibility was Chesterton, where I'd been on election duty the previous year and had done a fair amount of panda patrol since. It was a small town in itself, just under three miles northwest of the station. There was a mix of private and council housing, as well as houses owned by the National Coal Board occupied by miners from local collieries.

The council and NCB housing stood uneasily together on the Crackley estate, a couple of square miles of horribleness, which I say without prejudice as my own daughter lived there for a time in later, rather better days. The local council would house its problem tenants there en-masse, many of whom were feckless, unemployed, and unemployable. They were understandably resented by the hard-working colliers with the misfortune to be their neighbours. Bitter disputes between them were commonplace, as I'd already found out. This one estate and its population accounted for a sizeable proportion of the Division's crime statistics. As one of my Superintendents would remark a couple of years later, Crackley was an indictment on society.

Over the next few days, we visited the scenes of several burglaries in Chesterton, centred on Crackley. For these, Roy was taking his time, taking detailed statements and encouraging me to do the same. When I queried this he just said,
'We'll clear these up Tommy, might take a week or two but you'll see.'
By the end of the week, we had probably a dozen burglaries and assorted other thefts in the area to investigate. Roy seemed optimistic but was giving nothing away.
We went into a pub in the middle of the estate one lunchtime; the locals recognised Roy, and silence fell over the twenty or so people in the bar. Roy simply boomed out,
'As you were lads, we've not come for anyone', hushed conversation slowly resumed.
As we stood at the bar ordering drinks, a lanky young man with long, black, greasy hair and a thin moustache sidled over to us. He seemed familiar and looked at me with a hint of recognition, he turned to Roy.
'Hello Mr Ashley.'
'Ay-up Dennis, are you alright?'
'Yes thanks', he looked at me quizzically - a memory stirred. Roy said,
'This is Mr Tucker; we're working together for a bit.'

'Yeah I know, you took me to court in Kidsgrove last year.'

Now I remembered the 'master criminal' who'd been relieved of £5 by the magistrates.

'How's tricks Dennis, still living with your Mum?' asked Roy.

'Yeah, and that little shit of a brother of mine, I know I'm a bad lad Mr Ashley but bloody hell, he's much worse than me, you need to keep an eye on him.'

'What's he up to Dennis?'

'You name it, burgling, damage, robbin', nickin' from shops, everythin' and he's only twelve, he's bang at it, you need to stop him'

Perhaps Roy's optimism was well founded.

Maybe Dennis wouldn't have opened up to us so willingly if he hadn't been treated well last year, my colleague's advice had been good.

As we got back into the car, I eagerly asked,

'What do we do Roy, go and arrest him?'

'On the word of his toe-rag brother? No Tommy, we know who it is, but we've still got to put him there.'

Next morning as soon as we got into the office Roy said we were going out. Off we went in the van to Crackley.

'What are we doing Roy?'

'Looking for kids bobbing school.'

I looked at him curiously as he continued,

'Kids bobbing school are never up to any good, we might find out something.'

After half an hour or so of driving around we saw half a dozen boys about twelve years old, hanging around a block of derelict, graffiti covered garages. As we got out of the van they began to scatter, Roy called out reassuringly,

'It's alright lads, nobody's in any trouble, just want a chat.'

As the scattering subsided, we went and talked to them. Two of them were smoking,

'Where are the fags from lads?'

They remained silent and looked at the ground.

'They're nicked aren't they!'

After a brief interlude, where only the shuffling of feet could be heard, there was some nodding of heads. We started to look around the garage and found six packets of Players No 6 behind a cupboard.

'*We* didn't nick 'em', protested one of the lads.

'Who did then?'

'Lyndon, he had them from Birchhouse shops.'

Lyndon was the name we were hoping to hear. Result!

After checking their details, we sent them on their way, I don't think it was the way to school though. We'd later see them with their parents and obtain witness statements, all naming Lyndon as a thief.

We never arrested the twelve-year old Lyndon but interviewed him at home in the presence of his brassy, harassed single mother who had no control over him at all. He admitted to every burglary we'd been to and a good many more thefts particularly from the local shops, which had never been reported. We'd be putting through a report to the Juvenile Liaison Committee, they would decide whether Lyndon should be cautioned or put before the Juvenile Court. Over the next few weeks, we went to yet more burglaries on the estate which were clearly this lad's work even after we had caught him. Putting together the report for the JLC was like painting the Forth Bridge, as the list of charges lengthened daily; all of which Lyndon freely admitted without a shred of remorse.

The decision was taken to put him before the court. The magistrates put him into care, when sentenced he burst into tears; the first time he'd shown any regret at all, but only because he had been caught. He and his older brother Dennis still featured regularly in the court reports of the local press for years afterwards. Dennis, who fed me a good few snippets of useful information during the rest of my time at Newcastle has since died.

The big changes of the previous September had included the appointment of a new Deputy Chief Constable who would go on to be the next Chief Constable. Wanting to make his mark, one of his first actions was to establish the Force Support Unit (FSU), a select group of about twenty highly trained officers who could be deployed where reinforcements were needed, or just to assist Divisions on particularly busy shifts, usually at weekends.

One of their first appearances was at a Stoke City home match where they were proudly marched out onto the pitch as a display of strength in view of thousands of fans. They went on to be renamed the 'Tactical Support Group' but became universally referred to as *'The Muppets'* after the reaction of the football crowd.

They acquired a dubious reputation for turning up unannounced at high-spirited, but otherwise innocuous night-time revelry, sowing the seeds of mayhem and quickly disappearing to initiate havoc elsewhere.

One Saturday morning Roy and I were 'early' CID, coming on duty at 8am and responsible for dealing with overnight arrests. The only person in the cells was a young man of nineteen. He'd been arrested by a member of the FSU, who'd clearly lived up to their reputation a few hours earlier. There was no statement of arrest, no account of the circumstances, and nothing on the charge sheet giving the slightest clue as to why he had been arrested. Phone calls to the FSU's office went unanswered, so it was impossible to contact the arresting officer. The lad had sobered up and was nursing a hangover but was polite and cooperative.

The Station Sergeant insisted that we interview him, even though the obvious course of action was to send him on his way, due to lack of a scrap of evidence of anything at all.

Roy started the interview by asking him why he 'thought he had been arrested', the lad admitted that he had been drunk, and his behaviour was probably quite disorderly, but couldn't remember very much else. Without any account to hand, we couldn't help him to elaborate, it was a hopeless situation, and we had plenty more pressing things to deal with. Having decided to end matters there and then, Roy asked him quite innocuously, expecting a shrug, or a 'No',

'Is there anything else you want to tell us about?'

Suddenly the youth opened up to us and candidly admitted that for months he'd been stealing cash from his parents, in amounts that wouldn't be noticed but adding up to a substantial total. Instead of showing him the door, we returned him to his cell and visited his home.

His well-heeled parents conceded that they had missed small sums of cash but had put it down to forgetfulness. They were quite shocked by the situation and were more than happy for us to 'teach him a sharp lesson', as they put it.

That 'lesson' was very sharp indeed. On returning to the station, we charged their son with the theft of an unspecified amount of cash. At court he pleaded guilty. We were expecting a conditional discharge or probation as he had no criminal record. The presiding magistrate pronounced gravely,

'Exodus, chapter twenty, the Ten Commandments, 'Honour thy Father and Mother', three months imprisonment.'

We were expecting the word *suspended* to follow, but it didn't. We were as shocked as the young man, who a few weeks previously we'd wanted to release without charge. Three months meant three months in 1977, with maybe just a couple of weeks off for good behaviour. The stunned parents looked across at me and Roy angrily, as if it was all our doing.

To cap it all, the previously very cooperative young man made an official complaint that I'd assaulted him when I arrested him, although I'd done neither. My protests to Discipline and Complaints (the department's initials rarely used due to similarity to a gynaecological procedure) fell on deaf ears. I was served with the official forms and officially, officiously investigated, despite having officially been off duty when the incident happened. I made an official statement that I was in bed at the time and was officially told a few months (this was quick, sometimes it could be years) later that the complaint had been officially withdrawn. The Muppet who had officially arrested him, for whatever reason in the first place knew nothing of all this, although I later unofficially 'discussed' it with him.

The summer of 1977 was almost as hot as the previous one. Late shifts in CID always ended up with a tour of the town's pubs not, as some would imagine, a pub crawl but a hunt for information. One Saturday evening Roy was off, so I was paired with a wonderful guy, Detective Sergeant Wesley Fry, outwardly a down to earth, canny Irishman, but possessed of a towering intellect and very well read. He held a Master's Certificate and could have captained an ocean liner.

It was stiflingly hot, so I was eagerly looking forward to sinking a few pints of bitter to slake my thirst. The office was busy, so it was after nine o'clock when we eventually ventured onto the town and into the Super Star Inn. At the bar, Wes took his wallet out of his pocket,

'What's yours Tommy, bitter?' I nodded enthusiastically, the first one wasn't going to touch the sides.

'Two halves of bitter please landlord', chirped Wes.
WHAT? HALVES?

I needed more than this, I sank the half pint in virtually one swallow and Wes did the same, my round next, then Wes's and they followed in rapid succession. I learned a big lesson that night, halves go down much more quickly, so it's far easier to get drunk on them. I got my head down in a side office in CID for the night, ready to start a day shift on the Sunday morning, thankfully I had toiletries and a change of shirt in my locker. I've never drunk half pints since.

During the first week of nights in uniform after my CID attachment, I was sent to an incident in Chesterton where a young man had smashed an earthenware mug into his girlfriend's face during an argument, causing life-changing injuries. I obtained a very brief statement from her naming her boyfriend as the offender before she was loaded into the ambulance, leaving my statement form streaked with her blood. As luck would have it, Roy was the night CID officer and joined me.

'Let's go get him Tommy.'

We knew where he lived, and the lad drunkenly but quietly submitted to us. I told him that he was under arrest for causing grievous bodily harm with intent. This is known as a Section 18 assault, wounding with intent - the next most serious charge to murder. On arriving at the station, he asked to see his solicitor.

'Who's your solicitor?' asked Roy.

'Barrington Black', said our prisoner cockily, naming the celebrity lawyer of the day. Roy laughed loudly.

'Sonny, d' y' think Mr Black's going to drive his Jensen Interceptor all the way from Bradford at nine miles t' t' gallon for a little toe-rag he's never heard of who beats pretty girls up?'

As the youth was in drink, Roy and I arranged to return the following afternoon, to interview him when sober and prepare a file for the remand court. So, I was back in CID for the remainder of the week following this up with a file for the Crown Court, my most serious case to date. The Crown Court judge sent him to prison for a good while after he'd pleaded guilty.

From then on I spent a great deal of my 'in-station' time in the CID office, thinking that maybe a career there could beckon after the end of my probation. Roy and Wesley continued to helpfully feed the odd detectable case to me, which all went to enhance my personal standing; they both had my back for a long time afterwards.

In the same year, the late Queen's Silver Jubilee coincided with the annual Newcastle Carnival. By way of celebration, pubs could stay open from noon to midnight across the nation, extremely liberal for the time. Over the years it's become clear to me that the Great British Public are completely incapable of drinking responsibly, and this occasion amply demonstrated it. We were on night shift, a very hot and humid one. Unusually, we turned out in shirt-sleeves for the first half of the shift. Being a Monday night and not the weekend, the inflexible system dictated that we all patrolled alone - I was given a town centre beat. As I made my way through Ironmarket into the High Street I'd never seen Newcastle so full of people, even on market days. Not ordinary people out shopping, but a sweaty, uproariously drunken mass, many of whom had been drinking continuously for almost twelve hours.

A noisy group was walking towards me, clearly students from nearby Keele University, led by a very well-built young man, drinking from a pint-pot. I should probably have turned a blind eye but instead I asked him,

'Where've you had that glass from?'

'What's it to you boyo?' came the loud reply in a heavy Welsh accent.

'I'm arresting you on suspicion of stealing it, you do not have to…'

He threw the glass to the ground.

'Well, there's your evidence gone isn't it, boyo?' as it smashed into dozens of pieces.

He then pushed hard at my chest, I fell to the ground, taking him with me as I grabbed his arm. In the ensuing scuffle I managed to pull my truncheon from my pocket and struck him hard on his leg, the one and only time that I ever used it, just as assistance from two colleagues arrived from around the corner.

That was the first time I'd been assaulted on duty, but it wouldn't be the last. Assaults on police were viewed very seriously (as they still should be) by the courts in those days, and the student missed three months of his course - probably the rest of it for all I cared - whilst serving a prison sentence.

My second encounter with the complaints system came a few weeks later in the summer. A motorist had taken umbrage at a perfectly legitimate, legal overtaking manoeuvre I'd performed on the newly constructed Newcastle ring-road while driving to work. His assertion was that I'd overtaken on a pedestrian crossing, which I hadn't – there'd been a crossing there in the past, but it had been removed during improvements. He followed me to a nearby car park and a verbal 'altercation' developed and I walked off telling him to *go away*. I was in plain clothes that day, so nothing identified me as a police officer.

However, a few minutes later he presented himself at the police station counter to report a case of dangerous driving. The idiot behind the counter let slip that I was a police officer, so it became an official complaint against me. It was passed to a Sergeant to deal with, even though I'd done nothing wrong. Later that morning I was summoned to Elwyn Evans' office, he was bursting with glee as he served me with a Notice of Intended Prosecution, which I tore into eight pieces and walked out. He hated me, but I hated this vile man even more.

It would have been perfectly simple for the Sergeant to have visited the scene with the fool making the complaint, point out to him that there was no crossing there and send him on his way, but this wasn't the way the job worked. It would be nearly Christmas, and two interviews with a Chief Superintendent later before I was told that the complaint was unsubstantiated. It could, and should have been dealt with in minutes, not months.

Not long before my arrival at Newcastle, there had been a Sergeant on the shift, who for the purpose of this book will be named Falcon B'Stard. He was continually oppressive and abusive to the Constables and seemed to derive a great deal of satisfaction from exceeding his authority. After several months of this, in sheer desperation the whole shift had taken the unprecedented, highly risky step of adding their signatures to a report officially complaining about his conduct, citing the very many instances where it had become impossible to work under him. He'd been hauled before the Chief Constable, given a dressing down (after the HMI furore, I can imagine the scale of this), told that a huge mistake had been made when he was promoted to Sergeant and that he would never be allowed to be in charge of people again. He'd then been shunted sideways to a role in Courts Office where it was believed he could do no harm.

This was unknown to me until Bill Norman went to attend a three-month long course at Bramshill. In his absence we were to have an Acting Inspector, and it was to be none other than B'Stard - so much for the Chief Constable's promise. The whole team were outraged, but powerless.

For three months this Falcon B'Stard made my life an absolute misery, as well as everyone else's. Meanwhile Mel Cartwright, who'd become my rock was transferred away from the shift and replaced by another newly promoted Sergeant, Ian Holding, formerly a DC in our CID. He'd been selected for the Special Course at Bramshill starting the next January, following which he'd rise rapidly through the ranks, eventually becoming Deputy Chief Constable of Cheshire. I know from later experience that it's a difficult transition to be promoted amongst people you have previously worked with, and you have to be rather more firm than usual.

Therefore, we were burdened with a relentless bully of an Inspector and, by necessity, an authoritarian Sergeant; a complete change of mood from the nurturing, gently encouraging (discounting the hateful Welshman in the boss's office) environment in which I'd been learning my job. Every day B'Stard would take issue with over something I'd done, whether it be the way I'd dealt with an incident, or a mistake in some paperwork; he'd bellow at me,

'You want *stuffing* with a ragman's *trumpet*!'
Then,
'If you want to STAY in this job you've got to....'

I actually wondered if I did want to stay in the job, it was a very long three months, many were the days when I dreaded, rather than looked forward to going to work.

I was pressed into giving him a lift home at the end of a night shift once, which took me a couple of miles out of my way, but even then I had to endure yet more of his harping criticism.

As well as the incidents we dealt with, we were allocated outside enquiries – obtaining statements or performing interviews on behalf of other stations or forces. One of mine was proving difficult, every time I called there was a big, smelly snarling dog in the front garden; despite shouting 'Hello?' several times I'd been unable to attract anyone's attention. Like many people at the time, they weren't on the phone, so I couldn't make arrangements to see them. B'Stard was giving me plenty of grief over this, threatening all sorts if I didn't get it done. On my umpteenth visit the dog was still there. I shouted, no reply. In desperation I took my truncheon from my pocket and aimed it at the front door. It 'knocked' on the door with full force and then bounced off, the dog tried to catch it, but the heavy lignum staff hit it on the head.

The door opened - finally! The man I was to interview stood at the door, eyes switching between me, my truncheon on the garden path and his whimpering dog, Fortunately, he was a decent bloke who sympathised with my predicament; the enquiry was duly done and B'Stard's temper temporarily abated, while he searched for something else to harangue me with.

In September 1977 Arthur Rees retired. Predictably, given the favour he showed to his compatriots, one of his final acts was to promote any Welsh (and particularly rugby playing) members of the force who were qualified for advancement. Sometimes this was regardless of actual ability.

The Deputy Chief Constable took his place, as had always been the intention.

Around the same time, I returned to Ryton for a fortnight's Continuation Course. I'd been looking forward to it, an opportunity to catch up with some of the friends I'd made the previous year. I would be disappointed, not a single one of them was there and I was the only Staffordshire officer present. I'd taken time to bring my uniform up to scratch, bulled my boots and had my hair cut shorter than it had been for a long time. The first morning, we formed up as a squad outside the classroom and marched to the parade square. I was expecting to see the imposing figure of Sergeant Trickett, but he'd been replaced by the equally smart Sergeant Roger Wood, a thoroughly nice guy. He met us at the edge of the square, called us to halt and then in a loud, conspiratorial whisper,

'Piss off you lot, about turn, just go and hide, don't want to see you here again, got it?'

We got it, who were we to argue with the drill Sergeant? The course was a complete waste of time, all we did was sit around all day exchanging experiences, with a very laid-back Sergeant instructor whose interest in teaching us seemed to match our disinterest in learning. He probably enjoyed the time away from the parrot fashion teaching of new recruits. That's not to say that I didn't enjoy the course, a fortnight's break from the eyes of B'Stard and Elwyn Evans was extremely welcome, as well as lots of fun and laughter on the way.

The team heaved a collective sigh of relief as we welcomed our Inspector back from his course in the autumn. It would not, however be the last time I had dealings with B'Stard, who on the strength of his stint of acting Inspector, was promoted a few months later by the new Chief Constable and transferred to Hanley to perfect his bullying.

By November and nearing the end of my probation I'd decided that although I enjoyed working at Newcastle, my heart wasn't in it. My lack of local knowledge, and lack of connection to the area put me at a serious disadvantage; this would continue for a long time to come. The travelling costs were also a burden. Therefore, I decided to put pen to paper and request a transfer to Stafford, my home of twenty-two years. Although my bosses at Newcastle supported the move, the request bounced back at lightning speed from the desk of ACC Shepherd, stating that as my father was a senior County Council officer my presence in Stafford could lead to a conflict of interest. Ridiculous, as well as bullshit, but in those days an ACC's word was never to be challenged.

A few weeks later I stood to attention before the same man for the confirmation of my appointment, removal of my probationary status and a substantial pay rise. It was a formality as any unsuitable probationers were weeded out long before they reached the important two-year point.

I'd learned from various encounters with the ACC that he showed more respect for you if you stood up to him.

'Mr Tucker, tell me, why I should confirm your appointment?'

'That's a matter for you sir. You have all the reports in front of you recommending that you should.'

'Yes, but why do *you* think I should?'

I recalled the words of Noddy, my friend who'd had stood here twelve months earlier in the same situation.

'Because I'm good sir.'

This was the kind of boldness that he liked to see. A long pause as he made a show of looking through my file.

'Y-e-s, Mr Tucker, I *will* confirm your appointment. However, let me make it clear that for as long as I sit behind this desk, you will never, *ever* work at Stafford.'

'Thank you, sir, but you won't be behind that desk for *ever* will you?'

I thought I'd gone too far this time, but his stern look slowly dissolved into a tight-lipped smile.

'Time you got back to *Newcastle* I think. Dismissed.'

That was it, at last I was a fully-fledged Police Constable with a big pay rise.

Learning never ends though, it never should, I still only knew the basics.

11 – Planning Change

A few days into 1978 I was unexpectedly summoned to see Cuddles Wootton. I'd no idea what this was about, having last seen him a few weeks ago when he'd added his recommendations to my final probation staff appraisal.

Despite his fearsome reputation, he wasn't one for formality or ceremony and ushered me in, waving casually to a visitor chair. After initial pleasantries he pushed the latest copy of Force Weekly Orders in front of me.

'Look at that Order, with your good education, you should be applying.'

I looked at an advertisement for a three-month attachment to the Operational Planning Department at Headquarters.

'Yes, sir', I replied, somewhat puzzled.

His advice had been given in the form of an order, not a suggestion.

'Go downstairs and get it done, now.'

I did, handing my written application to the Inspector.

'I don't think this is a good idea Nick, you need more outside experience, but I think it may already be out of my hands.'

I didn't realise it at the time, but he was right on both counts. Within a couple of weeks, I'd been interviewed for the post by Chief Superintendent Jim Phasey, Superintendent Derek Fox, and a Bramshill flyer, Chief Inspector Paul Manning, known as 'Manning from Planning', who rose to be an Assistant Commissioner in the Metropolitan Police as well as a friend of the family.

On a Wednesday early turn before long weekend, Bill Norman came out on panda patrol with me for the second half of the shift; little did I know that it was to be the last time I'd work with him. He baulked at the sight of every dog we passed, his loathing of them very evident. His prejudice towards them was anathema to me as I'd always lived with a dog in the household. His hatred was more likely to be rooted in irresponsible ownership than the animals themselves.

Towards the end of the shift, we were sent to a street in Silverdale. The roads and pavements were icy and there'd been snow on the ground for a few days. An ambulance had been called to an elderly lady who'd slipped and fallen whilst out shopping with her small dog. She was badly shaken but didn't need to go to hospital, so we decided to see her safely home, a couple of hundred yards away.

'You drive her home Nick, put the shopping on the back seat.'

'What about the dog?' I asked as I helped the lady into the passenger seat.

'The dog is NOT going in the car!'

I put her groceries on the back seat and quickly sat at the wheel.

'Well, how's it going to get home sir, if we're all in the car?', I said, starting the engine.

'Ah, er....'

He'd painted himself into a corner, much to my delight.

I will never forget the sight. As I drove the lady home, looking in the mirror I saw the Inspector walking the dog along the road, sniffing at lampposts (the dog...) and leaving its liquid messages. He was holding the lead at a stretched arm's length, as if it and the dog were about to explode any moment. While he looked extremely embarrassed and uncomfortable, I found the situation absolutely hilarious. He caught up with us as I was helping the lady through her front door. He handed over the dog and we helped with the lady's shopping, ensuring that she didn't need any more help from us.

As we walked back to the car, he hissed,

'Not one word Nick, d'y'hear? Not one bloody word! Let's get back to the station.'

I kept his secret, revealing it only to his wife in a sympathy letter when he passed away a few years ago.

Back at the station I bumped into Superintendent Fox who was there on a disciplinary enquiry into missing property; yes, property was trouble, just as Mick had warned me. He looked at me hesitantly, said 'Hello' and asked the Inspector to join him in private. A few minutes later Bill Norman called me into his office.

'I'm not happy about this as you know Nick, it was out of my hands all the time. You start at Headquarters in Operational Planning on Monday.'

It was a late finish for me as I wrote up all my existing paperwork for handover, cleared my locker and drove away from Newcastle for three months, unaware that it would be sixteen.

Bill had been very good to me over the past couple of years. Despite infuriating me on many occasions, I realise that he'd kept a watchful eye on me, pushing me in the right direction all the time and keeping me out of trouble when my enthusiasm ran away with me. Despite the difference in rank, we got on very well together, a friendship of sorts.

I really can't imagine what my first two years would have been like without his guiding influence.

The next Monday, on the dot of nine o'clock I presented myself in Superintendent Fox's office. The formality of the interview was gone. Introductions were made; it was a small department with Chief Superintendent Phasey in overall charge of three areas, Operational Planning, the Command-and-Control Computer under development, and Communications. Superintendent Fox and Chief Inspector Manning were in charge of Operational Planning, and I'd be working with PC Glyn Oldfield. The two of us had an office at the back of the building, but as it wasn't heated we worked day-to-day in the relative warmth of the adjoining conference room when it was unoccupied.

After I'd settled, the Chief Inspector thrust a document of around thirty pages at me.

'This is your first project Nick, have a good read of this and join me when you've digested it, I want to know what you think.'

It was a completely new experience for me to be on duty, sitting quietly reading, no radio squawking in my ear and no background of constantly ringing phones. However, the paper I was reading was dynamite. It proposed the abolition of the manifestly dysfunctional Unit Beat system in favour of each station having a reduced number of panda cars. These would be renamed as Incident Response Vehicles - IRVs.

There was to be an *experiment*. Over the years, I saw many experiments; none were ever deemed unsuccessful, regardless of the actual outcome. The latest of these would be conducted at two stations, Hanley and Burton, each of which would have their vehicle fleet reduced by half. I was young enough in service to have not yet acquired the hardened cynicism of my older colleagues; although not seeing this for the cost-cutting exercise that it actually was, I was still flabbergasted. I knew from my short experience that the panda patrols at Newcastle were run ragged much of the time and a reduction was unthinkable. Knowing Hanley to be far busier than Newcastle, the thought of them managing with less cars than we had back at Newcastle seemed impossible.

I sought out the Chief Inspector later in the morning and shared my thoughts with him. He made it clear that regardless of resistance, it was going to happen; it would be my task over the coming weeks to produce the evidence in support of it. Even to my relatively naïve mind, it seemed a backward way of doing things.

A couple of weeks later, I walked into our 'cold' office to find a slightly built man of about forty-five sitting down looking through my paperwork.
'What are you doing?' I asked (There may have been an expletive there, I can't remember).
'I'm your new Deputy Chief Constable.'
We never got on.
He'd been a pilot in WW2 and despite it being a historical mystery, he proudly boasted that it was he who'd actually shot down Glenn Miller – it said a lot about him.

It was inevitable that one day I would come across Mr Shepherd, and sure enough I did, as he was coming out of his office, only a few doors down the corridor. It had only been about five weeks since I was last in his office.
'Morning sir.'
'TUCKER! Wha., j-just *wh-what* are Y-YOU doing HERE T-tucker at HEAD-QUARTERS?, he spluttered.
'Attached to Operational Planning sir, been here a week or two now.'
'Tell Mr Phasey I want to see him, straight away'
Tell him your bloody self, sir.
'Will do sir.'
I conveyed the message and ducked into Superintendent Fox's vacant office as Mr Phasey walked along to the ACC's door; I heard raised voices but could not make out the words. I came out of the office as the avuncular Chief Superintendent walked past, giving me a wink. It would be a while before I heard from Mr Shepherd again.

Having collated/manufactured the evidence in favour of the IRV system, despite obvious and overwhelming evidence *against* it, we then had to present the case to the

Divisions. A meeting was held in the conference room chaired by ACC Ken Gibson. All the Divisional Staff Officers (Chief Inspectors) together with our Chief Superintendent, Superintendent Fox and Chief Inspector Manning were present. Glyn and I were on hand to man flipcharts, overhead projector and to serve coffee. I'd never been amongst so many bosses before and felt quite nervous. Maybe it was because of my jumpiness that I accidentally tipped one Chief Inspector's coffee into his lap, to his great fury and my matching embarrassment.

The next afternoon I answered the phone.

'Operational Planning, PC Tucker.'

'Ah, PC Tucker, this is Chief Inspector Stoddard at Stoke, about yesterday's meeting...' He had a very clear, well-spoken voice with a mischievous tone.

'Yes sir...'

'Would you happen to be the clumsy constable who served extra coffee to my colleague?'

'Yessir, unfortunately I am. What can I help you with?'

'Nothing, I just wanted to say thank you I can't stand the bastard. There's a pint for you next time I see you at Stoke, bye.'

This was the start of a many-years-long association with George Stoddard, a wonderful man with an irrepressible sense of humour and a natural talent for dealing with people. He deservedly rose to the rank of Chief Superintendent, one of the finest bosses Staffordshire Police ever had.

The IRV experiment inevitably happened anyway. Within a year the system had been adopted force-wide, despite there never having been a post-implementation evaluation of the experiment. Some Divisions jumped before they were pushed. On paper – as with so many things - it *could* work, each IRV driver doing half a shift on response, and the other half either on foot patrol, paperwork or follow up enquiries while another driver took over the response work. In practice though, this depended on having the staff available to do it, which there rarely were.

I had one project which needed me to spend a few days doing research at Hanley's Courts Department. In charge there was a Chief Inspector who I'll refer to as 'Cutter', a name which many former colleagues will recognise and despise. The nickname apparently came from his time as a PC, when he proclaimed himself to be a '<u>cut a</u>bove the rest'. As well as his, shall we say, unpopular qualities, he permanently wore the most miserable expression imaginable, and was never known to ever crack a smile.

I was wearing plain clothes and went into his office to introduce myself on my first day. He couldn't have greeted me with less enthusiasm if he tried. As I left his office he asked me if I'd pick up a box of papers from the floor for him. As I bent down, my trousers split wide open. Nobody who knew him will believe this, but Cutter burst out laughing at this piece of slapstick, continuing to laugh as I walked into the corridor. One guy in the corridor looked puzzled, asking me,

'Is that Cutter?', and when I nodded,

'Naah, must be a stunt double.'

Other projects came and went, we did research into high-visibility clothing for Traffic Division, hazardous chemicals, contingency plans, firearms response and many other operational subjects. We also devised responses to changes in the law; such as Identification Parades. In order for us to comply with the latter, I designed a form to be adopted which extended to twenty-eight pages, and that was after cutting it down.

High visibility became a popular subject, and the relatively new hi-vis colour 'Saturn Yellow' became very fashionable. One day we were having a meeting in the office

170

of Mr Gibson, a straight-talking, no-nonsense boss who had risen steadily through the ranks of Staffordshire. He was very well liked and didn't suffer fools gladly; in fact he didn't suffer them at all. He wanted to talk about IRVs.

'I've been thinking, I want a new image for the IRVs, rather than the boring old blue and white it's time for a change, any ideas?'

I don't know whether it was me, or someone else present but someone piped up, tongue in cheek,

'How about making them Saturn Yellow sir?'

'Great idea.'

Within a few months, the panda car was extinct, the new IRV had been christened the 'Budgericar' by the local press. It had only been a joke, a joke which lasted for over ten years until the vehicle livery was changed.

My time in Operational Planning had been an experience, and I gained a useful network of contacts; however, it was detrimental to me, Inspector Norman had been quite right. I didn't even have enough experience to do my job at Headquarters properly, and I lost vital time needed to consolidate my training and gain true policing experience.

However, it did give me time to study and easily pass my Sergeant's Exam. I had a drink with Ian Holding while he was on a break from the Special Course at Bramshill, he encouraged me to go ahead with applying for the course, which I'd always intended anyway. (The photo accompanying my application is shown).

I gave some thought to where I wanted to be when I finished my ever-lengthening attachment, and still fancied

Traffic. Passing an Intermediate Driving Course could put me on the motorway, based at Stafford, Shepherd was about to retire so this wouldn't be a problem. However, the driving course coincided with the interviews and briefings for my Special Course application. I couldn't give my full attention to either and so was successful with neither. So it was therefore back to Newcastle, into the thick of an IRV system of which I'd been one of the reluctant architects, but keeping quiet about it.

I returned with three-and-a-half years' service, but only two years' experience and onto a different shift. Elwyn Evans had retired, so as to be able to spend more time with his obnoxiousness. We had a new Superintendent, Ken Ratcliffe, the Chief Inspector in Training when I joined. What a superb boss. He knew the job and the patch inside out, wasn't afraid to get his hands dirty, would join us on patrol, and call the troops in for a midnight brew which he made himself while enjoying some banter with us. Morale in the station was sky-high.

I still had my contacts at Headquarters and one night over a beer one of them asked me,

'How are you getting on with Mr Ratcliffe?'

'Great, he's doing a damn good job. He's very popular, particularly after Elwyn Evans.'

'Make the most of him mate.'

'Why?'

'He's back here next week in charge of Training.'

Not good news, but I had a bit of an 'exclusive', which I shared with the shift the next morning, they didn't believe me.

I bumped into the Superintendent in the station later on; not to put too fine a point on it we stood at the urinal together.

'Sorry to hear you're leaving us boss.'

'What do you mean Nick?'

172

'A little bird tells me that you're starting back at Training next week.'

'What? First I've heard. I'd know. You must be wrong.'

I ran into him again a couple of hours later,

'I've made lots of phone calls Nick, you're wrong, definitely wrong. I'm here for a good while yet, just as I want to be.'

'Very pleased to hear it boss, I must have had some duff gen.'

At the end of the shift, he was waiting as I came in off patrol and bundled me into his office,

'Where *did* you get that information from Nick?'

Touching the side of my nose, I joked,

'Can't reveal my informants boss!'

'Well, whoever they are, they're on the inside track, you're right, I'm back at HQ on Monday.'

That was the last time I ever saw this splendid guy; about a year later he took retirement and very sadly didn't live long enough to properly enjoy it.

It was probably the one and only time ever that a PC told his Superintendent that he was being transferred.

If only half our bosses had been of his calibre, the job would have been so much better – functioning properly and providing a decent service to the public.

Our new Superintendent was a high-flyer transferee from another force, in his early thirties, lacking experience in both policing and life. Quite a few of our number were former miners, including one Constable who bore the thin purple-black scars on his face from injuries where the atmosphere was laden with coal dust. It was quite common to see men in North Staffordshire with these 'pit-scars' which they proudly wore as a badge of honour.

The reaction of our new boss on seeing the guy's scars was,

'Constable, who's been writing on your face?'

So, the former miner, well-known for his blunt naming of digging implements, told him.

Although our new Superintendent was friendly and very approachable, his lack of understanding of the area and its people was telling. Over the next few months the high morale in the station steadily declined.

I have first-hand knowledge of a juvenile shoplifter who was arrested, but within an hour every single trace of the incident was expunged from records. The arresting officer - a probationer - was told never to speak of it again under threat of losing their job. The 'offender' had been accompanied by the children of a senior officer of the Sub-division, with whom they were spending the weekend.

I'd done the theory with much scepticism and unsurprisingly the new IRV system was a disaster from the outset. There simply weren't enough people to do half a shift responding, with the other half doing paperwork as imagined by the project. An IRV driver would be responding to incidents for the entire shift, sometimes without a break, or whatever break they had was curtailed by another incoming incident. Jobs created paperwork with little time to complete it properly. I used to take paperwork out with me to complete in the car, in whatever time I had to spare between incidents; it was unsafe insofar as security of confidential material was concerned, but there really was no other way to keep up.

At least each station now had a dedicated controller in addition to the Reserve Officer. However, it didn't help that controllers weren't allowed to use the discretion to properly exercise control; policy dictated that all incidents should be responded to straight away, regardless of urgency. Prioritising, or 'stacking' incidents for later response was frowned upon, so controllers wanted to absolve themselves of any responsibility for an incident and allocated an IRV or foot patrol to it straight away – 'job done' as far as they were concerned.

It was unsustainable. IRVs had designated patrol and response areas, but if a second job came in on an area where the IRV was already engaged, the controller felt under pressure to send another IRV to it, even if it could wait a few minutes.

One IRV would be dispatched to a job on their area. While they were committed on this job, another incident could come in on their area, so a second IRV would be directed off its area to deal with it, even if it could have waited until that area's IRV was free..

The first IRV would complete their job, and while the second IRV was still busy, an incoming job on the second IRV's area would result in the first IRV being dispatched from their own area to deal with it.

It was farcical, we'd frequently pass each other, two-toning and blue-lighting in opposite directions to incidents on each other's areas.

It would be many years before graded response to incidents became officially acceptable, although some bolder controllers (me included later on) would apply it anyway.

Despite its manifest failure from the outset, the IRV system lasted for over twenty years, almost double that of its ill-starred predecessor.

The flawed Yorkshire Ripper enquiry was never far from the front pages of the press; young women around the country were frightened, with some justification. One evening I took a statement from a young lady who'd spent a night out with friends in Leeds a few days previously and had felt very uncomfortable with a man who'd made advances to her. I took a detailed statement from her, description, accent and what it was about his conduct that made her feel uncomfortable. I was with her for over an hour. She was a very good, plausible witness.

I returned to the station and phoned the Ripper Incident room. Before I could explain the situation, I was asked,
'Was he a Geordie?'
'No.'
'Bin it then.'
I decided to send it to them anyway, very probably they binned it, but my conscience was clear.
The description she'd given me was a pretty good match for one Peter Sutcliffe...

The sixteen-month deficit in my experience became extremely telling. Within weeks I'd been selected as tutor Constable for a new recruit, I'd barely more than a probationer's experience to pass on to him. I was still learning myself and didn't make a very good job of it at all.

Had I remained at Newcastle for the third and fourth years of my service I could have been looking at being a Detective Constable by this point – those sixteen months at Headquarters, albeit enjoyable, had been a significant backward step.

The next few months of not being able to match my length of service with my experience were quite difficult, I won't dwell on them.

12 – On the move

Fast forward about eighteen months to 1981 and I was now at Hanley, the very busiest station in the county. My move had been precipitated in the spring by marrying another member of the shift. The force disliked married officers working together, although this was now irrelevant - my wife was on maternity leave expecting our first child, due in April.

I spent a very demanding few months acclimatising to my new surroundings and new colleagues, working the city centre and the three hard-pressed IRVs (previously six pandas), for which I kept schtum regarding my partial responsibility.

Hanley, being an inner-city area was completely different to the market town of Newcastle. It was significantly busier, the pace was hectic, and our work was different. For one thing, whereas Newcastle's residents were primarily white British people, a sizeable proportion of Hanley Sub-division's residents were not. Many didn't speak English as their first language, and we had little or no understanding of their varied cultures; at the time we were only just beginning to have the collective will on our part to learn about them.

There was a significant amount of what we now call social housing on the eastern side of the patch, which accounted for the majority of our work. Bentilee, in particular had been the largest 'council' estate in Europe at one time with over four-and-a-half-thousand homes; similar to a small town, with its own shopping centre, churches and a variety of pubs and clubs. Most of the people on this and the other estates were decent, honest, hard-working folk who didn't have much, and probably never would have.

However, a troublesome few were a different story and gave the area an undeserved reputation. It didn't help that, like Newcastle, the city council seemed to intentionally accommodate problem people and their families in particular streets. From the many streets on these estates, it was probably only a dozen of them that we were regularly called out to.

Some people would have empty pay-packets long before the end of the week, so they'd break the pathetically weak lock on the electricity/gas meter and take the cash. They'd then report a break-in, the 'burglar' having broken a window to get in. The invariable dead giveaway was that the broken glass was *outside* the building. The householder would protest loudly at being arrested but crumble when confronted by evidence of their fingerprints *inside* the meter box. These thefts became so prevalent that eventually we would deal with them on the spot; an arrangement entered into between the thief and the utility suppliers, who had little interest in the time and paperwork involved in a prosecution. We still had a clear-up, an offence admitted for the all-important crime statistics, which were being fiddled on an industrial scale anyway.

I had the most terrifying experience of my career on the Bentilee estate. In the middle of the night I was sent to a report of one of our regular customers having 'gone berserk.' In those days, at the insistence of our bosses, we always patrolled single-crewed, even on nights. Our leaders considered our safety to be of secondary importance to spreading us over as wide an area as possible.
I arrived and got out of the car, the man had indeed gone berserk and had smashed every pane of glass at the front of the house. He was at an upstairs window, shouting abuse and holding something. I shouted up to him,

'Ey-up Pablo, come on down to the front door, let's have a chat.'

As I walked up the path to the front door something whistled past my right ear. A crossbow bolt!

I ran for cover behind a wall, calling into my radio the urgent assistance call,

'10-9, Middlefield Road!.'

'I WON'T MISS NEXT TIME COPPER, FUCK OFF!'

Poking my head up momentarily I could see him reloading.

I was safe. I couldn't see him, and he couldn't see me. Within minutes the street was swarming with every other member of the shift, and the incident was resolved with nobody coming to harm, apart from our 'customer' sustaining a few minor injuries while being arrested.

I'd experienced a man threatening me with a machete a couple of years before, but this was very different, you can normally distance yourself from a blade, but not from something being fired at you. I'd been really absolutely petrified.

Of course, the shift, as usual, took the piss.

A recent riot in Shelton had led to our leaders insisting on visible policing there, twenty-four hours a day. One night it was my turn to patrol that area, although during the whole night I can't have seen more than ten people.

As I left the station, a scruffy dog approached and started to walk with me. Despite my many attempts to shoo him away, he followed me, three feet behind, all the way around the patch. I dodged down a few back-alleys and entries, but he always found me. I went into the all-night chemists on Stoke Road, bought some sweets, and asked if I could leave via their back door. The bloody mutt still found me a few minutes after I left.

I returned to the nick for my meal break. After an hour it would have been easier to have left via the back entrance to return to Shelton, but I didn't want this dog with me for the rest of the night. I used the front door instead, but when I reached Broad Street, there it was, and I was lumbered with it again. Eventually I was picked up by the Sergeant and rode around with him for half an hour. I asked him to drop me *nowhere near* he'd picked me up and thankfully I didn't see the dog again.

Within a few months I found my niche working in the very busy Control Room. Hanley was unique at the time as the Control Room had been moved away from its usual front office location to a purpose-built room on the first floor, with not one, but two controllers. It worked really well as the controllers could concentrate on the job in hand without the frequent distraction of having to help out at the front counter at busy times, then finding themselves unable to get away.

I was partnered with PC Gerry Hudson, a really experienced guy, very methodical with a sound, practical approach to getting the job done. Over the next twelve months we bonded as a team and our friendship grew, I learned a great deal from him, and we got on famously. Work was hectic, but we were part of a fantastic, hard-working, hard-playing shift and I looked forward to going to work every single day.

We had a steady inward flow of probationers, at Hanley they had to learn very quickly. One of them was Bryan Jones, a lovely guy, formerly a miner with a strong South Staffordshire accent, who quickly acquired the inevitable nickname 'Yo-yum.' He wore his heart on his sleeve and made no secret of the fact that he'd hated every minute at Ryton. Gerry and I cottoned onto this and on an unusually quiet morning before long weekend we thought of having a bit of fun. Most official communication in those days was via the Telex machine which clattered away incessantly in the corner of the Control Room, doing nothing but wasting triplicate paper most of the time.

We composed a fake Telex along the lines of:

TO ALL STATIONS
FROM HEADQUARTERS TRAINING

PROBATIONARY TRAINING – NATIONAL REVIEW

REGARDING THE ABOVE, IT HAS BEEN DECIDED THAT AN EXPERIMENTAL FOUR WEEK EXTENSION TO INITIAL REGIONAL TRAINING WILL BE CONDUCTED.

THEREFORE, SELECTED OFFICERS FROM THIS FORCE WILL ATTEND THE NO 4 TRAINING CENTRE AT RYTON ON DUNSMORE FROM *(whenever, but the week after next!)* FOR FOUR WEEKS.

AN INITIAL WEEK'S RESIDENTIAL COURSE WILL TAKE PLACE AT HEADQUARTERS FOR THE SELECTED OFFICERS PRIOR TO THEIR ATTENDING THE EXTENDED COURSE, COMMENCING ON *(the following Monday!)*.

THE FOLLOWING OFFICER(S) FROM YOUR STATION HAVE BEEN SELECTED TO ATTEND, AND SHOULD REPORT TO HEADQUARTERS TRAINING WING AT 9AM ON THE ABOVE DATE:

PC 3402 B JONES

MESSAGE ENDS

One of our Sergeants was in on the joke, we handed it to him to pass to Bryan just before going off duty for the weekend. We'd briefed the rest of the shift and they'd been endeavouring to make Ryton the main topic of conversation throughout the morning. Apparently, Bryan burst into tears on seeing the message and knocked on the Superintendent's door to plead intervention but was simply told 'If that's what it says, then that's what you've got to do son.'

Whether Bryan went to HQ the following Monday I don't know, but it was a Bank Holiday, the place would have been deserted.

It was four o'clock on an October Monday morning, our final night shift before rest days. The clocks had gone back the night before. Every station, for some reason managed to have a drawerful of various keys in the front office, Hanley was no exception. Amongst them were some very large, very old keys such as one could imagine would open very large, very old doors. Time for a bit of fun again! We called Bryan over the air,

'Kilo-alpha four-one over'

'Four-one, receiving just outside in Bethesda Street over.'

'Ideal, can you return to the front office and collect a key to the tower of Shelton church, it's our job to put the clock back by an hour and we were too busy to do it last night.'

A short pause followed by a nonplussed,

'Four-one, will do.'

Having been handed one of the old rusty keys, Bryan set off toward the church, about half a mile away. Ten minutes later he called,

'Four-one, I can't get the key to fit, over'

'Sorry four-one, we were just about to call you, you were given the wrong key, we've got the right one waiting on the counter for you.'

Bryan trotted back to the station from the church, collected another large rusty key and headed back. Several minutes later,

'Four-one, this key doesn't fit either, over.'

'Really sorry Bryan, we gave you the main door key, we definitely have the right one waiting for you now.'

Back to the station again, and yet again back down to the church, as he was about to walk from the road into the churchyard, the night shift Inspector from Burslem, riding shotgun in the Divisional IRV stopped and asked him what he was doing. Mark, the driver must have thought, *Now we're in the shit!*

'What are you up to son?'

'I'm putting the clock back on the church sir.'

The Inspector, Charlie Jones had a quite severe appearance which belied a compassionate nature and an absolutely legendary sense of humour. He clicked to the situation straight away,

'You'd best get to it then son, if the Chief Super sees the wrong time on that clock on his way in tomorrow morning, there'll be hell to pay.'

After a further trip back to the station to collect yet another 'correct' key, we put him out of his misery, he'd worked up quite a sweat going to-and-fro.

Bryan was a great lad with the potential to go far but couldn't settle in North Staffordshire. He resigned shortly after his probation ended, to go and work in a supermarket closer to home. I thought he was a great loss to the job and was really sorry to see him go. Happily, he later re-joined West Midlands Police, retired as an Inspector and is now a County Councillor. I'm very happy to still be in touch with him.

There was one facet of Hanley which dismayed me, this being that probationers from other stations who weren't making the grade were sent here as a last chance to prove their worth. A more appropriate course of action would be to move them to a station where they had colleagues with time to help them. Hanley was far too busy for this, everyone fully occupied with their own workload.

There wasn't a snowball in hell's chance that a struggling probationer would make the grade here if they couldn't do it elsewhere. The results were predictable, after a few months every single one resigned or had their services dispensed with.

One lovely guy was sent on his way after struggling desperately for a few months with his 'last chance' at Hanley. A former nurse, given proper support he'd have made a really good officer. Not long afterwards he took his own life. He left a devastated family but nobody in the force was ever held accountable in any way for this tragedy or ever expressed regret for it. It should have given pause for thought to senior management, but the brutal transferring of underperforming probationers to Hanley continued relentlessly. It was cruel and indefensible.

Complaints were an occupational hazard. It was often said that anyone who didn't attract complaints never did anything. It had some truth to it, the first tactic employed by a criminal caught 'bang to rights' was to complain, attempting to muddy the waters of their guilt. One incident had brought the Discipline and Complaints department to Hanley and the whole shift was being interviewed, one by one. Despite attempts to keep us apart, a good deal of conferring was going on and the complaint was destined to go nowhere. One of the lads, not known for phenomenal brain-power emerged from his interview and was telling us how it had gone. Glowing with pride he announced,

'They said I was very reticent.'

Then, noticing our collective bemusement,

'Er, what does reticent mean?'

Some people were eager for overtime, not me. There were some people I worked with who'd find themselves a protracted job before the shift ended, making themselves some overtime.

One guy on our shift was an overtime Ninja. His favourite caper was to find a fraudulent vehicle excise licence early in the day, then return to arrest the offender just twenty minutes before the end of the shift.

Some CID officers would strangely make their most arrests towards the end of their shift, such as 4.30pm on a day shift, or 9.30pm on noons..

Not me, when the end of a shift came, I'd do my utmost to ensure I was having a couple of quick 'wind-down' drinks before heading home to my family.

Three o'clock on a cold night, snow had been falling thick and fast. Heavy snow was an even bigger friend to us then rain, seemingly the world stopped. A brief, impromptu snowball fight started on the station forecourt as the shift turned out from meal-break. Gerry and I were watching from an open window, Gerry scooped up some snow from the windowsill, accurately aiming it at one of the lads below. This didn't go unpunished and before we knew it, a snowball sailed through the open window, across the room and landed on the computer terminal, of all places. There was a shower of sparks, but quick as a flash (no pun intended) Gerry reached for the mains socket and unplugged it.

A little more reticence with D&C looked very likely, but Gerry was completely unfazed. Fetching the toolkit from his car, he began to take apart the whole computer terminal, drying it out carefully with a hairdryer which one of the other Control Room staff kept in a cupboard. I fielded calls from Headquarters who were querying why we were not responding to messages being sent through on the computer, swearing blind that there must be something wrong on the network due to the snow.

Two hours later, having reassembled the dried terminal, Gerry gingerly plugged it in, we jumped clear as he pressed the switch... but it worked. Headquarters were told that we'd found a loose wire at the back of the terminal and plugged it back in.

Early in 1983 Gerry dropped a bombshell; he'd handed in his notice and was leaving to run a pub. We'd formed a great partnership, and I was devastated to see him go. I'd learned such a lot from him and had thoroughly enjoyed every moment of working with him. There's far more to being a controller than just answering the phone and sending patrols to deal with the calls. There is instinct involved, a feel for what is going on out there, taking decisions as to which jobs are the most important. An incoming call can seem innocuous but have huge implications. On the other hand, a report of a big fight may be of no importance at all; probably all over and the participants long gone when the police arrive.

Having only three IRVs at your disposal called for thinking on the fly. There was often no need to send a patrol at all, many matters could be resolved over the telephone, even if it meant promising the caller that you'd call them back when things are a little quieter. I learned all these skills from Gerry; a world away from the call-centre style of police contact today with which the public express so much well-justified dissatisfaction.

I'm going to digress. Computers: I'm a long-standing technophile and love to see technology being put to good, constructive use. However, I believe it to be one particular area where the service, certainly in Staffordshire took a wrong turning. The greater mobility of the Unit Beat system had the public accustomed to calling the police and having them arrive within minutes, regardless of the urgency of their call. This expectation was combined with a desire for reassuring 'bobbies on the beat', without the public realising that they couldn't have both.

Along came the Command-and-Control computer. I'm not criticising those who worked on its development, but those who decided on the basis of how it should be used. Its focus was entirely on just two of the many elements of policing, *incidents* and *resources*. It was in development at the beginning of my career, progress had been slow and by 1979 when it went fully 'live', both the hardware and software were already outdated. It was slow, unreliable and prone to recurrent long outages.

Incoming incidents were entered onto the computer, which replaced the Telephone Message Book. In case of computer failure, a paper form replaced the book, with the snappy heading 'Action Form.' For a time it was absurdly ordered that all incidents would also be recorded on this form, at Hanley this ridiculous instruction was completely ignored. Available resources were displayed on an incident's screen, with the intention that the nearest, most suitable resources could be deployed. Actions and results were entered onto each incident log and then it was finalised. Controllers could see at a glance which incidents were still unfinalized or 'open.'

Fortunately, reliability improved over time, but it seemed that the computer gradually became the de-facto measurement tool of a station's performance and the basis of how it should be resourced. Senior bosses around the county vied with each other as to whose patch was busiest. 'Busiest' became bizarrely conflated with 'most successful' whereas surely, effective maintenance of order and crime prevention would result in lower, not higher demand? A more realistic, telling measurement could possibly have been reported incidents per head of population.

This preposterous, infantile rivalry culminated in an angry memo from our Superintendent querying *why* another station was occasionally recording more incidents a day than Hanley. This dented his lofty reputation as Commander of the busiest Sub-division in the county. Incredibly, the (still allegedly having little to do) night shift controllers were ordered to create incidents out of thin air, recording them as 'late entry.' These could be anything, for example a HORT1 production at the station counter resulting in an offender being reported, a fixed penalty excusal, a warrants officer issuing doorstep bail, nothing was to be excluded. We duly complied, but the other station retaliated to this with even more farce. Thankfully, Headquarters noticed and quickly put a stop to it.

The computer inexorably led to front-line policing, in Staffordshire at least, becoming almost exclusively about responding to incidents; being reactive rather than proactive. Policing's essential element of the *prevention* of crime slowly began to disappear. This was a national trend amply demonstrated by the fate of the internationally acclaimed Home Office Crime Prevention Centre. For many years this had been based at Staffordshire Police's Headquarters, it moved away to Yorkshire in 1995 under a new name but closed down within ten years.

Senior managers became interested only in figures. Incidents and crime patterns could be measured; the value of visible patrolling police officers could not.

Back to 1983. I didn't enjoy working in the Control Room anything like as much after Gerry left. For several weeks I wasn't given a new, permanent partner. I'd often have to work with an inexperienced probationer who could neither operate the computer, nor deal with incoming calls appropriately. Training is vital, I was always willing to pass on my experience and knowledge to others. However, when someone is placed in an operational area to be trained, they should be surplus to existing staff, not a replacement. On days when I was partnered by such an officer, I couldn't have a meal break – and 'comfort' breaks had to be pretty brief too.

To compound this, at the same time as Gerry's departure, our shift Inspector, Barry Sheppard left the job to run a fish and chip shop. I'd had a great working relationship with him, he'd been constantly and unfailingly supportive. His replacement was newly promoted and anxious to make his mark. Unfortunately, we had an almost immediate clash of personalities, for no apparent reason. He was unsupportive, unapproachable and generally very difficult to deal with. However, by then I'd been joined by a permanent, very experienced partner, Don Holford, so began to enjoy work again. The Inspector clearly disliked both of us, myself in particular but neither of us could understand why.

Around this time, the Home Office had mandated that greater use should be made of non-administrative civilian staff to supplement day-to-day policing. Up to that point, their role in Staffordshire had been mostly operating switchboards. More staff were taken on to deal with the public enquiry counters; the idea being that this would release uniform staff for outside duties. It was an unpopular move, not least with the public who visited police stations with the natural expectation of being able to speak to a police officer.

Our first 'civilian' was a retired railway stationmaster, a lovely guy whose manner reminded me of Private Godfrey of Dad's Army. For the majority of a shift his only company in the front office would be the already fully (pun alert) engaged switchboard operator. He had no police experience at all and was constantly ringing the Control Room for advice, as we were the only people available to speak to him. This unofficial responsibility for the enquiry counter added noticeably to our workload so the whole setup was a failure. It wasn't our retired railman's responsibility, he was trying his very best to do a good job. About a year later he left and was replaced with a younger man, Trevor, who had experience of computer programming and operating. He quickly acquired the obvious nickname of *Clever Trevor*.

Our new leader had a bright idea, or at least he thought it was. Because Trevor had experience of computers this made him an obvious candidate to work in the Control Room, replacing either myself or Don. The fact that the clever young man had no policing experience, or any idea of how to make the most effective use of outside patrols was brushed off as irrelevant by the Inspector. He completely failed to understand that there was far, far more to being a Control Room operator than being able to type at a computer terminal. He decided that after meal breaks on night shift, either me or Don would (another pun alert) don our big hat and take it in turns to walk the streets. More officers on the beat at the very quietest time of the day – genius! This idiotic idea benefited neither the public nor the job but placed added pressure on the one of us left inside supervising Trevor. The only person to benefit was the Inspector, taking a perverse pleasure in pissing us off.

The battle of wills with the Inspector intensified, so once again enjoyment of my work declined considerably. There were constant arguments and stand-up rows. He was gunning for both of us despite our well-held belief that we were doing a good job. He wasn't the worst Inspector that I ever had, he didn't come close to that as I will reveal later, but he didn't inspire confidence, either in me and Don or the rest of the shift. The previously long-standing high morale of the team declined rapidly.

One Saturday we were taking over as night shift controllers from an extremely busy noon shift. Changeovers at the weekend could be chaotic, the noon shift controllers frantically updating incidents on the computer while at the same time trying to brief us. All this as Don and I were having to answer incoming phone calls, taking details on scraps of paper because the two computer terminals were already in use. It could be a quarter to half an hour into the shift before we were settled and up to speed with everything going on. Somehow, but predictably I lost one of my scraps of paper, and an incoming call I'd taken was overlooked in the bedlam.

I'd volunteered for a quick changeover to noons on the Sunday. During the shift the Inspector asked me to join him in the office. The forgotten call had resulted in a house burglary. I was absolutely mortified, I'd made a mistake which went against everything that I stood for as a police officer and held my hands up to it straight away. Our leader could barely contain his glee as he announced,

'I'm reporting you for this. You will have to answer for it *to the Chief. Your days in the Control Room are over. I 'm putting you back on the streets WHERE YOU BELONG!'*

It was a very low point for me, being 'sacked' from my position I could deal with, but I felt profound shame at having - albeit inadvertently and under pressure - forgotten such an important call. Nowadays, if the media can be believed such mistakes seem to be a daily occurrence and rarely, if ever, result in disciplinary action, being referred to as *'learning experiences.'* The resultant enquiry, despite my openly admitting a basic mistake rumbled on for almost a year. Eventually I was summoned before the Chief Constable. In an apparently rare moment of wisdom, he understood the pressure which had caused this genuine error and administered a slap on the wrist. It later transpired that Glenn Miller's alleged nemesis, the same man who I'd found searching my desk a few years before, had recommended that I be required to resign. Thank goodness this was not taken up by the wiser of the two men.

Going *back on the streets*, to quote the Inspector, was like a breath of fresh air – there was so much less pressure. I started to enjoy going to work again, but dark times were just around the corner, not just for me but for the whole service.

13 - Donkeys

The WW1 epithet *lions led by donkeys* was still relevant in the police service sixty years later.

During my initial training I'd gained the impression that the higher ranks in the service were infallible, god-like beings, to be revered and treated with the greatest of respect. It came as a shock when I joined the front line to see the sheer contempt in which some of our senior officers were held. The many reasons for this became very clear, very quickly.

The very best, most effective and respected bosses in any walk of life are those who show their staff the same respect that their staff give to them. I worked for many superb ones; experienced people who led from the front, made firm decisions and stood by them. They'd show respect for those following them and would back them to the hilt if things went wrong, even if they made a mistake.

The job didn't have nearly enough of them though.

I've worked under some so stupid that I wouldn't trust them to run a bath. Some covered their incompetence with well-developed bullying and blustering, plus shedloads of weapons grade bullshit, the deplorable Elwyn Evans being a prime example. It's difficult to understand how some of them got to where they were; maybe they cosied up to the right people, maybe they were promoted out of harm's way, or possibly they did just the right thing to climb the greasy pole without showing any actual ability.

Nowhere was this more evident than the tragedy at Hillsborough in 1989, where the force's senior management made an incomprehensibly reckless decision. This was to put a newly-promoted, inexperienced Chief Superintendent in command of policing what would be by far the season's highest profile football match. That there would be disorder was an odds-on certainty, the conduct of the visiting supporters was a known factor which clearly hadn't been properly accounted for in planning the operation. The tragedy in which so many people lost their lives, and the brazen cover-up which followed showed in granular detail how incompetence and bluster can cause so much harm. I'm sure that in the public sector the service is not alone in having highly paid senior managers of such staggering ineptitude.

Shortly before my appointment, the country was having electricity cuts on rota as a result of industrial disputes. There had been a fatal night-time crash on a major road in the north of the county. The road, normally lit, had been plunged into darkness by the blackout. The local Chief Inspector arrived at the scene, to find a force photographer who'd started setting up his lighting. The boss strode over to him,

'Eh, yo, what am yo dowin' with all that stuff? '

'I'm setting out the lighting so that I can photograph the scene sir.'

'I dunna want yo dowin' that. I want yo to tack a photograph of 'ow d-a-rrk it is!'

He was in charge of policing a town of twenty-thousand people.

There was a time when each officer had a 'worksheet' to track the flow of their paperwork through the system. Despite Headquarters having given clear instructions to the contrary, worksheets were quickly seized upon as an opportunity to measure how hard an officer was working.

One afternoon I was summoned to the Chief Inspector's office at Hanley.

'PC Tucker, I've been tackin a leowk at thay workshate…'

'Yes sir?'

'Well for the last six months there's been nowt on it, nobody arrested, no mawtorists repowted, absolutely bugger ow '

'That's right sir.'

'But why? Wot bloody yose are yow ter us if you're not lockin' any bugger up or stopping any cars. WHY?'

'Perhaps you haven't noticed that I'm one of the eight people who work in the Control Room sir, in fact I've never seen you in there, do you know where it is?'

Thinking about it, I'd never seen him out of his ground floor office, let alone the Control Room upstairs.

'LESS OF YER SMARTARSE TOKE, GET ITE!'

It was the same Chief Inspector, now second-in-command of the busiest station in the county.

In 1986, as part of the National Garden Festival there was to be a military parade through the city centre. A huge security operation had been planned, rest days and annual leave had been cancelled. Quite how, armed with wooden sticks we could protect soldiers carrying Kalashnikovs escaped me.

Our Divisional Commander, six feet seven inches of donkey, held a briefing parade in the police station yard. We all lined up and stood to attention while he stood on a (carpeted, really!) orange box, not that one was required, spouting twenty-four carat bullshit orders. Amongst us was Sergeant John Sharpley, renowned for his sense of humour and contempt for senior ranks. Every time our boss paused for effect, John shouted, 'Bollocks', without moving his lips.

After wincing a couple of times when it happened, the Chief Superintendent bellowed,

'WHOEVER THAT MAN IS - STOP IT AT ONCE!'

Undeterred, John repeated this another couple of times. Those of us around him knew it was him, we were chewing through our tongues trying not to laugh - very difficult.

'SERGEANT SHARPLEY!'

(You could feel everyone thinking *'Shi-i-it, he's spotted him!'*).

'Y-y-yes sir?'

'FIND OUT WHO THAT MAN IS!'

The urge to laugh was overpowering, as John loped along the ranks like Groucho Marx, a wicked grin on his face, hands clasped behind his back, appearing alert for more interruptions. John continued to fill the tall man's pauses, straightening and looking around each time he threw his voice. We were concentrating so hard on not falling about laughing that the stream of bullshit from overhead went almost unheard. After another few interruptions,

'SERGEANT SHARPLEY!'

'Yessir?'

'CAN'T YOU FIND OUT WHO IT IS?'

We were breaking out into splutters; we couldn't take this any longer.

'No sir, can't find him anywhere!'

Returning to his position, John apparently decided that further interruptions would be unwise. We were dismissed, none the wiser for the briefing, but at last able to break into laughter.

An officer's wife had ruined some of his uniform shirts by accidentally washing them with dark colours. He wrote a report explaining what had happened, requesting to be issued with new shirts, going so far as to offer payment for replacement. The report was returned to him by the Superintendent, requiring that his wife *'report hereon the reason why this carelessness had occurred'*!

There is a story that one of these 'leaders of men' had to send a confidential fax. He sealed it in an envelope marked 'Confidential' before putting it through the machine.

We had a Deputy Chief Constable (not the asserted Glenn Miller killer) with an archaic, extremely disciplinarian approach. He was a loud, oppressive bully, and as someone put it, 'built like a block of flats.' One of his first acts on appointment to the post was to give a lecture on the subject of discipline to all supervisors while they stood before him. It was an epic rant, in the style of a fire-and-brimstone sermon, with inspiration from the Nuremburg rallies. Not only did he seek to inspire the fear of God into those present, but the entire polemic was video-taped. Every officer in the force was instructed to watch it, having to sign that they'd done so; the sight of this huge man ranting away on the small screen was absolutely comical.

About a year later I was on a regional management training course in Birmingham. The training centre had asked the DCC if he'd be kind enough to send them a copy of his video-nasty. Believing that it would be a shining example across the region, he'd been only too pleased to oblige. It was certainly used, but as an example of exactly how a leader should *not* behave. Our fellow course members watched, incredulous that such a man could be one of the leaders of our force. While we cringed with embarrassment, they expressed their sympathy.

The same man had joined the force as an ACC a couple of years earlier. In the early hours one morning he was visiting police stations around the south of the county in plain clothes, probably seriously disrupting a good few night shifts. He strutted into Aldridge police station, which bore the county crest in stone above the front door and rang the bell. The weary station PC ambled to the counter. The conversation reportedly went along the lines of:

'Yes mate, what can I do for you?'

'**MATE?**' He thundered,

'**DON'T YOU KNOW WHO I AM?**'

'No, should I?'

'I AM YOUR ASSISTANT CHIEF CONSTABLE!'
'You may be *somebody's* Assistant Chief Constable, **mate**, but you're not mine.'

Aldridge had once been in Staffordshire, hence the (redundant) county crest, but it had been part of the West Midlands for over twenty years.

The failure to identify someone he didn't need to, on the part of this PC led to another daft decision. Framed photographs of the force's 'Executive Officers' were issued to each station, with orders that they should be displayed prominently on every ground floor corridor. The intention was that the self-proclaimed VIPs would be recognised and shown the appropriate respect on one of their rare forays from Headquarters' top corridor. At Longton someone (okay, it was me, they can't touch me for it now) enhanced the monochrome displays with red 'blob' stickers on the noses. It made for some hilarity until the Superintendent, stifling a laugh of his own, ordered reversion to black-and-white.

On one of the final residential courses of 1990, a male and female officer had been found *in flagrante delicto* in the residential accommodation at Headquarters. Oblivious to changing times, the same DCC had been scandalised by this laxity in the morals of *his* force.

I was on one of the first courses of the new year, not at Headquarters but the new Weston Road complex, about three miles distant. At 9am on the first day, all of us on courses at the site were loaded onto two coaches and bussed to Headquarters. There we joined the Headquarters residential courses in the gym. We stood to attention for twenty minutes or more as the DCC launched into an intemperate, thunderous tirade expressing his disgust at the lack of morality in *his* force. He spelled out the intended consequences should anyone choose to stray from the path of righteousness, despite not one of us having been involved in this scandalous episode.

At the front of the gym was a group of cadets, who'd only started a few weeks before. A young girl in the front row was so nervous that she gave a completely unintended giggle, he ripped into her viciously in front of the hundred or so of us who were there.

Some leader!

When I arrived at Newcastle in 1976, it was like stepping back into the early 1950s, apart from radios, everything seemed so antiquated.

Arthur Rees was a very well-liked and immensely respected Chief Constable – his maxim was *A happy policeman is a good policeman*. On his retirement in 1977 his successor swept through the force like a breath of fresh air, dragging us all, sometimes willingly, sometimes not, into the 1970s.

However, we stayed there in the 1970s – for all his tenure of nineteen years; the average tenure of a Chief Constable is around three to four years, his was five times that. In the first four years the force bubbled with the flow of new blood, but his remoteness and autocratic style led to a slow decline in morale. He clearly didn't believe in his predecessor's maxim.

He had a marked reluctance to promote people, which showed an apparent lack of confidence in his own decisions or in the ability of his people. Instead of people being promoted into positions which fell vacant, the posts were instead filled for lengthy periods by acting ranks. This resulted in at least one acting Sergeant or Inspector on just about every shift in the county, as well as in Divisional senior management. Acting ranks were only ever intended to cover short term situations, temporary promotion should actually have been used but would have been more costly. 'More actors than equity', was a commonly heard phrase.

Promotion under this Chief meant the loss of any specialist role held, and a move to an operational front-line shift at a different station. This could be some distance away, sometimes requiring a house move. One Constable was promoted to Sergeant and transferred to a station several miles away, this would have needed him and his family to move house. He pleaded that he'd prefer to be closer to his home, where his wife had her job and where his children were settled at school. He was then told that he'd be transferred, but without the promotion. Our Chief's word was absolute.

Whether on promotion or not, a transfer to another, maybe distant station became a regular feature of visits to Headquarters. There was no stability at all, family lives were disrupted by house and school moves, and partners had to find new jobs. Shifts had new members joining all the time, replacing long-standing colleagues who were there one day and gone the next, often without warning. Team spirit suffered as we no longer properly knew the people we were working with - whether it was them joining our shift, or one of us joining theirs. It was only when the Police Committee criticised the burgeoning cost of removal expenses, and newspaper headlines such as, *'Join Staffordshire Police and See the County'* that the constant movement of people started to slow down.

Maybe in connection with this, it became force policy that in future we'd be expected to work within fifteen miles (as I recall) of our homes. The cost to the public of removal expenses decreased, but officers' daily commuting costs rose, but obviously at no expense to the force.

I believe the rationale behind this constant churn of people was to prevent people from becoming too familiar with each other, thereby avoiding the possibility of corruption taking hold. To me this was further evidence of the Chief's lack of faith in his own decisions and in the integrity of his people.

Police Regulations required the Chief Constable's permission to buy or rent one's home, giving absolute control over where force members lived. Permission was regularly denied, and no reason had to be given. Living outside the county boundary was completely proscribed; probably due to collusion between the force and the council to maximise income from rates/poll tax/council tax.

A policy was introduced that any home-owner joining the force would be compelled to sell up and move into a police house; these were shabby and very poorly maintained at the time. The location would be decided by the force and could be far from where they were already settled. Having made a start to family life in a home they owned, it's beyond me why any mature, eminently suitable candidate would be attracted to a career which treated them so appallingly from the outset.

A celebration of a promotion to Inspector had ended with a tragedy on the road. In a knee-jerk reaction, it was ordered that all future off-duty gatherings must be attended by an officer of at least Inspector rank, to keep things under control. It was met with justified derision, not least from the national press. At the same time, promotions from Sergeant to Inspector became 'temporary' for one year, similar to a Sergeant's twelve-month probation.

Even a Constable promoted to Sergeant could have spent a long time at multiple locations in the acting rank before being promoted to a probationary Sergeant – for me it was twenty-seven months, so by the time promotion was confirmed I'd already done over three years in the rank; for some it was even longer. Promotion to the more senior ranks went at a glacial pace; as earlier mentioned, vacancies were filled by acting ranks for lengthy periods. The command structure of the force began to lack consistency and continuity, with no apparent succession planning in place. The never-ending interchange of leaders impacted heavily on morale.

Our Chief became virtually invisible, only to be sighted very occasionally at Headquarters or following in the wake of a Royal visitor or other VIP, surrounding himself with a 'Praetorian Guard' of yes-men (and they *were* men). I saw him just four times in his nineteen years as Chief, even though I spent over a year of this at Headquarters. By comparison, I would see his successor often during the four years I served under him.

A 'Force Executive' was formed, made up of the five officers of ACC rank and above, and the Head of Finance. At the same time an 'Executive Suite' was created on the 'top corridor' of the Headquarters building. This had always been a thoroughfare, used by all Headquarters staff who'd regularly encounter and mix with the senior officers along the corridor. The creation of the suite closed the area to everyone except the 'Executive', their staff, and visitors with appointments; giving a stark impression that the Executive were intentionally cutting themselves off from the people they were supposedly leading.

The Chief been a state pensioner for some months before he was finally persuaded to retire, still insisting that he had more work to do with the force; but maybe more to do with waiting for a knighthood which never materialised. It was proposed that each of us have £5 deducted from our pay as a retirement gift; this would have totalled around ten-thousand pounds on top of the six-figure lump sum he would draw on top of his pension. Needless to say, fierce opposition put a stop to this fawning gesture.

He had his devotees, maybe you've realised by now that I wasn't one of them.

Good ideas came and went, came again, went again and came again, the wheel of change in constant rotation. A much-vaunted shake-up of the force in the early 1990s had resulted in an increase in the number of Divisions (for example, Stoke-on-Trent's two Divisions became four).

Like other bright ideas (e.g. IRVs), it worked fine in theory but not in practice. Each new Division was under the control of a Superintendent instead of the higher rank. It was chaotic, for one thing there was neither enough office space nor sufficient support staff to meet the basic administrative needs of each new Division.

I've now been retired for longer than I was a police officer. Policing has changed beyond recognition over those years, so I no longer feel qualified to make judgment on today's policing. It does, however, seem to have an even deeper crisis in leadership than when I was working. Donkeys are still in charge, and, it seems, more of them than ever. Time and again, Chief Constables, their Deputies and Assistants fail to lead or support their people properly.

Shortly before I wrote this, an Authorised Firearms Officer (AFO) from the Met was cleared of a murder charge, twenty-five months after shooting a dangerous man, suspected to be armed. Those many months will have been sheer hell for the officer and his family, with no certainty for their future.

The dead man had a string of previous convictions for gang related violence and had shot a man twice in a nightclub, captured on video. On the judge's direction, this was not put to the jury during the trial.

It was only *after* the not-guilty verdict that the Commissioner spoke out against the injustice faced by his officer, criticised delays and roundly criticised the Crown Prosecution Service (CPS) for having brought the charges in the first place. The gutless Commissioner at the time of the shooting did not speak out at all. The same scenario has played out after every other shooting in the past, no support whatsoever forthcoming from spineless police leaders for their officer until court proceedings have ended.

The system was loaded against the AFO from the moment he fired; it will happen again and again until senior ranks show true leadership and give proper, visible support to their AFOs from the moment they pull the trigger.

Should AFOs become disenchanted by their treatment, they could all 'down tools', as they are volunteers; they are not under orders to be armed. The consequences for public safety would be unthinkable.

Furthermore, on the subject of AFOs, later in service when I was a traffic patrol Sergeant I attended a seminar on the actions to be taken in the event of fatal shots being fired by one of the AFOs on my team. It had been decided by the donkeys that as Traffic Sergeants, our responsibility would be the preservation of evidence at the scene. I disagreed, pointing out in the clearest of terms, that I saw my overriding responsibility as being the welfare of my team member. More evidence of the *equus asini* being far removed from reality.

Officers on Traffic Division were encouraged to qualify as AFOs. I was disqualified due to wearing spectacles. Together with this and the well-known lily-livered management of those who have had to fire, I can't personally begin to imagine how I'd feel after taking a human life. I would never have wanted to be an AFO, but I have the greatest respect for those who volunteer for this potentially life-changing role.

Cut after cut has been made to the service over recent years to which these people have raised little or no objection.

New laws are passed to satisfy the demands of the electorate, with no thought to the practicality of enforcement; again met with silence from police leaders, who should be considering the impact on the workload of their people.

Donkeys prefer instead to bow to their political masters in the hope of a lucrative sinecure upon retirement. When, as is usually the case, this expectation is unfulfilled they round on the government and the Civil Service with well publicised, damning criticism of their policies on policing, law and order.

True leaders would put their opinions to good use **during** their service. Transparent spinelessness.

Nothing's changed for the better in police 'leadership' in the half-century since my standard of education was first remarked upon.

To the donkeys, their rank means just one thing – STATUS.

Maybe loss of that status is why many of them stay on long after they could have retired.

14 – The Job Isn't Finished Until the Paperwork's Done

Paperwork was the most significant burden in our work; its demands grew exponentially despite constant efforts to achieve its reduction. For every form that disappeared, it seemed that two more took its place. Almost everything we did required some form of paperwork.

It's probably clear by now that I viewed a significant amount of paperwork as a waste of time and effort that could have been put to far better use – *and it was!* It didn't seem to occur to our 'leaders' that every few minutes spent on form-filling or report writing was an officer away from the front line; the total number of those minutes must have been colossal. If only the public knew, they'd be outraged by police being needlessly away from the front line for so long.

Our bosses wanted to see us constantly out on the streets, whilst at the same time demanding to see our reports promptly on their desks. Finding time to deal with paperwork in the daytime, when the very same bosses who required it perambulated around the station could be very difficult.

A Superintendent walked into the parade room at Newcastle where four of us were diligently writing up our reports. He thundered,

'What are you men doing in the station?'

One of our number courageously replied,

'We work here, sir.'

'GET OUT, ALL OF YOU!'

Idiot. He and his kind were always asking why reports were submitted late.

I've already mentioned the Form 12, sudden death report. It was only in the North Staffordshire Coroner's area, on Mr

Hails' insistence that this had to be completed and typed up in full on every single occasion. This was required by him even if a death certificate was issued before or while it was being typed up, a shocking, costly waste of time. Elsewhere in the county, after ensuring that there were no suspicious circumstances, the officer attending would arrange for the undertaker and leave; the Coroner's Office would take up the enquiry the next morning. Not one of our senior officers had the courage to approach Mr Hails with a view to ending this absurd situation in North Staffordshire. That being said, a sudden death could be very welcome on a cold, wet shift, as the length of time taken to deal with it was never questioned.

One useless, unnecessary piece of paper was Form 65F, a Fire Report. For years, the Fire Brigade expected the police to attend every incident they went to. In a rare outbreak of common sense, somebody at HQ finally put an end to both the form and our attendance, years after it should have happened. Yes, there were occasions when the police would be needed, but not every time.

The 65F (and the ubiquitous Book 1 and night report) had to be completed for just about every occasion, date, time, location, cause of fire, persons injured, damage caused, number of appliances and firefighters attending.

WHY?

Surely this was exactly what the fire brigade would be recording, so it served no useful purpose at all. It would be written up and filed, never to see daylight until the day it was destroyed.

A road accident would be written up on an HORT7 with its attached driver and witness statements, in the station's Book 1, typed up for the 'Night Report', and then eighty percent or more of them filed away and eventually destroyed. So much work, of no value at all except for the prosecution of a few errant drivers, or for insurance companies to occasionally make enquiries.

Crime reports wasted an incredible amount of time. I'd already learned from Roy Ashley that statements were purely for use at court, having no other purpose other than force policy's insistence on them being obtained from all crime victims, but this senseless waste of time and paper went on for years.

Attending a crime required a statement, an entry in the Book One, sometimes a pro-forma Telex circulation and an unofficial Form 34 pro-forma. On this we'd include details of the crime, attach it to the statement/s and submit it to a Detective Sergeant who decided whether it would be officially recorded as a crime and complete an official Form 34 (crime report). You can imagine how many times the details of one single crime were written down.

If a Division's detection rate wasn't too good, it was possible for some Form 34 pro-formae and their attached statements to become 'lost', in the sense that they had never existed. A rigorous inspection by an HMI at another Division in 1978 exposed this as an all-too-common practice. As a result a new *Book* 34 was introduced into which all crimes were entered by Control Room staff immediately on being reported. The books had numbered pages for an audit trail. It was no coincidence that every Division's detection rate suddenly fell quite dramatically.

A great deal of other paperwork was purely administrative. It should never have required front-line officers to complete, but it was. For example, an assault on a police officer was a recordable crime, so was a detected crime for the statistics. Although a purely administrative task, clerical staff would send a memo to the assaulted officer asking them to complete the paperwork. At one station I returned the requests, telling them to stop wasting my people's time.

We may have been one force, but each Division had its own way of doing things. Later you will see that I had a couple of spells at Stoke just a mile and a half from Hanley; both stations were doing exactly the same job in a similar environment, but the paperwork required was completely different. For example, one afternoon at Stoke I sustained a slight accidental injury. All injuries, no matter how minor had to be reported - on paper of course - so I submitted a report detailing the circumstances.

Next day I had a call from Sub-divisional office,

'Your report is very good, but *we don't do it like that here...*'

The words in italics seemed to follow me around whenever I made a move

'...we have a special form for it.'

'Does my report contain all the details you need?'

'Yes, but not in the right orde...'

'But nothing, I've reported it, end of.'

It was bizarre that each Division, doing exactly the same work had its own unofficial forms. Headquarters instructed that there were to be no unofficial forms, those used by Divisions would require Headquarters' approval and be adopted force-wide. Despite this, every Division, and different stations within it had unofficial ones, invariably invented by, and for the convenience of administrative staff.

Every station had its own offence report format. An arrest for crime at Newcastle, for example, would be written up completely differently just three miles away at Hanley, together with much more duplication.

Non-criminal offence reports (such as drunkenness) however, were very straightforward. A front page would have details of the offence and offender, statements would be attached with a list of previous convictions, it could be as little as three pages in some cases.

The advent of the Crown Prosecution Service (CPS) in 1986 introduced a national standard reporting system. Eradicating all regional differences, offence reports would be written up the same way across the whole country. The format was agreed in partnership between the CPS and senior police representatives. However, the police officers must have been asleep at every meeting, with the result of a plethora of new forms which had to be completed for *every* case. This added a considerable burden to the officer reporting. For example, the offender's name and personal details had to be written down multiple times in *every* file. Previously, handwritten reports had been universally accepted by prosecutors, but the CPS insisted that every file should be typed. The force simply didn't have the staff to undertake this huge task.

Consequently, despite now having a clear national standard, our paperwork load increased significantly. Specialised units for file preparation were eventually set up with additional typists being employed but diverting funds from the already stretched front line. I later become the manager of one of these units. A drunkenness file made up to CPS requirements passed across my desk, instead of the handful of pages of years gone by, it extended to over fifty. The printers in my department were using upwards of ten reams of paper every week, most of which passed to the CPS.

There are so many more examples I could give, where unnecessary paperwork demand took operational police officers away from the front line, I could write a book about that alone – in triplicate of course.

15 - 1984

It must be clear by now that my political views are at odds with those of most of my colleagues; views expressed in this chapter will probably not be shared by many of them. Although electorally bribed by Thatcher's promise of a pay-rise in 1979, I made no contribution to her increased majority in 1983. The battle of wills between a confident Thatcher and the reactionary Arthur Scargill led to the infamous Miners' Strike of 1984 which was a tragedy for British industry, for the trades union movement, for the police service, and the public.

Thatcher had firmly locked the unions in her sights even when in opposition. It's indisputable that they wielded excessive power, but in no small part due to the incompetence of company leadership. For example. British Leyland couldn't make a profit because they were producing competing models aimed at the same market sector. The dearth of profits resulted in poor wages, while soaring inflation led to inevitable demands for wage increases which simply couldn't be afforded, inevitably leading to strikes. Strikes impacted on productivity and in turn, profits – a vicious circle. With the firms unable to make money, in fact losing it, funds weren't available for investment in new models or technology. In a few short years, the British public were attracted to imported cars with greater reliability and durability, with lower running costs. They were made even more attractive by having standard features which were optional extras on British cars, so quickly began to dominate the market. Unprofitable British manufacturers had nowhere near the resources needed to compete, so began to fail inexorably despite being given generous support from the taxpayer.

At the same time the communist inspired Scargill and his union had placed such a stranglehold over the mining industry that, like the rest of British industry, it couldn't compete on the global market. Scargill's rationale for the strike was the prevention of large-scale pit closures which he firmly believed the government intended, but which they falsely denied.

I believe that Thatcher actually *wanted* the strike, evidence points to her government having made meticulous advance preparations for it. However - most importantly - she envisaged a swift, crushing ending, showcasing her apparently unassailable power to the unions. Humiliation of Scargill would be a catalyst for the emasculation of the wider trade union movement. Apart from there being no early end to the strike, she was successful, but at the appalling cost of the decimation of British manufacturing industry and the tsunami of unemployment and recession that followed.

Scargill's assertion of pit closures has since been vindicated and shown to be entirely correct. However, he haemorrhaged public support with his increasingly intemperate ranting. He made two major mistakes in my view:
- Firstly, by failing to call a ballot, almost universally viewed as undemocratic. This alienated public sympathy and aggravated tensions between working and striking miners. He would almost certainly have lost a ballot, something the government was extremely eager to make political capital from.
- Secondly, by calling the strike at the wrong time strategically. Winter was all but over, and the government, having made detailed preparations for the strike, had a massive stockpile of coal for power stations. The impact of the strike on the

country, such as power cuts wouldn't be noticed for over a year, if ever.

Scargill was rendered deaf and blind by his own rhetoric. He ignored public opinion and didn't take it on board; the outcome could have been very different if he'd done so. He made the perfect opponent for Thatcher; she knew it and seized the opportunity.

I've always been convinced that the policing of this strike was, for the first time, politically driven from the outset. A National Reporting Centre, staffed by senior police officers from across the country was set up to coordinate policing of the strike at national level. This reported to the Home Secretary, who in turn briefed senior ministers; it's not unlikely that briefings would have gone up the chain, with orders from Downing Street coming down it. It's clear to me that Chief Constables were under orders from the government not just to keep the peace, but to break the strike by any 'lawful' means possible. This has been strenuously denied, both at the time and over the forty-odd years that have followed.

We were briefed on the legislation covering industrial disputes, which we were already well aware of, but in 1984 it was being given a different spin. Now, the meaning of the law on picketing was being stretched in such a way as to essentially prevent it. I recall briefing sheets being handed out with the wording, '*if a Constable **apprehends** that a breach of the peace may occur then he may...*' It was suggested to us that this legislation, over a century old, gave carte-blanche to stop and compel any vehicles to turn around if we had the very remotest suspicion that they had travelling pickets in them. Furthermore we were assured that the legislation empowered us to use forcible restraint against pickets while working miners were escorted past a picket line. The ethical independence and impartiality of the service was totally compromised.

Politically driven or not, this strike was going to be policed far more robustly than any previous industrial dispute - maybe the strike to end all strikes. Until now, our neutrality had been paramount to all industrial disputes; we would have enabled pickets to make their case to their fellow workers, and provided this was done peacefully, our duty had been to maintain order, nothing more. This time, the word *impartial* and its synonyms were doing some serious heavy lifting. Pickets were prevented, often by 'lawful' force from putting their case at all, their working colleagues (or *scabs*) being bussed past them under police escort, sometimes at alarmingly high speed. With each passing shift, the perceived prevention of picketing increased the hostility from the strikers towards their working colleagues and the police, eventually leading to disorder and missiles being thrown. In extreme cases, this frustration manifested itself in unconscionable attacks on the homes of those who continued to work.

Apart from some minor skirmishes, the strike passed off relatively peacefully on the picket lines of Staffordshire's collieries. However, away from the pit entrances the rift between working and striking miners became horribly evident; neighbours and even families were in deep conflict; cars and homes were damaged while savage fights broke out in what had always been the congenial atmosphere in pubs and clubs. Some of my colleagues had been miners prior to joining the service, and just as many had miners in their own families.

Community officers from the outlying areas of Bucknall, Bentilee, Abbey Hulton and Milton were taken away from their normal duties to police the picket lines with the rest of us. Many mineworkers, both working and striking lived in those areas, so the community officers were actually needed on their patches more than ever, donkeys' decisions again.

The strike started in Yorkshire on my twenty-ninth birthday and quickly spread, the first Staffordshire pit affected was Littleton Colliery, on the outskirts of Cannock. Two personnel carriers were sent from our Division to add to the already strong police presence on the picket line. Bryan was with us; you'll recall that he'd been a miner, but also at this very colliery. He should not have been here and was very conflicted. A shrewd supervisor would have kept him back at Hanley, but the decision had been made by our newly promoted Inspector. We disembarked the carriers some distance from the colliery and marched in formation to the pit entrance in an attempted display of intimidation. The already rowdy tone of the picket line stepped up as they saw this and they started jeering at us,

'Parasites!...''Maggie's army!'... 'Police state!'...

Then suddenly, as we came closer…

'Ay-up! It's Broyan! Yo'm o'roite mite?'

The tension was defused immediately. We struck up an instant rapport with the 'mob' and there was no trouble; peaceful picketing with us chatting to striking and working miners alike. Our Inspector stood aside, fuming at this turn of events. However, as everything remained peaceful our lawful obligations had been achieved.

In the belief that the strike would be short-lived, massive resources and funds were put into it, the government promised a blank cheque to the police to deal with it. Officers from neighbouring forces were drafted in to assist. We were routinely working twelve-hour shifts and longer. The early shift for most of us started at 4am to cover the 6am shift changeover at the collieries. Night shifts started at the usual time but ended at 10am, a few times I worked a double shift into the afternoon. It was shattering, my home life consisted merely of sleeping between shifts, rest-days were just that, when not in bed I was feeling like a zombie. I had a two-year-old son by now and seriously missing out on quality family time. On one occasion I walked into the house without having seen him awake for three days; he burst into tears - it broke my heart. While some welcomed the overtime I was not one of them, my family was always my first priority.

Whenever possible I stayed behind on IRV patrol, dismayed by the oppressive way we were expected to police the picket lines. There was a gung-ho attitude in certain officers, some senior enough in both service and rank to know better.
One day as we approached the Hem Heath colliery picket line, one guy sang to the tune of the number from 'Oliver',
♪ ♪♪...*You've got to pot a picket or two boys, you've got to pot a picket or two*...♪♪ ♪
To many it was a joke, but it spoke volumes of the attitude of many police officers towards the striking miners. To them, the miners' strike was a battle, with strikers seen as the enemy; a mindset possibly originating from the way in which we had been briefed.
The singer was an Inspector from another station, in charge of us and responsible for our conduct.

Despite the government promising virtually unlimited funds to police the strike, it would appear that our Chief Constable decided to go it alone and operate within his existing budget. A rumour circulated that this was because he believed his fiscal restraint would be rewarded by his being able to add a knighthood to his existing gongs – anyway, it didn't.
As the strike continued beyond its anticipated short duration, cutbacks were made to stay within budget. Our leaders - mostly unsuccessfully - encouraged us to claim overtime as time off in lieu. Although regulations gave us the right to a fixed Subsistence Allowance while away from

our stations, we were ordered to claim only the actual expenses incurred. Legitimate claims were summarily rejected, with the Police Federation doing nothing at all to support our position. Those attempting to press the issue were warned of the potential risk of deadly career damage or an unwelcome transfer.

Maintaining the budget for the strike apparently hit the force's coffers very hard. For several years afterwards we were driving run-down vehicles maintained on a shoestring, using pattern parts and cheap batteries, resulting in some very embarrassing breakdowns. Can you imagine a police officer in a marked car asking you for a push? It happened. You'd always try to make certain to park facing downhill, should a rolling start be required.

As I've said, it was mainly peaceful in Staffordshire. During the first few weeks the pickets were turning out in force, and we responded in ever greater numbers. One morning we were policing a picket line at Holditch colliery in Chesterton. There were over a hundred pickets and about sixty of us. It had been good natured, if boisterous - until the news broke that Arthur Scargill had been arrested in another force area.

Shunning any last vestiges of impartiality, some of my colleagues, including Sergeants and Inspectors cheered loudly, totally unprofessional and provocative. I was disgusted.

Unsurprisingly, the pickets reacted with hostility to this inflammatory behaviour. Scuffles and shoving broke out. At one point I had to momentarily push a man back with the flat of my hand on his chest, to prevent both of us from falling over. The man and I spontaneously apologised to each other and shook hands. The push was witnessed by some of the crowd who started loudly protesting at 'police brutality',

A Superintendent, naturally positioned as far away from the action as possible, heard the shouting and came over. The pickets were rowdily claiming that I'd assaulted the man, despite his protests to the contrary. The donkey took me aside and we stood just a short distance away, in full view, and possible hearing of the pickets.

'What the hell happened there, what have you done?'

'I pushed the man away with the flat of my hand, it was instinctive self-defence and we both apologised straight away, it's a storm in a teacup.'

'Doesn't look like it', said Eeyore, 'You shouldn't have done it, see how they've reacted? *You're* responsible for this situation.'

He stupidly started wagging his finger as he spoke. Twenty yards away, the pickets saw this and started jeering.

I was furious.

'What the fuck do you expect me to have done, just stand there and get trampled to the bloody ground?'

'Remember who you're talking to. Now get back to the picket line.'

The pickets continued jeering at me.

'You're bloody joking! You've just given me a bollocking in full public view, they all saw it, look what they're doing now! I'm going to report this conversation and plenty of my colleagues have witnessed your behaviour.'

Force Standing Orders prohibited any officers from 'admonishing' their juniors in public or in front of their colleagues; to do so in any setting is a sign of a very poor manager.

I was enraged, and feeling very uncomfortable, as the pickets continued to jeer.

'Get back on the picket line now PC er.', looking at my shoulder, 'one-four-four-one or this will be dealt with as a disciplinary matter. I am *ordering* you.'

'Bollocks, **sir**. Those pickets will give me loads of shit, all because of you. You haven't a bloody clue have you?'

I stormed off towards the carrier, with him braying after me,

'You haven't heard the last of this!'

I sat in the carrier, wrote up the incident in my pocket-book and spent the next hour reading.

I *had* heard the last of it though.

Cretin.

We had an Inspector in the force who bore a striking resemblance to Arthur Scargill, but a lovely guy with a far more genial nature. His presence on the picket lines of Staffordshire was a subject of great amusement, both for us and the miners.

The strike dragged on, and picketing dwindled to a handful of miners at each colliery, as did our response. A carrier of officers from each Division covered the shift changeovers, just by taking a few from the normal shift for an hour or two. However, this still resulted in us having very few front-line patrol officers at various times of the day. With annual leave, courses, court and other absences it was quite normal for a shift to be reduced to less than a handful of officers, whereas a couple of years previously we had been turning out a dozen or more.

I started one afternoon shift at Hanley completely alone, no Sergeant, no Inspector, just the keys to a car and a radio to communicate with the solitary controller upstairs. Until the rest of the shift returned from the picket lines at about 4pm, I was the one and only uniform patrol at the busiest police station in Staffordshire.

The NUM failed to support its members financially during the strike, exacerbated by the government's sequestration of all NUM funds in December 1984. As 1985 dawned, striking miners were starting to drift back to work with little intervention from slowly decreasing picket lines, both in numbers and hostility. It was either return to work, or penury for most of them.

Additionally, the National Coal Board and the government, aided by biddable press and TV, engaged in a propaganda campaign to encourage striking miners back to work. Offers of back pay, holiday pay and bonuses were extended. The media put out figures suggesting that strikers were returning in droves.

A few days short of the first anniversary of the strike, facing imminent defeat the NUM ended the strike. Miners had always been a proud breed, so instead of acknowledging a humiliating climbdown, the striking miners marched back to their pits, bands playing, banners unfurled, and heads held high. Most humiliated of all was Scargill, his grip on the industry and trades union movement lost.

The only thing Scargill got right was that all of his predicted pit closures happened.

Littleton Colliery, the scene of my first picket line duty of the strike now lies underneath a sprawling housing estate. Like the sites of the other five collieries in Staffordshire operating in 1984, it shows little sign of its previous industry.

Families had been split, neighbourhoods divided, and many working men's clubs slowly closed down, former strong alliances between the working people of the city irreparably fractured.

The consequences for the police service weren't a reward from the government for a job well done. Instead it was questioned why we needed our present resources, having apparently - but not actually – coped with many less people on the front line for the past twelve months. Following the strike, the number of officers we turned out on a shift progressively decreased, while more and more civilians were taken on.

There are those who boast about the money they made from the strike, referring to their 'Scargill holiday', their

'Arthur extension', their 'Maggie' kitchen. I'm not one of them, I didn't want the overtime and shunned it whenever I could, I valued time with my family above all else; I enjoyed being on the patch doing proper police work, preferring not to be doing the bidding of politicians.

That year of strife gave nobody anything to be proud of, a shabby, shameful chapter in our history which changed the country for ever.

16 – A Bumpy Ride

As I'd endeavoured to keep away from the picket lines wherever possible, I'd become one of the mainstays of the front line on our shift and was enjoying it. The Inspector had thought that putting me *back on the streets* was something that I wouldn't cope with. He'd been wrong but at least acknowledged it when the time came for my annual appraisal at the end of 1984. He was surprised that I'd adapted so well and acknowledged that I was one of the most useful, experienced members of the shift. He reported on me very favourably, and the animosity that he showed towards me when I was in the Control Room faded away somewhat.

He even said he was sorry for having had to report my lapse. I still didn't trust him though.

The Chief Constable had announced some time ago that he wouldn't consider promoting anyone with less than ten years' service to Sergeant, regardless of ability. Although I was qualified and had sat before a couple of promotion boards I wasn't going anywhere yet. Maybe as I'd now spent nine years in the job it was time to take promotion a little more seriously.

Taking it seriously was difficult. The first stage was held annually, a locally held 'Divisional Promotion Advisory Board', chaired by a Chief Superintendent from another Division together with a Superintendent and a Chief Inspector. If successful you went on to appear before a Force Promotion Board. It was loaded against you from the start; you'd be sent down ever-deepening rabbit-holes, tricked into giving wrong answers, and generally humiliated.

At one of these sessions was a Superintendent with whom I'd worked a few years ago. The last time I'd seen him he'd been bald on top with a Bobby Charlton combover. As I marched into the room and threw up a salute, I almost choked as I looked at him, a full head of hair, a very obvious wig, far too long and untidy to go with his uniform, grey with a non-too subtle pink tinge.

I was so distracted by his rug that my answers were well wide of the mark, and at the end of the interview I knew it had all been for nothing when the chairman said,

'We couldn't help noticing that for the entire duration of this interview you've had a ridiculous smirk on your face Mr Tucker, you clearly haven't taken it seriously, could you tell us why?'

I told them.

I left the room knowing that it would be a whole year before I would be looking at any possibility of promotion again.

On 17th January 1985 the unthinkable happened. I arrived at Hanley at 5.45am to the horrific news that two members of the night shift had been killed in a crash on the A500 half an hour ago. They were PC's Graham Whitehurst and Bob Owen, who'd been a good friend. I've never known a day like it, the usual busy, chattering atmosphere, punctuated by outbursts of laughter was hushed and leaden. None of us had the first idea of what to say to each other. The job still had to be done, but today there would be none of the usual mickey-taking and ribaldry that saw us through. Not one of us even had the heart to play the customary frame or two of snooker at our meal break. It was a bitterly cold day, but despite this I was glad to be allocated foot patrol for the morning as my thoughts weren't on the job at all. Motorists parking illegally in the city centre that morning were shown no mercy.

The next day was very different. My wife had gone into labour in the night, but the contractions were a long way apart and I didn't have a lot of time off owing to me; I decided to go into work at 6am and return when the contractions became closer, this could be some hours away yet. On arrival at Hanley I explained the situation to the Inspector, who suggested I do a spell in the Control Room; he appeared an hour or so later and told me to go home, saying that the books would show that I'd worked a full shift, very good of him, just for once. By lunchtime I was the proud father of a sister to my nearly three-year-old son.

I took a fortnight off; I couldn't believe how much harder it was to care for two children compared to one. When I returned to work, the unusually cold winter really sapped my strength. Night feeds when I was on early turn led to no sleep at all. After a few weeks, totally drained I came down with a particularly unpleasant dose of bronchitis and was off work for four weeks.

When I returned, we had a new Chief Inspector - B'Stard! So much for the former Chief's declaration that he'd never again be in charge of people. My staff appraisal interview was overdue, and it was to be with him. We hadn't seen anything of each other for about seven years, I thought that he may have mellowed; I was wrong. After initial unpleasantries he read through my Inspector's glowing report on my work.

'Hmm, very impressive PC Tucker.'

'Thank you, sir.'

'But your Inspector hasn't known you as long as me, has he?'

'Known me as long? You and I haven't crossed paths in seven years! I think he knows me a lot better than you and better placed to comment.'

'And you've been off sick for the last few weeks...'

'Yes, but that's not a measure of my performan...'

'Now look, Tommy...'

'I left that nickname behind at Newcastle *sir*, if you don't mind...'

'Let's face it, *PC Tucker* you were always a problem for me as a probationer...' this was going to end badly, I had to stand up for myself.

'*Always* a problem? You supervised me for three months out of two years! You're the one and only person who ever had anything negative to say about me. Every other report during my probation was good, if I was as bad as you think then I wouldn't have got through would I? Anyway, my probation's ancient history. Seven years ago, how's that relevant to my performance over the last twelve months?'

'I haven't seen anything that suggests you've changed, you're still as bad as when you were a probationer. You've got no ability at all.'

I was shaking with anger.

'You're not looking very hard are you? You've only been here a week! Perhaps you should look at my record and base your conclusions on the *evidence* instead of your bloody-minded prejudice. I'm wasting my fucking time here.'

(There may have been one or two more 'f's in my last bit).

I stood, turned my back on him, walked out and slammed the door.

I wasn't going to allow this turn of events to derail me. After arriving home, I phoned my Superintendent (B'Stard's boss), telling him how unhappy and angry I was. He suggested I put my thoughts to paper and hand it directly to him; he'd include this with the appraisal when it went to the Divisional Commander.

I'd been involved in a minor collision outside the police station and as was always the case, my driving permit had been suspended pending a retest, so for a few weeks I was on foot patrol in the city centre. I wasn't too bothered about getting retested as the change of pace was quite welcome. Then a vacancy arose for a community officer at Bucknall, No sooner had I said that I *may* be interested than I'd upped-sticks and was stationed there. Another change of pace, and

224

I was still in no hurry at all to get my driving permit back. The shifts were less exhausting too, 8am-4pm and 10am-6pm days, and nights was 6pm-2am. It didn't last long though. Read on.

After the debacle of my staff appraisal, I was summoned to see the Divisional Commander, the six feet and seven inches of donkey referred to in an earlier chapter. As I waited in his secretary's office, she warned me that he was 'very formal.' *Pompous* would be more appropriate

As befitted the occasion I was in my best uniform, boots polished, hair and beard trimmed. After being bid to enter I marched in, turned, stood to attention and saluted him. He didn't motion me to stand at ease, sit down, or to take my helmet off.

After five minutes of strained conversation standing to attention, he told me to take a seat, the visitor's chair was positioned a good eight feet away from his desk, clearly aimed at making me feel as uncomfortable as possible. As I sat, I put up my hand to remove my helmet, but his face indicated that this would be a mistake. It felt quite ridiculous, sitting nearly three yards away from this pompous ass, still with my hat on.

It was a full twenty minutes before he relaxed the tone a little and invited me to take off my hat and sit more comfortably. Naturally he wouldn't overrule B'Stard's damning comments but said that in the interests of my career he would arrange for me to work in CID for a few months, but I could forget any thought of promotion or even being given a spell of acting Sergeant for at least two years. I was determined to prove him wrong.

Commuting from home in Kidsgrove to either Hanley or Bucknall was a chore. I'd bought a moped, it made travelling to and from work cheaper and quicker as I could carve through the glacial city traffic. It was, however, more dangerous, as I found out when I came off it one day whilst off-duty, breaking my left arm and gashing my chin, meaning three months off work. It was a beautiful summer though, and I loved being able to spend more time with my children as they played in the garden.

I returned to work in September, but there had been problems with my arm, it hadn't healed properly and was going to take time. On the police surgeon's orders I was placed on restricted duties, back in the Control Room, and there I stayed until the following summer, even after I'd been signed off as fully fit.

In the spring I'd applied for another Ritual Humiliation Board. It was best uniform, polished shoes, saluting and all the usual bullshit, all intended to drain your confidence and make you look subservient. As I'd been on holiday when the main thrust of the boards was being held, I had to travel to Lichfield for one that had specially convened for me. It was being chaired by Paul Manning, now a Chief Superintendent. As I waited in his secretary's office he walked through; I made to stand but he waved me to sit down,

'Nice to see you Nick, are you alright? Be with you in a few minutes, sorry to keep you waiting.'

A few minutes later I was called through. The usual march, stand to attention and as I put my hand up to salute, Mr Manning said,

'Just sit down, Nick, okay. Welcome to Lichfield, we've tried to make the atmosphere as oppressive as possible so that you feel at home...'

We all laughed, the board went very well, a friendly chat and quite the opposite of the bullshit I'd been used to.

I returned to Hanley feeling quite confident.

The next Wednesday night I paraded as usual at 10pm and a memo from Headquarters was thrust into my hand. I was appointed acting Sergeant, at Biddulph, for three months -

with effect from two days ago. I was due on duty there at 2pm the next day, I'd never been near Biddulph - I didn't even know how to get there. I spent the next few hours writing up my very substantial workload to be handed over, went home at 3am and tried to catch a few hours' sleep. Before I started in the afternoon, it would be a good idea to visit Biddulph that morning to meet my new boss, Inspector John Cooney. At least I'd proved the tall donkey wrong and had a lot to thank Paul Manning for.

Around 11 o'clock I found my way to Biddulph, only four miles from home, but completely alien territory to me. I met another acting Sergeant, Steve Birch in the front office. He referred to my new shift as the 'Legion of the Damned'; *Shit... why?* I went upstairs to the Inspector's office and tapped on the door. John Cooney looked up from a massive pile of paperwork,
'You must be Nick, you'd best stay out there a minute or two, I've just farted.'
I'd never had such a down-to-earth boss, we got on famously for the next not three, but almost six months.

I arrived back at the station for 2pm, met and paraded my new shift
Biddulph was a section of Leek Sub-division. My Sub-divisional commander was a recently promoted Superintendent - B'Stard! *Again! Shit! Why does it have to be me?* Not far into the afternoon he rang me. Without anything that resembled a welcome to the station, he asked me about a local event that I knew absolutely nothing about.
He exploded.
'Call yourself a Sergeant? You don't even know what's going on in your own Division?'
'I've been here less than an hour sir, twelve hours ago I was on nights in the city centre, five hours ago I was in bed.'

It wasn't a good start. One consolation was that the B'Stard's office was ten miles away.

I was on a precipitous learning curve, my new patch was a small town surrounded by rolling high moors and countryside. Other than the odd incident attended on behalf of Newcastle's RPUs when they were otherwise engaged, I'd never worked outside an urban area in my ten years' service; or out of a small building with only four cars in its fleet. I'd had no time to mentally prepare myself for the very sudden jump from a PC in a large team in the inner city, to being the Sergeant in charge of a small team and, when John Cooney was off-duty, a town's police station. I still hadn't had my driving permit returned but now really needed to be mobile. After arranging a retest, my driving permit was returned to me; until then I'd spent the first few days being driven around by members of the shift which meant I could get to know them better.

The learning curve was made steeper by the local accent, totally different from the 'Stokie' dialect even though the city was just a handful of miles away. I was on foot in Biddulph High Street one afternoon with one of the team. He asked if I minded him popping into the bank, no problem - until a member of the public came over to me. He may as well have been speaking Martian, I couldn't understand a single word he said. Fortunately, my colleague came out of the bank to my rescue; it would be a few weeks before I could understand the locals properly.

I was so disoriented that on my third day at Biddulph I answered the phone,

'Good morning, Cheadle police, can I help you?'

'Come on Nick, I know you're on earlies but when you don't even know where you are....' A good thing it was someone I knew, it was embarrassing enough as it was.

The 'Legion of the Damned' weren't a bad lot really, one very experienced and nearing retirement, another who I knew already, being a DC at Hanley a few years before; I knew I could depend on them both. There was another PC with a constant conspiratorial air about him, a great guy with his own way of doing things which nobody else understood, but very hard-working and he got the job done. He hated being at such a remote station and wished he could be transferred to Hanley. I'd gladly have swapped with him.

Finally, there was a PC, notorious for being well beyond the control of anyone. I understood that he'd previously been an English teacher, but his paperwork was barely literate, with handwriting like a nine-year old's. He lived in a cottage in an idyllic spot in the country from where in his off-duty time he indulged in every field sport imaginable, mostly of dubious legality.

In my first week we were riding in the car together, he said to me,

'I have no ambitions whatsoever in this job, I've no intention of staying in it.'

'You're being paid to be a PC, regardless of your plans you'll work properly and it's my job to make sure you do', was my response.

He applied for a vacancy on the force Poaching Squad. I minuted his application saying that I couldn't support it. I contacted the Inspector in charge of the squad who roared with laughter as he said,

'We've been trying to catch that sod for ages, and he wants to join us? No way!'

The PC wasn't happy.

He regularly approached me with a situation he was having difficulty with, usually having been derailed by his ineptitude.

Years later I learned that as a manager, if someone comes to you with a problem, you should imagine that they have a 'monkey' with them; a good manager will make sure they still have the monkey with them when they leave but feel better about it.

Whenever he came to me with a problem his first words were always,

'What *you've* got here is...'

Handing the monkey over at the very start of the conversation just wasn't on!

He gave an impression of constantly being very busy, without actually doing anything useful at all, and any resulting paperwork was rarely forthcoming. He'd find himself inconsequential, protracted jobs or enquiries which would take him away from our normal day-to-day work, again with no paperwork generated. Once, this involved using a rubber dinghy and grappling hooks in a small pool, allegedly having received information that stolen property had been dumped there. This took him a whole early shift, nothing was recovered.

We were eating kebabs on a town centre car park in the middle of the night; when he finished, he casually tossed the wrapper out of the car window.

The job didn't need him, or anyone like him, as my first problem PC he was an absolute nightmare. He'd have taxed any Sergeant, let alone one with my limited experience in the rank.

He left the job the following year, damn good riddance too.

It was a Sunday late shift, B'Stard strode into the front office, demanded tea and went through the books with a fine toothcomb. He asked me questions on everything and anything, most of which had happened during the seventy-five percent of time that I was off-duty, which I couldn't possibly answer. This was the by now familiar to me scenario of B'Stard deliberately trying to make me feel inadequate by not having answers for him; it took me back years. In his familiar intimidating fashion he made me feel personally responsible for everything, seizing on every single tiny mistake made by others and over which I had no control, but blaming and bollocking me for them. I was silently and in vain wishing for an important job to come in to take me away from the evil bully. The torture lasted for an hour and a half, I breathed a heavy sigh of relief as he left the station and walked to his car, leaving no donation to the tea fund.

It was only then that I noticed his wife had been waiting in the car all the time. If he treated his wife like that, nobody else had a bloody chance.

A twelve-year old girl had gone missing from home after a row with her parents. It was a regular occurrence, and she'd normally return home within a couple of hours. However, she had mental health issues so had to be treated as a vulnerable missing person, regardless of the time she'd been missing - an hour so far today. I asked the shift to make a sweep of the area while I visited the parents. The door was answered by the girl's older brother, he had a milky glaze in his eyes. It was obvious that he couldn't see me properly; although I was in uniform I had to tell him I was the local police Sergeant. A call came from the father in the living room,

'Come in Sergeant, we're through here. I'd heard there was a new Sergeant in town, it's good to meet you.'

In the lounge was an obviously blind man in his early forties. As he welcomed me and asked me to sit down, a call came from his wife in the kitchen,

'Would you like a cup of tea, Sergeant?'

Is the Pope Catholic?

As the kettle boiled in the background, I spoke with the man about his daughter. After a few minutes, cups clinking, his wife came through from the kitchen.

My cup of tea arrived on a tray – placed across the arms of a wheelchair in which the lady was seated. Not long afterwards the daughter came in through the back door, oblivious to the alarm she had caused.

The father's blindness resulted from a hereditary genetic disorder which had caused him to have lost his sight in his teens; the gene had passed to his son, who would lose all his sight within the next couple of years. The mother had advanced multiple sclerosis and had lost the use of her legs several years ago. The daughter, with her mental health issues had special educational needs.

I stayed for an hour or more. For all their terrible afflictions, it was one of the happiest homes I ever visited, full of warmth, love and optimism; they didn't complain at all about their incredibly difficult situation. Neither of them were able to work, but they put a great deal of energy into raising money for charity, in the firm belief that as society was supporting them they should give back as much as possible.

Inspirational people, I felt humbled to have met them.

We had a significant triumph when we caught two Liverpudlian criminals red-handed one evening, burgling a house. They went on to admit many house burglaries across a wide area of the North-West and North Midlands. As I was busy at the scene with the team, the station PC functioned as custody officer until my return. One of the miscreants had concealed an item of jewellery while being searched and it was later found hidden in his cell. Not a big problem, but B'Stard got wind of it and made a huge issue of it, focused, of course, on me. The merest thought of congratulating me and my team for a job well done never occurred to him. He'd search for something to criticise and make a huge issue of, in everything and anything.

At the end of my time at Biddulph, John Cooney reported well on my work. Before leaving I'd met with the Divisional commander who had praised me on a job well done. However, B'Stard signed off the paperwork, still basing his thoughts on his unwarranted opinion of me from years before, making his own dislike of me very clear and deeming me unsuitable for promotion. Having him as my Superintendent meant I'd been doomed career-wise from the moment I started there.

Thankfully, that was the last time I ever had to deal with him whilst in the job. Some years later, after I'd retired I came face to face with B'Stard whilst out shopping in Hanley. The *hail fellow well met* smile he greeted me with quickly disappeared from his face as I gave him both barrels and then some, just as he had with me, so many times. It felt good.

Back to Hanley for a few weeks, back on IRVs and amassing a pile of paperwork. Just as my workload reached its peak, another Headquarters memo was thrust in front of me at the start of a Tuesday noon shift. I was to be acting Sergeant at Stoke, with effect from the day before. Again I was completely unprepared. I had to spend the rest of the day writing up my paperwork, again. Putting my stripes back on, I headed down the road to Stoke the next afternoon.

My bosses at Stoke weren't very impressed by my having been missing in action for two days, as if it was my fault. This was at a time in the force when you were deemed responsible for all your failings, mostly those over which you had no control, or even had any knowledge of. As somebody had bravely noted on a computer log around that time, *to err is human, to forgive is contrary to force policy*.

Nevertheless the Chief Inspector, Ray Willard took me to his office and welcomed me effusively. He constantly got my name wrong though, calling me Nigel, Norman and Neil, but never Nick in the course of our first meeting.

A few days later, I sent two PCs to execute an arrest warrant for failing to appear at court. I was custody officer for the afternoon and awaited their return. When they arrived at the cell block with their prisoner I was expecting a straightforward booking-in. Switching the video recorder on I went into the usual routine,

'Can you tell me why this man has been arrested?'

Before either officer could speak, their prisoner said, in a state of great anxiety,

'I'm PC Matlock from Northern Traffic Sarge, I've been fitted up for shoplifting.'

My bowels momentarily turned to water; I'd certainly not been expecting this. Unbeknown to me, the two officers had been diverted to a report of a shoplifter at Tesco, alleged to have stolen a bottle of whisky.

I booked him in, finding it very difficult to have a fellow officer before me, but knowing that I must carefully follow proper procedure to the absolute letter. Surely there had been a mistake though - this couldn't possibly happen.

On being asked if he wanted anyone to be informed of his arrest, he nominated his Chief Inspector. Deeply shocked at learning of the situation, his boss told me that he was one of his most highly regarded and hardest working officers.

Enquiries had to be made, and statements obtained, so there would be a delay before he was dealt with, and he'd have to go in a cell. Closing the cell door on that guy, instinctively believing in his innocence was the most difficult, painful thing I'd done in my service.

The case was handed over to a Detective Sergeant. As the afternoon wore on it became obvious that soon-to-be ex-PC Matlock had not been fitted up at all; he was putting forward a risible defence and had committed a brazen act of theft.

There were all types in the service, we didn't all get on, we didn't know everyone we worked with. What we *did* do though, was to work across the service as a united team, with a common bond of belief in the honesty of everyone we worked with. That afternoon my belief was shattered by this thief.

By the end of the shift, he'd been charged with theft and written out his resignation, effective immediately.

The body of a newly born child had been found in a public lavatory in the city. Such tragic incidents always attracted attention from the public. It was common to make media appeals for the mother to contact us as she *may need medical help* (which roughly translates to *detectives would like to speak to her)*.

We had a call from a lady saying that she had found an afterbirth, there may be a connection.

It was in the middle of the road outside the Mr Kipling cake bakery in Trent Vale. The IRV had arrived before me, and the crew had already coned off the area. CID and Scenes of Crime officers were en-route, although the officers told me they were very dubious as to what we were dealing with. The lady who'd found it was in a state of some agitation, seeing my stripes she rushed towards me,

'Thank goodness Sergeant, it's an afterbirth. These officers won't believe me. I *know* it's one, I'm a cleaner at the maternity hospital, I've seen lots of them. I *KNOW*!'

I went to take a look at the 'afterbirth' which was bright red, semi-transparent and had small light flecks in it.

'It is, isn't it? I'm right, aren't I Sergeant?'

'It's like no afterbirth I've seen duck, and I've seen the ones from my own kids, they're grey. Did you say you worked in the maternity hospital?'

She looked offended. I'd had enough of this.

We were outside a cake bakery!

To the lady's gasps of horror, I bent over it and as I did, a sweet smell drifted into my nostrils. To gasps from the assembled crowd, I started to prod my finger in the object. I scooped up a fingerful, put it to my lips and tasted it.

Our informant came towards me, furious, 'What do you think you're doi….'

235

'This is strawberry jam duck; those bits are the pips. It must have spilled from a tanker going into the bakery.'

The lady flushed, turned, melted into the crowd and vanished as I radioed for CID and SOCO to be cancelled.

I'm relieved she wasn't one of the hospital's medical staff.

17 – Bumpier, With Potholes

My time at Stoke was short-lived. A relentless many-months-long, downhill slide started.

One Sunday afternoon I answered the phone in the front office, a furtive male voice said,

'I want to speak to the Detective Chief Inspector.'

'Sorry, he's not on duty, can I take a message?'

'No, I've got to speak to him, can you ring him at home?'

'That's not how we do things.'

'Ring him, he'll speak to me'

The line went dead, and I thought nothing more of it. Calls asking for senior officers were commonplace, often with abusive intent. If they were off-duty, force policy was to take messages and certainly not to disturb them at home other than in the most exceptional circumstances.

A wise Sergeant had told me some time ago, 'If in doubt, do it by the book, then nobody can criticise you.' On this Sunday I inflicted catastrophic career damage by following his advice and correctly following force policy.

The next morning, I heard that the DCI was on the warpath. One of his informants had called the station and hadn't been able to speak to him, it had been very important. How was I to know? I didn't want to place the whole of my team under suspicion, so believing honesty to be the best policy, I went up to the DCI's office. I introduced myself and explained what had happened the previous afternoon.

It seems that honesty was not the best policy where this particular detective was concerned.

'We don't do it like that here.'

I was back at Hanley, minus stripes the very next day.

To err is human...

It didn't end there; it seems that the wrath of the DCI was only partially assuaged. A few days later, a Superintendent's memo was pushed in front of me on noon shift parade. With effect from the following month, I was to be moved to another shift.

The memo named two other officers for shift changes, but they were permanently seconded to other duties meaning that for them it was purely a paper exercise – in all probability they weren't even aware. It was obvious that this was at the behest of the angry DCI, as it was focused on just me, the other names added as a badly executed smokescreen. Nobody had troubled themselves to discuss it with me, sadly typical of the indifferent way our senior officers had come to treat us. It was a clumsily implemented, malicious punishment for following force policy to the letter and having had the honesty to having said so.

This was very bad news indeed and extremely demoralising. I'd worked with the same shift (apart from the two spells of acting) for seven years. It wasn't just the people I worked with on the shift but the network I had with others across the city on the same shift pattern; it helped us all to work effectively as we could regularly call upon each other for the odd favour.

I put pen to paper protesting at this treatment but there was no right of appeal, it was a done deed and was going to happen, come what may. One senior officer 'advised' me to leave it, 'while you've still got a career.' I took my revenge by claiming all the overtime incurred by the changes in shift pattern caused by my sudden moves to Biddulph and Stoke and back. I had a bit more money, but I was on a different shift, with different people, and very unhappy. The memo had said that the movement was necessary to balance out skills and experience between shifts. Absolute bullshit, even with my experience and seniority I was treated as a spare part on my new shift and regularly allocated outlying foot beats and jobs that nobody else wanted to do.

I'd been on the shift a few weeks when a 'complaint' came out of nowhere, allegedly from a member of the public.

I wasn't officially informed, never interviewed and all efforts on my part to find out what was going on were stonewalled. It was many months later that I was called to the Divisional Commander's office for a bollocking for what still remained a mystery even after I left the room. On asking him what the exact nature of the complaint was I was told to 'let sleeping dogs lie.' Someone had conspired to make my life as uncomfortable as possible, and I'd a bloody good idea who it was.

One evening I was doing football duty at Port Vale when I was suddenly violently sick and had terrible abdominal pains. It subsided but I didn't feel at all well, the Sergeant took one look at me and sent me home. The next day I went to the doctor, still suffering dreadful pain. I was given a prescription and sent on my way. I followed the medication but over the next two days the pain become worse, and I became quite unwell, so I went back to the doctor. Within an hour I was in a hospital ward being prepared for emergency surgery.. The surgery never happened, but I was in hospital for almost two weeks being poked, prodded, having scans and X-rays – as well as the everlasting bog-stopping (the hospital's bog this time) white-shit barium meal again. The final diagnosis was that a small gallstone had slowly passed through and lacerated my bile duct. Whatever it was, it was very painful and made me feel really ill.

Two weeks later I was back at work feeling much better but one evening soon afterwards I was walking down a dark alley - a spare part yet again - stumbled into a pothole and turned my right foot over. The pain was excruciating, I could hardly walk but somehow managed to hobble the hundred yards or so back to the station, file an injury on duty report and ride home. A good thing I was on my motorbike, as I don't think I'd have managed to operate the brake of my car with my foot as it was.

Little did I know it then, but that was to be my final shift as a PC at Hanley. The next day my right ankle was swollen to double its size and black all over - off sick again, this was not going to look good on my personal record. Physio and rest slowly improved the situation but with the emphasis on 'slowly' the weeks went by and I was still not able to return to work.

Eventually I was summoned to see the police surgeon; quite normal for anyone who had been off sick for any length of time, or so I thought.

'Ah, Mr Tucker, come in, take a seat. Do you know why you're here?'

'Probably routine, my sickness record has taken a battering doc. I'm hoping to get back to work very soon', which by now was indeed the case.

'Er, not quite', he pushed a report from my Inspector towards me and let me read it. The report expressed great concern at the length of time I'd been off work and had been minuted by the Divisional Commander, who recommended that I should be medically retired. During the time I'd been incapacitated there had been not one single word of contact from Hanley, nobody had visited me, phoned me or discussed future plans with me. I was horrified, as was the doctor when I told him so. This callous treatment spoke volumes of the quality of our senior management. The doctor examined me, concluding that apart from an improving dodgy ankle I was completely fit for duty, and that would be his recommendation.

Staffordshire Police's - Hanley's in particular - atrocious people-management didn't end there. A week later I decided that I would be able to return to work after my shift's present rest-days. However, a local PC knocked on my door to inform me that as of the previous day I'd been transferred to Burslem. I went to Hanley and spoke to my (by then, former) Superintendent who denied all knowledge of what was going on, bare-faced lying which I couldn't prove. This move should have been discussed with me in advance by a senior officer, rather than me being informed by another PC and having had to instigate the discussion.

Thoroughly dejected by the latest crushing treatment, I cleared my locker. I'd reached rock bottom.

I phoned my new Superintendent, John Chawner who I'd known for some years, a very fair-minded, approachable man. I made an appointment to see him the next day. Welcoming me to the Sub-division, he commented that I had a lot of ground to make up. I couldn't help myself, I told him that to my mind at least I'd done nothing wrong: B'Stard had bullied me at Biddulph (I would easily have had an official grievance case against him had this been a few years later), I'd been sent back to Hanley from Stoke for sticking to the rules and telling the truth, Hanley's senior management had treated me despicably, and my health issues were down to pure bad luck. He seemed sympathetic and said he would keep an open mind.

Moving to Burslem at this extremely low ebb actually marked a sharp upward turning point in my career, I loved working there. It was a small, very cramped station but with great people and a really friendly, relaxed atmosphere. It was busy enough to stave off boredom, but with enough spare time to generate our own work and make enquiries. At Hanley, those of us on IRVs could have a caseload of up to twenty-five crime reports, with five of them possibly detectable and needing arrests, plus half a dozen car crashes to investigate - all this on top of the daily incoming work. There was never enough time to do it all properly, with constant broken appointments, no time to complete paperwork and no sense of fulfilment. We were mainly concentrating on stopping the wheel falling off and keeping out of ~~the shi~~ trouble. Burslem was quite different, it took only a week for me to realise that I'd never felt more contented in the job. With the exception of Stuart Austin, the shift's controller, I was the longest-serving on the team and gained a great deal of pleasure from helping the less experienced members. They were great people with lots of very eager youngsters amongst them.

I still had a fight on my hands as I'd had a less than complimentary annual appraisal from Hanley. I was summoned to Headquarters to see the head of personnel, Chief Superintendent Turner. The department was popularly known as 'Turner's Tours', because many visitors to his office were uprooted and moved somewhere, but I was determined not to be one of them. I strode into his office, stood to attention, and saluted. He wordlessly motioned me to sit down and for several minutes he sat in silence, ignoring my presence; sifting through what appeared to be my personal file with an occasional sigh, the odd tut and shake of the head. This was blatant intimidation and by now I'd had a bellyful of being mistreated by the force. I was having none of it and stood up.

'I can see you're busy sir, I'll come back another time.'
'SIT. DOWN!'
He finally looked up, realising I wouldn't tolerate being messed with. Without a further moment's delay we began to discuss my appraisal, based on just two months' work on my 'new' Hanley shift and the reports from Biddulph and Stoke.

'It looks like you've been going through a purple patch.'
'You could say that, the last twelve months are nothing to be proud of, but I don't think I've been fairly treated. In fact I think I've been well and truly shit on from all quarters.'

I told him the same story I'd from my meeting with Superintendent Chawner a few weeks before.

'Well things have got to change, I'm sure you agree.'
I nodded in full agreement.
Some changes in the behaviour of senior management were needed too.

'What are we going to do with you? I think a change of policing style could suit you, how about a rural patrol unit?'

I put forward emphatically how I'd just settled in at Burslem. I was enjoying myself, working hard and already achieving results, I certainly didn't want any more upheaval. He made a show of thinking hard for a few moments.

'Very well, you can stay at Burslem, but I'll be asking Mr Chawner for a report on your progress in three months' time, hopefully we won't have to move you.'

As if being moved was an inevitable force of nature.

18 – Taking Off

The three months passed.
I stayed at Burslem.

I was really happy there, of all the stations I worked at it was by far the most enjoyable and rewarding, as well as sometimes very challenging. I had a shock coming though. I'd worked some 'difficult' council estates, Crackley, Bentilee and Abbey Hulton, but I'd yet to experience the mother of all sink estates – Chell Heath, which bordered on our patch.

Their proximity meant that the Chell Heathens occupied plenty of our time. One evening I had to take a prisoner with one of my young colleagues, Phil to search the man's home on the estate.

As we pulled up outside there was a boy, no more than two to three years old, dressed in filthy clothes playing at the kerbside, he took one look at us and exclaimed,

'Fuck off pigs.'

That was my welcome to Chell Heath; I'd hazard a guess that this youngster's future prospects wouldn't see him as CEO of a major company.

It was an unwritten rule that you *never, ever* left your car unattended in Chell Heath, so Phil went into the house with the prisoner while I stayed with the car. Within moments the prisoner shot out of the front door with Phil close behind. Without a second thought I joined the pursuit, and we caught our man within seconds. He'd given us false details; he was actually a wanted man making a run for home. On returning to the car, I patted my pockets for the keys and couldn't find them - then a dreadful squeaky-bum moment when I remembered that I hadn't taken them out of the ignition when I leapt out of the car - they weren't there now. It was a minor miracle that the car was still there, and - thankfully - my briefcase containing my paperwork.

I asked Burslem to send someone to us with a set of spare keys, but Sod's Law dictated that none could be found. Another car arrived and headed back to Burslem with Phil and the prisoner. I couldn't leave my car as someone in the slowly growing crowd of spectators had the keys and would have had some real fun with it. I had to sit alone, locked in the car, surrounded by a hostile crowd who were delighted at having got one up on the 'pigs.' They spat at the car constantly; there was nothing I could do but sit and stare into space as green Heathen snot dribbled its way down the windscreen. This lasted for over half an hour, it felt much longer, until the breakdown truck from Northern Traffic Group arrived.

The driver dropped me off at Burslem, there was plenty of the usual piss-taking as I walked through the front office. Our acting Inspector, Malcolm Jones took me into his office – he was understanding, but in view of all the fuss that had been created he'd have to commit the matter to paper. I'd committed a cardinal sin by leaving the keys in the car. Fair enough, Malcolm had no option, but I made a point that the lack of spare keys was a very serious issue too, needing urgent attention.

Next afternoon, rather than wait for the call I decided to confront the issue head-on and see our Chief Inspector, John 'Taff' Thomas, a tremendous guy who'd also been my Chief Inspector at Biddulph – the poor man had B'Stard as his boss there. A few years earlier he'd survived a parachute jump when his parachute hadn't actually opened.

'Thought you might want to see me sir?'

'Come in boyo, come in, shut the door.'

Oh shit, shut the door...

'It's about last night, stupid thing I did, caused lots of trouble and made us look bad, it won't happen again.'

'I'm sure it won't son. Look, you jumped out of the car to go and help your mate, it went tits-up, but I can't criticise you for that or anything else. Put it down to experience. You're making a name for yourself here, keep it up.'

Brilliant! I volunteered for a bollocking and came out with Brownie points!

I was on a course for the machine used for the station breath test procedure, the Lion Intoximeter. Unusually this course started at 2pm and lasted for 24 hours. During the afternoon we were shown how to operate the machine as well as how alcohol metabolises in the body; more interesting than it sounds actually and would probably need a separate book to explain fully. Briefly, even if you have several drinks in rapid succession, it can be an hour or more before it's absorbed into your blood. It's quite possible that someone could neck four pints of beer during half-an-hour in the pub, drive home and easily pass a breath test if stopped on the way. An hour later, it would be a different matter. I don't recommend it, but on an empty stomach it's feasible that you could drink half a bottle of whisky in half-an-hour and none of it would be absorbed into your bloodstream for an hour or more.

We were encouraged to put theory into practice, *game on!* During the evening we were drinking (to excess) in the bar and periodically testing ourselves on the machine. It took four pints and a couple of large whiskies in the space of an hour and a half before I touched the legal limit, and even then I could hyperventilate (a way of beating the machine if you're bordering on the legal limit) down to a figure well below it. The next morning however was a different matter. At 9am, after a good night's sleep on site I tested myself – I was nearly double the legal limit, and it was after lunch before I could safely drive home.

4am. Hanley were dealing with a murder at Bucknall. The suspect lived on our patch, they asked us to visit his home and arrest him. I went with Malcolm to the address they gave. It was a beautifully kept old, detached house in Milton. The circumstances didn't quite fit, the house was far too upmarket. We checked with Hanley and having been assured that this was the correct address, we knocked on the door. The curtains were all open and the house seemed empty. No reply, we checked with Hanley, the Inspector there ordered us to force entry to the house.

Having smashed a pane of stained glass in the front door we let ourselves in. and had a look around. The house was spotless, tastefully decorated with chintzy furniture and carefully arranged, twee ornaments. It was obvious that nobody was in. As we started to climb the stairs, Hanley called to admit a mistake, the address was wrong, something we'd been well aware of all the time. Having been given the correct address, we left another patrol to look after the lovely, but now insecure house. We went a hundred yards or so along the same road to a ground floor council flat, this was more like it.

Malcolm stood behind me as I rapped on the door. Movement from inside and a man answered the door, looking unsurprised by our turning up in the middle of the night.

I confirmed his name and began,

'We have had a report of a murder at Buck…'

Suddenly Malcolm pushed in front of me, continuing,

'…nall which you are suspected of. I'm arresting you on suspicion of murder.'

First time I was about to arrest someone for murder, and Malcolm pulled rank and snatched it away from me! As he would say, 'Swine!' Smashing guy actually, we had some great times over the years.

One Saturday early turn, I arrived at Burslem and was sent back to Kidsgrove to stand in for the early-turn controller, who'd phoned in sick. Kidsgrove was very quiet at that time of day, so I had little to do for the first couple of hours. It began to get a little busier, but still not very – the phone would ring about once every twenty-five minutes, maybe it was going to be a stress-free shift.

At 9am the Chief Inspector arrived. Howard Poole, a giant of a man who I'd known for years. After I'd explained to him that I was filling in, he looked through the books and went to his office, across the corridor from the Control Room. Every time I ended an incoming phone call, Howard would come into the room.

'What was that about?'

I'd tell him.

'Well, you need to… and … and don't forget …'

After this happened a few times, I put my coat on and put my head into his office. He roared,

'Where the bloody hell are you going?'

'Well, you seem to know what to do without any help from me boss, so I'm back off to Burslem.'

I could see the rage momentarily build in him, and then quickly subside,

'Okay Nick, point taken. I should know better, you've been in the job long enough to know what you're doing, I'm sorry.'

We got on famously from that day onwards. Howard was a fearsome boss, but very well respected. He liked the type of people who stood up to him and would willingly acknowledge when he was in the wrong, which was very rarely. Another boss of the calibre that the job really needed, but in pitifully short supply.

Burslem was a town dominated by many pottery factories, which sadly declined to zero over the next few years when outsourcing labour to other countries became widespread in British industry. At the time Thursday nights were busy, it was payday for the workforce who ventured out with their newly found, ephemeral wealth, falling out with each other after too many drinks. Although Thursday was a hectic night, Fridays and Saturdays, unlike the City Centre were fairly quiet.

One Thursday night, we all raced to a fight in the town centre. Two middle-aged men were knocking each other about and ignoring our requests to calm down, so we were forced to arrest them. As I was putting one of them into the car he fixed me with a stare,

'Get this you bastard', and head butted me.

The next thing I knew I was coming around lying on the ground with my colleague Mandy's worried face hovering over me. Having been taken home, I was off work with headaches and blurred vision for three days. Obviously, the man was charged with assaulting me.

A few weeks later we were in court, he had pleaded 'Not Guilty' to both the assault and being drunk and disorderly. The Crown Prosecution Service lawyer took us through our evidence, after which he buried himself in the paperwork for his next case, oblivious to the defence lawyer's cross-examination.

'Officer, is it possible that the defendant *accidentally* caught your head as he bent down to get in the car after you arrested him?'

'No, he said...'

I was trying to say what my attacker had said to me before the head butt.

'No officer, I put it to you that it is possible, anyone who gets into a car has to bend their head forward.'

'Yes, they do, but this was deliberate, he said...'

'No further questions your worships.'

'Thank you officer, you may stand down,' said the magistrate without offering me the opportunity to complete my sentence.

The defence solicitor had been determined that I shouldn't repeat the words I'd already said in my main evidence, I'd been desperately trying to catch the CPS lawyer's eye to intervene, as was Mandy, but to no avail.

The magistrates, as they often did, swallowed the lie and the thug walked free from court. Mandy was just out of her probation, and this was her first (probably of many) experience of a travesty of justice - she was outraged. I committed my thoughts on the negligence of the CPS lawyer to paper, but nothing appeared to come of it.

We had a regular customer in Smallthorne, a middle-aged single man who'd lived with his mother. He had mental health issues and should have been receiving appropriate care from the proper agencies, but as was often the case, it fell to us to shoulder the burden instead.

He was an absolute pest, constantly reporting non-existent incidents, which became a daily occurrence following the death of his mother; he was now on his own in the house.

One day a neighbour called us as he hadn't been seen for a few days; it could be the usual case of searching the house for a body. At least I didn't have to kick any doors down this time as the neighbour had a key. As I went in, the house didn't have the anticipated scent of death, but I was still apprehensive as I cautiously went from room-to-room downstairs, calling his name.

Having found nothing downstairs and still calling his name, I climbed the stairs, the tension building with every step in the deathly still, silent house. I went into the main bedroom; there wasn't the expected body in the bed but suddenly, in my peripheral vision I saw a trousered and shoed leg poking out at the side of the wardrobe - I jumped out of my skin.

Fuck me, he's playing hide-and-seek!

I could hear my heart pounding. As I recovered my composure,

'Come on Eric you dickhead, stop playing games!'

No reply, the leg didn't move. Then I remembered,

He's got a wooden leg!

This was it, complete with shoe and trousers that he had taken off, but without Eric attached.

He wasn't in the house, several phone calls later (getting some satisfaction at running up his phone bill), it turned out that he was safe and well in hospital, having called an ambulance in the middle of the night a couple of days ago. I don't think I saw him again after that, maybe he finally received the care that he should have had for years.

Car parking at Burslem was virtually non-existent, so I was still commuting by motorbike, parking it in the station yard by the side door. I returned to the station at the end of a noon shift to find the night shift Inspector's Mini parked where my bike had been, I couldn't see it anywhere.

I went to his office,

'Where've you put my bike boss?'

'What bike? I haven't done anything.'

He was a bit of a joker, so I didn't believe him at first.

'C'mon boss, I want to get off home, a joke's a joke but…'

'Honestly Nick, I haven't seen it.'

My motorbike had been stolen from right outside the back door of the nick - I couldn't believe it. It was recovered about half an hour later, wrecked by the Chell Heathens. Naturally, the scumbag who'd taken it couldn't keep quiet about his accomplishment of *robbin' a pig's motorbike,* so the word soon reached CID's ears. The next day he was arrested and charged. He proudly pleaded guilty (to give him even more 'street-cred' probably) but had to pay compensation for my insurance excess.

Some calls we received from the public were an absolute waste of time, a good controller could filter out most of them without a patrol having to be sent but some slipped through the net, and we ended up being sent to many LOB (Load Of Bollocks) jobs. It was up to the officer attending whether to deal with a genuine job officially, to *give suitable advice* or - to use the vernacular - *cuff* the job if it had little or nothing to do with the police. The more experienced you were, the easier it was to see that an incident was a waste of time and to cuff it, knowing that would be the end of the matter. With fourteen years' service behind me, and as the most experienced outside officer on the shift I became known as an 'ace cuffer' by Stuart, who would send me to incidents, eagerly anticipating whether and how I would cuff the job.

One busy Sunday afternoon I was on IRV patrol in Norton, and he radioed me.

'Job in from the ambulance, they've had a 999 saying that a lad has hit his mother with a bottle, and she has a head injury.'

After I'd confirmed I'd attend, Stuart sent a quick burst,

'Cuff that mate!'

After blue-lighting to the address in Ball Green, I radioed Stuart less than five minutes later.

'The son is nine months old...

'The bottle was his feed...

'In a tantrum he has struck his Mum with it...

'She has a half inch superficial cut to her scalp.'

Stuart replied incredulously,

'That's your best cuff yet Nick!'

He never did believe me. It was a complete waste of our time and that of an emergency ambulance crew. The public can be incredibly stupid.

Late one night I went to a crash on Waterloo Road in Cobridge. A young lady had stepped out of the offside door of a private hire car, started to cross the road without looking and was struck a glancing blow by a car driving towards Burslem. She was sitting on the kerb being attended to by the ambulance crew who would be taking her to hospital.

I talked to her and obtained her details, intending to visit her for an interview after she was discharged. The young man driving the car was very shaken. After he'd given a negative breath test and I made sure he felt able to drive home, I made an appointment to interview him when I was back on daytime shifts.

An hour later I was tucking into a bag of chips when Stuart called me,

'Your girl from the RTA, she's in intensive care, she's critical.'

I was astonished, she'd been fully aware and chatting to everyone only an hour ago. I arranged for my colleagues from NTG to join me at the scene but there was nothing of value to an investigation. Normally Traffic Division would take over a fatal RTA or potential one, but I decided that this was an opportunity for me to prove myself once-and-for-all by dealing with it.

On my rest days Malcolm Lloyd, the duty Inspector at Burslem phoned me to say there was no possibility that Donna, the young lady, would survive. He suggested that I come back on days instead of noons on the Thursday; he'd already arranged for the car to be examined, and no defects had been found. An appeal had been made for witnesses.

I came back on the Thursday morning to a list of witnesses who'd come forward. I also had a message to contact the mother of the young man who had been driving the car. They were clearly a caring, respectable family, and she was deeply concerned about Donna, as well as her son. I arranged for her to bring him to the station for interview later in the day, with a solicitor if they wanted one.

I visited Donna's devastated husband in Hanley, spent some time with him and explained how I'd be dealing with the enquiry. There were no Family Liaison Officers in those days, witness and victim care was entirely down to the investigating officer - me. I told him that he could contact me at any time, for anything at all.

Then I set about seeing some of the witnesses. One thing quickly became obvious, all of them had consumed large quantities of alcohol on the night. Although there were common threads in their statements, because of their intoxication the Coroner would not be fully satisfied with their accounts. However, it was all I had.

I interviewed the driver of the car at length in the afternoon. He was extremely upset, a decent lad. From what I'd already learned from witnesses, I seriously doubted that his driving had caused this tragedy.

The next day Donna's husband came to the station, very distressed and asking to see me. Donna's life support machine was going to be switched off as she'd been found to be brain dead; I still couldn't believe that this was a young lady I'd been chatting to only a week ago, apparently only slightly injured. He had no family to support him and asked if I would take him to the hospital, I was more than willing. It also meant that I could have the necessary identification done for the Coroner.

He identified Donna to me as she lay there with the medical staff gradually taking all the tubes away; tears stinging my own eyes I stepped back, leaving the young man alone for a final few moments with her as she quickly, quietly slipped away. They were both only in their twenties, absolutely heart-breaking, a scene that I have never forgotten.

Over the next few days, I interviewed and took statements from all the witnesses, every single one of them had consumed alcohol – a fact that had to be included in their evidence, but it was crystal clear that the young man driving the car was blameless, there was nothing he could have done.

I called on Donna's sister, who'd been with her at the time; she was a pleasant enough but hard-faced, careworn young lady with cheaply dyed hair, smelling of patchouli oil and chain-smoked Old Holborn roll-ups. She was alleging, quite insistently that the car had been travelling at a very high speed; understandable as everyone tries to find someone to blame in these situations. Meanwhile the Coroner's Office had contacted me to say that the identification was unacceptable as the 'deceased was still alive at the time'; by a few seconds maybe, this was ridiculous as well as cruel, but they insisted on a further identification. I couldn't put the husband through it again, I'd called on him earlier that morning and he was falling apart by the second. Her sister was prepared to do it though, so I decided that after taking her to identify Donna's body at the hospital mortuary, I'd visit the scene with her to get her version of events. It would be useful to take her step-by-step through the fateful incident where it had actually happened.

We stood at the scene, and she showed me exactly how they had got out of the private hire car, where they had walked, and where her sister was struck. She was still adamant that the car, as she put it 'came out of nowhere.' I got back in the car with her and using its odometer I measured the distance from the scene to the point where visibility was lost. I then showed her simple calculations to show that for the car to have suddenly appeared it would have had to be travelling at over 150mph. The car was a 1.3 litre Vauxhall Cavalier, she still wouldn't accept it.

I had to trace the driver of the private hire car; all I knew was the name of the firm, an outfit with which we had many dealings, and for all the wrong reasons. Their driver had moved off immediately the car doors slammed shut, either ignorant of what followed or, quite likely, not caring. I phoned the firm to ask who the driver was but was predictably met by their characteristic lack of interest or cooperation. I asked to speak to the owner, *he's out boss,* still no interest, so I said I'd be there within the hour to inspect their (mandatory but in all probability non-existent) records.

As if by magic the driver presented himself at the station in less than a third of that time and was duly interviewed. As well as being of little help, he wasn't remotely concerned that one of his passengers had received fatal injuries just seconds after handing over her fare. Despite being summoned, he didn't even bother turning up at the inquest, the Coroner was furious.

After many interviews, taking of statements and writing up, my enquiry was complete; for a Divisional IRV driver to complete a fatal enquiry was a big accomplishment. From the low of the previous year, I felt on top of my game and able to tackle anything. My Divisional ritual humiliation board that year went much better than usual too.

Donna's family were still seeking someone to blame, although the tragedy had been entirely caused by the two young ladies, both drunk, alighting from the car carelessly. There were angry scenes at the inquest, they were gunning for the innocent young man whose car had hit her. One by one the witnesses gave their evidence, and I could see the Coroner, John Wain (Frederic Hails had retired) becoming increasingly aggravated by the constant buzz of hostility from the family. Eventually his anger boiled over. I'd known him a long time and was quite surprised to see him slam his papers down on the desk, then shout angrily at the family,

'What on earth do YOU know? You were ALL **DRUNK**, including the witnesses! The only people involved in this who weren't drunk are this young man (pointing to the unfortunate driver) and the police officer! If there's one more sound from you. I will have you all removed!'

An uneasy silence followed. I had to escort the young man and his mother to their car and see them safely on their way after the verdict of 'Accidental Death' had been recorded.

Cobridge was part of my regular patch, for many years it had been a hotbed for street prostitutes, it still is today. One of the streets that they infested had the appropriate road-signs *Humps for 800 yards*. No matter how many times you arrested them they kept coming back. I arrested my fair share of them, but I would often just park my marked car in a highly visible spot at the centre of their 'operation' while doing my paperwork; they hated it. I'd also follow their pathetic kerb-crawling clients; this could be quite entertaining as they followed ridiculously labyrinthine routes away from the area before being stopped and providing a pathetic explanation for their behaviour. I've always loathed the 'ladies of the night', but over the years those who had been just doing it for money had been replaced by wretched drug addicts who had turned to this 'profession' to feed their habit. It was nothing short of slavery; most if not all of them were being pimped by a man who as well as being their dealer was supplying drugs to all and sundry. The prostitutes had now become victims.

The pimp-cum-dealer lived in a first floor flat, the front bay window had a panoramic view of the area of Waterloo Road where the prostitutes under his control displayed their wares. There was a twenty-four-hour stream of addicts to the rear entrance of the block. As well as having a menacing physique he was a very clever, intelligent man, constantly one step ahead of the game and living behind reinforced doors in the belief that he was untouchable. Until a major operation could be launched against him, he was just that; all that we could do was to frustrate his business as much as possible by keeping his women off the streets.

One Saturday night there'd been a dispute between one of his slaves and her 'client.' The pimp had intervened, culminating in him firing a handgun at the client from the window of his flat; fortunately he missed. A seriously overdue decision was made to launch a full-scale operation to arrest him on the Sunday morning. Firearms and the Tactical Support Group (TSG, formerly the FSU) were brought in, his flat was raided and searched; he was arrested and a string of charges followed. During the subsequent lengthy jail sentence he passed the time smoking cannabis. The clever, sharp-witted man emerged from the prison gates as a free man, but a jibbering idiot, pathetically potty from persistent pot smoking. He's still in the area, but the former local criminal mastermind, whilst still troubling the courts is now ridiculed as a village idiot. I've seen cannabis produce other psychotic wrecks like this man, anybody who thinks it's a harmless recreational drug is seriously deluded.

An RSPCA officer had been called one morning to a report of a neglected dog at a mid-terraced house in Middleport. They'd discovered a matter of even greater concern which I had to deal with.

Looking through the ground-floor rear window of the house, I could see the dog and three small children, the oldest apparently about six years old. I coaxed him to unlock the back door for me; he was a bright little lad. He, his three-year-old brother and two-year-old sister were alone in the house. On the floor of the living room were a couple of bowls, a packet of Kellogg's Ricicles and a bottle of sterilised milk. Talking to the boy, I discovered their parents had left for work at about 7.30am and would not be back until 4.30 in the afternoon, this was all the food that they had been left, and he was 'in-charge.' It seemed this was a daily arrangement during school holidays. I wondered whether any arrangements had been made with neighbours, but after knocking on a few doors it seemed nobody was aware, and nobody know where the parents worked. The RSPCA officer took the dog away. After changing the stinking nappy of the two-year old. I bundled the children into the back of my car to take to the station.

I settled them in front of the TV in our lounge with one of the office staff looking after them. They needed feeding, so my next stop was the Vine Inn across the road where the landlady made some sandwiches for them. Meanwhile, my colleagues in the station managed to trace the mother to the pottery factory where she worked. After she had been brought to the phone, I instructed her to come to the station *immediately*, the factory was ten minutes' walk away. Whilst awaiting her arrival I made another call, to Social Services.

'Immediately' was almost three-quarters of an hour later, when both parents arrived at the station, completely insensible to the seriousness of the situation. They were so utterly pig-ignorant that they had no realisation of what they had done wrong, believing it perfectly acceptable that their small children should be left alone in a house, with all the attendant dangers.

One thing they said left me absolutely dumbstruck.

'We thought they'd be alright with the dog there.'

Social Services obviously though it was alright too. Following interviews with both parents and much discussion they wouldn't support a prosecution for neglect; they allowed the children back into the 'care' of their parents. The RSPCA wouldn't let them have the dog back though – says a lot.

Those kids are probably leaving their own children unattended now, and it's happening all over the country. Nothing ever seems to be done about these situations until lives are lost - even then only maybe.

The dog probably had the best prospects of all.

The ambulance service, like ourselves were always under a great deal of pressure but seemed to believe that we had limitless resources which we could place at their disposal. We'd often receive calls from them asking us to 'check out a call for us', or in other words attend an incident that they couldn't or wouldn't go to. It was ridiculous but, unlike other services, we were never able to say 'no', for fear of a disciplinary enquiry following.

Early one morning following a 999 call which the ambulance wouldn't attend, I was sent to a house in Sneyd

Green, where an elderly lady had fallen out of bed. Her partner, also elderly, was too frail to help her back. I gently helped her back into bed and ensured she was well and comfortable before I left. Some weeks later, the Coroner's Office contacted me, the lady had since died in hospital from pneumonia after being admitted with a broken hip, suspected to have been caused by the fall. They demanded my explanation; somewhat impolitely I suggested they should be directing their questions at the ambulance service for their failure to attend.

Far too often we were expected to take on responsibility for matters which were the duty of other bodies, particularly Ambulance, Mental Health and Social Services; to then be blamed for the outcome. The police service was the agency of last resort, constantly taking a kicking for the lamentable shortcomings of others.

Although things were going well at work, my ankle was still troubling me. The police surgeon helpfully suggested I use my BUPA membership to see a consultant, who found badly torn ligaments in need of major surgery. This was done in the summer of 1989, so I was out of action for a few months, wanting to become fully fit as soon as possible. I came out of hospital with a huge, heavy plaster cast on my right leg for the first two weeks, then a lightweight cast for a further month. In the hot summer weather, the sweating and itching from the cast was terrible, but I did have the bonus of once again being able to spend the summer holidays as quality time with my family. A couple of weeks after the cast was removed, I was back at work but placed on restricted duties by the police surgeon for a few weeks while I had physiotherapy to complete my recovery.

I'd been involved in another minor 'toucher' (which all police vehicle collisions were named, regardless of their seriousness). I passed a driving test but was also given a fortnight's refresher driving course, my first course at MTC for over ten years. Despite initial reservations I thoroughly enjoyed it, proudly coming away with my driving greatly improved. I was given the grade I'd sought on my Intermediate course a decade ago, and a recommendation that I go forward to an Advanced course. Another career option opened up for me. Traffic had been my ambition in my early service and was now within my reach. Having become exasperated by the grinding, humiliating promotion process, I decided to apply for a transfer. However, I was soon putting my acting Sergeant's stripes back on and heading for Longton.

I spent the best part of a year at Longton, enjoying it tremendously. I had a great Inspector and mentor, Tony Ellis who constantly backed me to the hilt as well as giving me many useful pointers on how to succeed. Every single member of the team was dedicated and incredibly hard working; they played as hard as they worked too. There was always a drink at the end of a shift, even nights sometimes. While I was at Longton I was interviewed, and accepted for Traffic, my recent fatal investigation having made a good impression – this was, however subject to my passing an Advanced driving course.

It was while I was at Longton that I became aware of the phrase every Sergeant dreads to hear from one of their team.
'Basically Sarge…'
When you heard this, it almost invariably meant that you both needed to sit down, as the *basically* could extend to half-an-hour or more.
My sense of humour runs away with me sometimes. One young PC approached me one morning in the busy front office.
'Can I have a word Sarge?'

'Er, *prehensile*...okay?' I replied.

He didn't understand why everyone else in the office laughed.

I have already mentioned Charlie Jones and his legendary sense of humour, he was now my Chief Inspector, an outstanding boss who led from the front and was hugely respected by everyone.

We had a probationer who was very fond of Panda pop, which seems to have a very high gas content, in his case it resulted in regular loud farts and belches, sometimes within the hearing of the public area of the station. I'd asked him several times to be more careful, but it continued. I thought I could deal with this in a light-hearted way, so in a rare Longton quiet moment I quickly put together a mock report, detailing the guy's 'constant loud gaseous eruptions and explosions' and my concern at the poor impression this could make on visitors to the station. I handed it to Tony, who minuted it,

Ch.Insp. Jones, Forwarded for your 'special' attention.

A couple of hours later I was summoned to the Chief Inspector's office, the PC was standing to attention in front of him. Another PC on the shift - in on the joke - was there as his 'friend' and Tony was in there too, Charlie spoke to me in a severe tone,

'Sergeant Tucker, I'm looking at your report about PC *[name withheld]*. I'm very concerned about it.'

He looked very seriously at me over the top of his spectacles, and I thought that maybe this time my joke had misfired, he went on,

'You talk here of 'loud eruptions' and 'gaseous emissions' which the Constable denies; do you not think you're being a bit unfair on him?'

I caught the merest hint of a twinkle in his eye and thought, *in for a penny, in for a pond,*

'Well, what with the belching and the farting sir, it's like sitting in the middle of a brass band sometimes!'

The Chief Inspector eyed me sternly for what seemed like an age, I thought I really had overdone it, and suddenly he was in fits of hysterical laughter. Everyone joined in, our boss's uproarious laugh was infectious. As it died down, the PC said to Charlie,

'Sir, will you let me call the Sergeant a bastard?'

'Yes, but only this once.'

'You're a bastard Sarge.'

The wind eased significantly after that. There's more than one way to deal with a problem.

On a more serious note, one afternoon I was sent to an end-terraced house in Heron Cross; home to a couple and their three children, clearly living in abject poverty. Outside was a JCB, as well as a bulldozer and a tipper truck, together with a team of heavily-built workmen who were there to demolish the house.

It seemed that the couple had been renting the house from a private landlord, a property developer who'd subsequently offered to sell it to them. The 'mortgage' payments were made direct to him, but they'd defaulted for two months,. Their creditor had sent the demolition crew round in a flagrant act of intimidation. Having obtained their details I swiftly sent the crew on their way, pointing out that their continued presence would constitute a criminal offence.

The whole situation was a scheme that the notorious Peter Rachman would have applauded; my subsequent investigation was an excursion into uncharted territory. The title deeds were still in the name of their 'landlord', he didn't have a licence under the Consumer Credit Act to act as a mortgager and his use of the demolition crew amounted to blackmail. It was part of my sworn duty as a police officer to protect this vulnerable family from this man's cruel, criminal exploitation of them. I was absolutely determined to do something about it.

After overcoming several avoidance tactics on his part, I interviewed the loathsome man at length in the presence of his solicitor. He denied any wrongdoing, purporting that he was 'only trying to help people.' He gave evasive answers which had clearly been drilled into him by his only slightly less odious solicitor, with whom there were several whispered exchanges during the interview. I put together a file for the CPS to consider.

Not deterred in the slightest by my quest to hold him to account, he continued to make threats to the family. I made it clear to the impoverished family that they had no legal contract with the contemptible man. I suggested they allow him to evict them, then put themselves in the hands of the council as a homeless family. They were very fortunate and within a few weeks were living in a spacious council home in a decent area. Life had begun to seem a little brighter for them and they appreciated the efforts I'd made on their behalf. Home ownership, sadly, would be forever beyond their reach.

The CPS agreed that several offences had been committed but they were *at the lower end of the scale*, and it was *not in the public interest to prosecute*.

If sending a heavy mob and plant to demolish a debtor's home is 'lower end of the scale', who knows what could constitute *further up the scale* and *in the public interest* in the eyes of the CPS. Too much like hard work for them was a more plausible reason for their attitude, I saw it far too often.

Hanley had Bentilee and Abbey Hulton, Burslem had Chell Heath, but Longton had Meir, a large council estate with pockets of private housing - invariably referred to as not just Meir, but ***The* Meir**. I wouldn't say it was as 'rough' as Chell Heath, but parts of the sprawling estate were dominated by two rival criminal family dynasties who, together with their associates had a disturbingly malign effect on everything that happened there. It seemed every call to incidents *on the Meir* resulted in fights and arrests. Blood-soaked prisoners were brought into the cell block, without a single one ever complaining about how they came by their injuries.

My regular stints as Custody Officer brought challenges. One particular prisoner, a *Meirite,* had admitted several offences of burglary. After he'd been charged I had to make the decision whether or not should be bailed. As he was already on bail for other burglaries, it was out of the question. I announced my decision that he would remain in custody and be put before the next available court.

He protested.

'But the Detective Inspector said I'd get bail if I coughed the burglaries.'

Oh, S-H-I-T!

This had huge implications, both for the admissibility of the evidence against him, as well as the integrity of the officers dealing. The exchange had been captured on video and even the most useless of defence solicitors could make a major issue of it. The case officers shrunk away visibly, knowing that a potentially serious breach of the Police and Criminal Evidence Act had occurred. Although I'd been placed in an invidious position, I stuck to my decision.

The man was returned to his cell, protesting loudly. I spoke with the case officers,

'That's right Sarge, the DI said to bail him if he admitted them.'

'It's not the DI's decision to make – it's *mine*! How can I possibly grant bail to someone who's already on bail for the same offences?'

Despite pressure from the detectives, I stood my ground. Phone calls were made and the Superintendent, as required by PACE in dispute situations, was called upon to make a final decision; he upheld my position. I wasn't flavour of the month with the DI, but if the man had offended again on bail then it would have been my head on the block, not his. This was a move up the learning curve for me, making an unpopular but correct decision, and sticking to it.

An absolute harridan in her forties, life on the Meir having added over twenty years to her appearance, was presented to me at the start of a night shift. Why she'd been arrested I don't remember, but she was extremely agitated. I called for a female officer to search her, and while being searched the woman became increasingly aggressive. Suddenly she stripped off every stitch of clothing and stood there stark naked - not a pretty sight at all.
'Right, where else do you want to fuckin' search?'
We finally got her into a cell, and she banged on the door continually.
Longton was an ancient station, a 'shithole' to quote the Superintendent when I started there. It was to be demolished and replaced very soon, preliminary work had already started. Unusually, the female cell was in the same corridor as all the others. Female officers or a civilian 'matron' had to be present when the cell door was opened, but I had to walk past every time I checked on the male prisoners. We'd brought in one of our matrons to attend to her during the night.
It was about 1.30am, our guest had finally worn herself out and I was checking on the male prisoners. As I passed her cell door,
'Psst!'
I took no notice,
'Psst, Sarge!'
I still took no notice.
'Sarge, I need to talk to you.'
Of course, there could be something wrong.

'Come to the door!'

I did and could see one eye looking at me through the spyhole.

'What's the matter? I'll get the matron to come to you.'

'I don't need anything.'

'Well, what's the matter then?'

I was rapidly becoming sick and tired of her.

'Do you want a fuck?'

'What did you say?'

'You heard me, do you want a fuck?'

I paused, and replied,

'Well now you come to mention it, yes...'

'Open the door then.'

'I might have one when I get home in the morning.'

'You BASTARD! I'm clean, what's wrong with me?'

'I wouldn't know where to start duck, the night ain't long enough.'

Nice lady - all the grace and sophistication of an unflushed toilet.

I returned to the office, my 'rejection' had made her start shouting and banging on the door again, waking the other prisoners who were clamouring for her to shut up. Tony Ellis came by,

'What's up with her Nick?'

'She wants her leg over boss.'

'She's in for a bloody long wait then.'

Thursday nights in Longton were much the same as Burslem, there were still a good number of pottery factories with a local workforce. They would take their bulging pay packets for a walk around the pubs, returning home with those packets de-bulged, probably after a good old ruckus too.

I stood on The Strand in the early hours one Friday morning, bloodied drunks were being loaded into the backs of police cars and driven away, while others were being encouraged to either make their way home or enjoy our hospitality. I couldn't help noticing the seemingly never-ending sound of breaking glass coming from all directions, near and far.

If I ever have to pack this job in I'll set up as a glazier in Longton, I'd make a fortune, I mused.

The number of boarded up shops in this town at weekends had to be seen to be believed. Thirty years later they're boarded up because they're no longer in business and the pot-banks are no more; most of the pubs have gone too, how times have changed.

We had a change of Superintendent while I was at Longton. I'd known and got on very well with Ken Powell for many years, since my early days at Newcastle when he was a very helpful, capable, down-to-earth Detective Sergeant. I had a great deal of respect for him, he was extremely good at his job. Senior management were itching to promote him, but he hadn't taken his Inspector's exam - maybe he hadn't wanted to.

In the mid-80s he took and passed the exam, rocketing up the ranks, Inspector to Detective Inspector, then Chief Inspector and Detective Chief Inspector before finally landing at Longton as Superintendent, all in about four years – for once the Chief had found the confidence to give someone rapid promotion. Ken had spent many years as 'one of the lads', but this wasn't the way he was now. As he'd risen so quickly – just like his former Newcastle CID colleague Ian Holding - he could only carry off his rank by being extremely firm, which he most certainly was.

He went through the station like a dose of salts, I thought the previous Superintendent had run a tight ship, but it now felt as if it had been barely afloat.

He found a seriously overdue crime report in the locker of one of my shift. As this lapse had happened on my watch I was just as responsible as him, so we both sweated for a couple of days. Eventually Tony Ellis told me that the Superintendent would not be taking it any further as he had no wish to damage to my career. I was to administer a stern bollocking to the PC and record it in my pocket-book as if I'd discovered the matter myself.

I was very relieved; this could have finished me. I passed our new Superintendent in the corridor a day or two later,

'Thanks boss.'

'No more favours Nick, okay?'

A few weeks later, bearing in mind what he'd said, I really did think I was finished. I'd been dealing with a police vehicle crash involving a stolen car. The driver had run off from the scene but a few weeks later was in custody at Longton for another matter, so I'd be able to interview him about the crash. He was perfectly cooperative as I booked him out of his cell. The antiquated station's sole interview room was not in the secure custody area. As I led him from the cell block, he pushed me to the floor, was off down the corridor like a greyhound out of the trap and shot out of the back door. By the time I'd picked myself up, raised the alarm and reached the door he was nowhere to be seen.

An escaped prisoner was a serious disciplinary matter, I could be in deep trouble. Superintendent Powell was phoned and came to the station. After Tony Ellis had been in with him for a few minutes he came out, sending me in. I thought I was going to be back at Burslem within minutes.

'Are you alright Nick?'

This was encouraging.

'Yes, thanks boss, I'm gutted that this has happened, I'm so sorry, CID must be furious with me too.'

'Not your fault. I've been pissed off about security ever since I got here. This is what happens when HQ don't listen.'

He told me that he'd been pleading for security improvements, but funds were being refused because of the station's forthcoming demolition and replacement.

Accountancy had trumped critical operational need, something which had become disturbingly commonplace.

He continued,

'Obviously I'll have to report this to Headquarters, but I've been waiting for this to happen. It'll be carefully worded as being their fault, with no blame attached to you at all.'

To say I was relieved was an understatement. However, the escapee was on the run for several days and I felt I'd let my colleagues down by the escape. It would have been quite acceptable, and much easier for me to have marked up my accident file that he'd 'refused to be interviewed' without even bothering to ask him.

Wednesday of nights week was a turning point where my body clock did a 'flip.' I'd feel completely drained on the Wednesday night but then be fine for rest of the week. One such shift, I dozed off in my armchair during meal break. The next thing I knew there was a hand on my shoulder,

'Sarge?'

'Uh…wha..?'

'It's quarter past six', said someone from the early shift.

The sods had left me there for three hours and gone home.

'Sleep well last night?' Tony quipped as I arrived at the station on Thursday evening. I thought he may have made an issue of it, but didn't, bless him.

After I'd finished at Longton and taken off my stripes I did an Advanced driving course. An error had put me on a six-week course, intended for standard grade drivers. My driving grade meant that I should have been attending a four-week course. I'd been really looking forward to the course but as it progressed, I felt my driving ability begin to slide backwards. The harder I tried, the worse it became. As my instructor put it afterwards, I'd been the best driver in the car at the start of the course but had 'peaked' far too soon.

The final driving tests were with the Chief Instructor, a route of about eighty miles, at very high speeds, concluded by a mock pursuit situation.

They were carried out in alphabetical order, I was the last on the list. All tests except mine were done on the final Thursday; I was the sole candidate the next morning. The eight others had passed and were enjoying an alcohol fuelled end of course 'do' that night; I had to remain stone cold sober and get a good night's sleep. The next morning, I was a bag of nerves and just couldn't concentrate enough on the driving; although I flunked the test, I managed to keep my intermediate grade. It was devastating to be told that I'd failed, by just one mark, but the Chief Instructor promised me that I would be given another - four-week - course as soon as possible.

Back to Burslem, and onto a different shift but I soon settled in. Once again I was senior PC and found myself having a busy time alternating between PC and unofficial acting Sergeant to cover absences. By now thoroughly disillusioned with the promotion ladder, my heart was set on a move to Traffic Division

I was enjoying being back at Burslem again though, it was pleasantly relaxing to be just one member of a team, instead of having to supervise one.

One morning I was called to a children's home on the patch, one of the residents had assaulted a member of staff, a fairly common occurrence. The assaults were minor and there was rarely any wish for charges to be brought, mainly to avoid souring the fragile relationships between the staff and the kids. However, the staff wanted these incidents recorded for their own protection. Some of these children were very troubled and troublesome, and needed to be managed very carefully and firmly.

Two social workers were in the room with the boy, including the one who had been assaulted, fortunately uninjured. The lad was in his mid-teens and fairly well built. After I'd been told what had happened, I turned to him and asked him to explain himself. He appeared extremely agitated, almost hysterical and without warning launched himself at me. To stop him and bring him to his senses I slapped him twice on the face, hard. He calmed down immediately.

Eventually he apologised to me and to the social worker who he'd attacked. I made a record in my pocket-book so that I could record and write off the crime report.

The other social worker in the room had remained strangely silent; two days later I discovered why. She was the boy's personal caseworker and made a complaint of assault against me on his behalf. This was serious, and for a while it looked as if I could be facing criminal charges.

However, when our Discipline and Complaints department went to obtain a statement from the boy, he couldn't even remember the incident, so the enquiry collapsed. It had been a very anxious time for me but ended with a trip to Headquarters with my Superintendent for 'advice' from the acting Deputy Chief Constable, Dave Rowley, followed by a very friendly chat; we'd known each other for a long time.

The next time I'd see him would be on a promotion board.

A few years later, a scandal erupted regarding sexual abuse in children's homes in Staffordshire. This was centred around, although not confined to the Riverside School (actually a home) near Uttoxeter. Here, children had been abused on an unimaginable scale; after a far-reaching police enquiry, several staff members were jailed. The extent of the abuse was such that children were threatened with horrible consequences should they even think of talking about it to anybody.

Children were repeatedly absconding from this home and others; in retrospect it's perfectly obvious why. They'd be reported missing, usually found with their parents or local friends and driven back to the home. Once handed over to the home by the police, the abuse would continue until they fled the home again. Children's homes across the county slowly disappeared from the landscape as enquiries continued.

By seeking out and returning these troubled youngsters to the place where they were being abused, we were unknowing active participants in allowing the abuse to continue. It makes me shudder, even now, to think about it.

One guy on the shift at Burslem was absolutely bone-idle, nobody wanted to be paired up with him, but I had the misfortune to spend one night shift with him. We were called to an all-too-common theft from a vehicle in Smallthorne. A ridiculously easy way to break into a car at the time, particularly a Ford, was to bend back the top of the driver's door and reach in to unlock it. The car's owner was very keen to point out a clear set of fingerprints on the window. Surprisingly, given his idleness, my temporary partner had got out of the IRV first and was dealing with him. He should have called for a minor Scenes of Crime exam.

He shone his torch over the prints, made a show of examining them and turned to the owner,

'Show us your hands'

He shone his torch over the man's fingers for about thirty seconds and proclaimed,

'They're *yours*, you must have touched the window earlier.'

He wiped off the prints with his sleeve.

I reported this to our Inspector, I don't know what the outcome was, but the job didn't need people like this idle uniform-carrier.

Whenever staff appraisal times came around one thing I was told, year on year was that I didn't conform. I argued too much and questioned established, sometimes quite absurd 'norms' within the job; I rocked the boat and made waves. It was valid comment, but I couldn't help myself, that was the way I've always been. However, although I challenged existing practices, I always suggested alternatives. Change was coming though; the large scale 'review' of the force mentioned earlier was taking place, new ideas were being taken on board. Everything and anything about the force and the way we worked was to be examined and questioned, it was a new *vision*, it even had a name – 'Towards 2000.'

I was put forward for yet another Divisional promotion board in the spring but didn't even try. As I'd lost interest I gave open, honest answers to my inquisitors, even spiritedly arguing with them over several matters. For once they were impressed, despite my intention having been the opposite. Accordingly, I was to be given one final spell of 'acting' to prove myself once and for all.

Before I knew it, four years after having been 'busted' there, I was back at Stoke. A baptism of fire on my first day, an early shift where I was the one and only uniform supervisor in the station for the whole morning.

This time, a change happened within me when I came to realise that I was thinking like a Sergeant, rather than *trying* to think like one, despite my lack of interest in promotion.
Maybe, just maybe, I should be seeking promotion?
Nah!
Another great shift to work with, some of them I knew quite well already; a good mix of experienced and younger officers who worked extremely well as a very tightly bonded team. However, I did face the challenge of two probationers having difficulties.

One was a cocky youngster with an unshakeable belief in their ability. Their slapdash approach to dealing with incidents and lamentable paperwork told a different story. Furthermore, well-intentioned advice from more experienced colleagues was rejected. A progress report was due soon after I arrived at Stoke, so I sought the views of previous supervisors and older members of the shift. After I'd written up the report and discussed it with them, they still wouldn't admit to having a problem, strongly, and quite insolently asserting the opposite. I did my best to bring them on, attending and reviewing incidents, discussing what was done well and what could have been done better. Before I left Stoke, I was able to give at least a 'satisfactory' mark on their appraisal.

The other was the total opposite, someone whose performance was actually very good, but doubting their own ability. Some more self-confidence would make them more decisive and effective. As with their colleague, I went to incidents and discussed them afterwards, making sure to emphasise the strong points of how they'd dealt with them. When it was time for me to move on, I was able to mark their final report as 'excellent' in all respects and recommended confirmation of their appointment.

My Divisional Commander at Stoke was George Stoddard, now Chief Superintendent. He actually retired while I was there – the force review was gathering pace, and the number of his rank was being greatly reduced – only to be increased again within a year. Stoke City were playing one of their first games of the season, an evening match at the old Victoria Ground. I wasn't earmarked for duty at the match, but Mr Stoddard called me to his office shortly after I'd started my noon shift,

'Inspector [*whoever*] has reported sick, he was supposed be ground commander tonight, I'd like you to do it Nick, do you think you can?'

It was not an offer to be declined, it was both a compliment and a test. That evening, as a PC who was acting Sergeant, I was doing an Inspector's job, in charge of PCs, as well as acting and substantive Sergeants and the Constables working in the ground. It was a quiet match which passed off peacefully, fortunately, and nobody questioned my authority. Another move up the learning curve.

While at Stoke, I spent four weeks on another Advanced driving course. This time I flew through it. There comes a point where suddenly you realise, 'Yes, I can do this', and your driving changes forever, this happened during the third week as I was barrelling down a B-road in Lincolnshire. It was a glorious open road with sweeping bends and visibility far into the distance. I was commentating,

'.... I can see that after we've reached the bottom of the hill the road bends gradually to the right and then gently uphill. I'll take a third gear for flexibility and to climb... '

Clive, the instructor put his hand over the gear lever,

'It'll only do a hundred in third Nick....'

A split-second glance at the speedo, I was doing almost thirty miles an hour more than that, I felt like I'd been doing about eighty.

After the final test drive, and being told that I'd passed, the adrenalin that I'd been running on for four weeks finally stopped pumping into my system – for the next forty-eight hours I found myself sweating constantly, just as if I was having drug withdrawal symptoms.

I spent a few more weeks at Stoke but I could finally move to Traffic. As the doors of Stoke police station closed behind me, I headed for my dream transfer, to Central Traffic Group at Stafford.

19– Flying!

I'd finally achieved my ambition of many years previously, working on the motorway. My induction day at Central Traffic Group (CTG) was 9am—5pm, to meet the bosses and visit HQ stores to be issued with my additional uniform and kit. The trip to stores was a 'rite of passage', being every new CTG officer's first solo drive in a patrol car, a 3-litre Vauxhall Senator.

The shine of the experience was somewhat dulled. After driving to Headquarters from CTG's base at Weston Road, I visited Mick Ryan in the stores, he issued me with a plethora of new kit, correct hat size this time. After I'd loaded it into the car, the engine wouldn't turn over. I asked unsuccessfully around HQ for help, the subsequent phone call to base asking for someone to come with jump leads was rather humiliating.

On the subject of kit. I was required by the force to wear spectacles for driving, in fact I couldn't see properly without them. For safety we had to wear *force approved* glasses, so everyone who wore them had identical frames. They weren't at all bad actually, the frames were stylish and very durable. Once you moved to Traffic you were issued with sunglasses, or flip-up clip-ons if you wore specs. It's just a pity that the clip-ons didn't fit the frames, no matter how hard you tried.

Once back at CTG I was shown around, met the staff and my new Divisional Commander, Superintendent Jim Pountney, a lovely guy just a few months away from retirement.

The people on my new shift would be working noons that day. At 2pm in the modern briefing room at Weston Road I took my seat and met my new colleagues. At a normal Divisional station, shifts are made up of people who have been posted there whether they like it or not, sometimes as a punishment or 'last chance', so there was always a mix of happy and unhappy people in the team. Everyone in this room was exactly where they wanted to be; they'd applied for their posts, been interviewed and, like me, gone through courses to achieve their ambition. The atmosphere was entirely different from what I'd always known. My partner for the foreseeable future would be Bob Thompson, a couple of years older than me, with a little more service. He was an extrovert with superb people skills, a carefree manner and as keen as mustard. I couldn't possibly have found anyone better to work with. My time working at CTG, both with Bob and in other roles was by far the happiest time of my entire career.

The group worked mainly the motorway between junctions 10 and 16 of the M6 and out to junction 3 of the M54. They were also responsible for the trunk roads, A34, A5, A51, A518, A519 and A449 in the centre of the county. For motorway patrol we had a fleet of Jaguar XJ6 4-litre saloons. I'd always loved Jaguars, so this was a real treat for me, where speed was concerned, in a straight line they were amazingly fast for their day, but their soft suspension, coupled with the massive amount of kit in the boot made them something of a handful once off the motorway. We used Vauxhall Senators for trunk road patrol, as well as Mobile Armouries, of which more soon. These were superbly capable patrol cars.

The rest of the day was taken up with introductions, showing me around and getting to know the kit we'd be using. Bob and I headed out in a Senator for a ride around the patch for an hour or two until it was time for me to go home.

The end of a very different day, I felt as if I was walking on air.

Next day was our first day on the motorway together. After briefing at Weston Road, it was time for the weekly speedometer checks on the rolling road. Then it was off to the M6 and our main centre of activity, Doxey Post on the outskirts of Stafford, with its own unmarked junction off the motorway. Here was also the base from which the highways department maintained the county's motorways, and a Department of Transport test area where we had access to a very complex, accurate weighbridge. As we made ourselves a brew before heading out onto patrol, our Sergeant, Paul Heeks joined us, he turned to me and winked,

'Best kept secret in the county the motorway Nick, you're going to love it.'

He was absolutely right. Motorways, contrary to what the public believe, are by far the safest roads in the country and serious incidents are a relatively rare occurrence; most crashes were rear-end shunts involving only damage. The advent of so-called 'Smart' motorways has changed that though, I'm glad I don't have to work on them; the most serious crashes always happened on the hard shoulder; now that in some places it no longer exists, people in stranded vehicles are extremely vulnerable.

Because actual incidents were infrequent, we generated most work ourselves and worked very hard at it.

First job was to escort an abnormal load north to the county boundary at junction 16, an easy start, sitting at a safe distance behind with strobes flashing, making sure following traffic overtook safely. On the way back south, Bob spotted a rigid wagon which was low on its rear.

'We've got a weigher Nick.'

We stopped the lorry and told the driver to follow us to the weighbridge at Michelin in Stoke, a mile or so off the motorway. The wagon was indeed overweight, the driver was reported, but allowed on his way as the overweight was not excessive. Had it been more than a certain percentage overweight they would have been issued a prohibition notice and would have had to transfer some of his load off the vehicle, a very common occurrence.

Less scrupulous operators would routinely run their fleet as overweight as they could get away with, it reduced their costs, in all likelihood they still do. I would have to attend a four-week specialist Traffic Patrol Officers' course before I could deal with weight offences myself.

Back onto the motorway we dropped in behind a Vauxhall Cavalier, and followed it for a short distance at 90mph, we put the strobes on, but the driver was concentrating more on getting to his destination than looking in his mirror and observing the traffic around him. Eventually he saw us, slowed down and we followed him onto the hard shoulder.

'This is how you deal with a speeder Nick.'

Bob got out and trotted to the stopped car in front of us, an unusual trot which quickly becomes an acquired art for all motorway officers - a sort of side-on run moving forwards whilst always looking at the traffic coming from behind. You *never, ever,* turned your back on the traffic, not even for a split second, absolutely essential. The noise of the traffic is incredible, the hard shoulder on a busy motorway feels a very hostile place to be Standing to the front of the driver's door, Bob asked the driver to come and sit in the back of our car.

'Okay sir, now we're out of the noise, I have to tell you that we've followed you for a mile at 90mph. Do you know what the motorway speed limit is?'

'Seventy.'

'I'm going to have to report you for speeding, but I can deal with it by way of fixed penalty...'

Bob then explained the fixed penalty system to the hapless company rep and did the necessary paperwork, as the weeks passed I would recognise the relief with which someone many miles from home, having been stopped by two big police officers in a powerful car, was finally sent on their way with a slip of yellow paper and nothing more serious. Completely different from reporting motorists for offences on city streets, where most miscreant motorists argued the toss.

We always told them how to move off as well, very important.

'Imagine you're on the slip road joining the motorway, build up your speed on the hard shoulder and merge with the traffic in lane one...'

It was fortunate that we'd stay on the hard shoulder with lights flashing to warn other drivers, as our advice was rarely followed; most would move off as if they were pulling away from a kerbside parking space in town.

Speeding 'reps' were very common. They worked to targets set by their company. If they achieved one month's target, the next month's bar was set higher, and so it continued. They could only keep their jobs by speeding as much as possible. Most that we stopped would already have at least six points on their licence. Some had nine, so such a stop meant court, a ban and unemployment. Every so often we'd hear,

'I hope you realise you've just lost me my job.'

It didn't seem to occur to them that they'd lost their job themselves by breaking the law.

Target setting by companies eager for profit never seemed to take road safety into account.

As the months went by we had more than our share of speeders, but were fairly tolerant and although we stopped many, we wouldn't generally issue tickets or report anyone for speeds under 85mph unless the conditions were poor. There were more than enough above this speed to keep us busy anyway, and most already had points for speeding on their licences.

Some of their excuses were laughable, but it was astonishing to see that despite travelling at high speed, their observation was atrocious; we could follow them mile after mile with blue lights before being noticed.

After any situation where we issued a ticket or reported for summons (if the speed was really excessive) we'd try to make sure the driver was calmed down and in the right frame of mind to continue their journey, so we'd have a brief chat.

One question they'd often ask would be go along the lines of,

'Okay, I know I was speeding, I deserve the ticket, but there are loads of others doing the same. Why did you pick on me in particular, what made you notice me?'

'Well, it was when you overtook us....'

In a marked Jaguar patrol car!

It happened so many times; the look on their faces said it all. There was no better wake-up call for someone to realise that their driving drastically needed improvement..

Many people don't understand there is no such thing as a 'fast lane' nor is there a 'slow lane'; all lanes apart from the left one are for overtaking. I quickly lost count of the number of people we stopped to advise about poor lane discipline, most of them were just too stupid to have the slightest understanding of what they were doing wrong, saying after well-intentioned advice,

'I still don't know why you've stopped me, I wasn't speeding.'

As if speeding was the only reason to ever stop people.

At night, people hogging the middle lane on an empty motorway would say, 'I thought I'd be safer in the middle lane in case I fell asleep' -incredible.

Poor lane discipline is the cause of a lot of serious congestion on motorways.

Lane-hogging is now a fixed penalty offence – with points, and about time too, even if there's hardly anybody there to enforce it anymore.

Back to my first day on the motorway. We'd stopped more cars and lorries than I normally would in a month. Several speeders, vehicle defects which were dealt with by fixed penalty, or the Vehicle Defect Rectification (VDR) scheme. This gave a driver time to fix the problem and have this certified at an approved MOT garage, if they didn't they'd be summonsed.

Tachograph charts were examined, drivers reported and ordered to take an overdue rest break. One was reported for exceeding his hours and ordered to stop for his daily break at the next service area, a mile away - despite being only half an hour from home.

I was very surprised by the number of people not wearing their seatbelts, they were shown no mercy, there's no excuse.

The ample performance of the Jaguar was regularly called upon, to catch up with speeders, or to get to the occasional incident quickly. Something could be happening a few yards away on the opposite carriageway, but it could be a twenty-mile drive or more to get there once you had turned around at the next junction. Thus, driving at well over a hundred miles per hour was common and frequently necessary. Sometimes, instead of going all the way to the next junction to turn, we'd reverse a mile or more along the hard shoulder – this wreaked havoc with your neck muscles, and you had to watch for the engine overheating due to the different airflow. You could cover a huge mileage in a shift, two hundred or more was quite normal on the top or bottom sectors and used almost a full tank of fuel.

We had four patrol sectors. Sector one, 'top' from junction 15 to 16, sector two from junction 14 to 15, sector three, 'middle' from junction 14 to 12 and sector four, 'bottom' was junction 12 down to the county boundary near Walsall, in practice this extended into the West Midlands area at junction 10 where we had to go to turn around; it also included the newer M54 from its beginning to junction 3 at

Tong in Shropshire. This was my least favourite sector as even in the early 1990s this section of the M6 could be horrendously congested all day; Friday was busiest, when it was possible to spend most of the day driving with extreme caution along the hard shoulder.

As we were on the top sector we took our meal break at Keele services. When Sir Charles Forte introduced his motorway service areas to the public, he declared that on-duty emergency service workers would dine at them free of charge. Chief Constables had said this would not be proper, instead agreeing that a nominal charge should be paid. This was now fifty pence which was still outrageously low compared to grossly inflated menu prices.

The quantity of food which we would routinely load onto our plates was ridiculous, but it was an enjoyable perk, which I believe is now history. I'd brought sandwiches today, but Bob dined amply. I wouldn't bother with sandwiches when we were next on 'top.'

On Saturday mornings at summer holiday time, me and Bob would load up our plates as usual, bacon, sausages, eggs, tomatoes, mushrooms, fried bread and toast. We'd then hand over 50p each at the till, while astonished onlookers with their families had to choose probably less food for the whole family than we had on each of our plates, which would cost them twenty pounds or more.

The days turned into weeks, the weeks turned into months, I'd never been happier; despite a long, somewhat costly commute between Kidsgrove and Stafford. Driving home on the motorway was challenging though, particularly in the middle of the day; the change of mindset from being 'in charge' in a marked Jaguar to joining motoring morons in my own car took some coping with, I'd arrive home enraged by the antics of my fellow motorway travellers.

I was really contented to be working with a bunch of really great people, there was a great team spirit, and we all helped each other. Out on the road I felt the mustard-keenness of a newly appointed probationer, even though I now had over sixteen years in the job.

Part of the force review process had been to rename the traffic groups. Suddenly, no longer were we Central Traffic Group, but Traffic Support South (TSS), little did we know it at the time, but this was the first small, insidious step towards the slow death of traffic policing in Staffordshire, following a national trend.

Armed Response Vehicles (ARVs) were in their infancy. For reasons best known to the force hierarchy, two ARVs were put out from TSS, but only at weekends. These were crewed by officers from the TSG. On weekdays, the middle sector motorway car was designated as a Mobile Armoury (MA), a patrol car loaded with firearms in locked safes – basically an ARV but without AFOs. In the event of a firearms incident, the MA would be driven to the location, then joined by the AFOs. Like most plans, it only worked on paper.

Monday, 8.30am, we were driving the MA and were directed to rendezvous at Codsall police station for a developing firearms incident. On blue lights it took us twenty-five minutes to arrive, although it was another forty-five minutes before the AFOs arrived. I was flabbergasted to see that they were the TSG ARV crews from the night shift, who I'd seen going off-duty less than four hours ago. How on earth could they possibly be expected to make life-or-death, rational decisions after working a full night shift and having had so little sleep?

Fortunately, the incident was resolved without shots fired or our patrol car leaving the police station yard; Bob and I spent several long boring hours at Codsall though. We were most concerned, not only at the physical and mental suitability of the AFO's, but also the period of at least an hour and a half between the initial report of the incident to being ready for deployment.

I then hoped that I would never find myself looking at the wrong end of a gun-barrel.

Locations on motorways are expressed by marker post numbers, every hundred metres along the road. For anoraks the numbers are the distance in kilometres from Staples Corner at the beginning of the M1 in London, followed by a slash and tenths of a kilometre. There would then be an 'A', or a 'B', A for northbound, B for southbound. So, marker post 236/2A is 236.2 kilometres from London on the northbound.

We used the emergency phone box numbers as the location reference in the case of speeders; they are every mile along the motorway, the numbers being the marker post number, minus the slash, plus four-thousand for a reason I've long since forgotten. Hence box 6336B was at marker post number 236/6B, or in plain language, near Stone in Staffordshire where I now live; it isn't there any more (the box, not Stone) as this is now a so-called 'Smart' motorway.

I've mentioned the Jaguar's very soft suspension which could easily rock you off to sleep, this didn't fit well with my struggle with Wednesday nights. In the small hours of a Thursday I'd nodded off in the passenger seat and Bob jabbed me in the ribs, we were on the hard shoulder, a stationary car in front of us.

'Your turn Nick, 92-94 mph…'

'I shook myself awake and walked to the car, as it was very quiet I decided to deal with the driver through the passenger door. After going through my spiel, I started to fill in the ticket and suddenly realised I hadn't the foggiest where we were, it was a pitch-dark moonless night; I needed to put the location on the ticket. We were midway between marker posts too, so using one of those wasn't an option.

'Excuse me a minute, will you?' I trotted back to the patrol car.

'Bob.... where the fuck are we?'

'6368, you daft sod.'

I went back to the driver and continued writing out the ticket,

M6, 6368...,

Shit, I thought,

I don't even know which bloody carriageway we're on.

In the enveloping darkness this stretch of motorway was absolutely featureless. If I went back to Bob again I'd never hear the last of it so, I asked the driver conversationally,

'Where are you heading for at this unearthly hour?'

'West Bromwich.'

South of here!

I continued writing,

*M6, 6368...**B**.*

The Jags were very thirsty; if you accelerated hard or drove at a constant high speed you could see the needle of the fuel gauge moving. It was 9.30pm on a busy Sunday, we'd been on top sector and were heading back towards Stafford to end our shift, eager to get home as we were on a quick-changeover. As we neared our turn-off at junction 14, we were sent to a crash just south of junction 16 on the northbound carriageway. Including turning round at junction 14 this was about twenty-two miles away. We were already down to less than a quarter of a tank of fuel. Blue lights on and away I blasted to the scene with the speedo well into three figures, the fuel gauge needle visibly and relentlessly creeping towards red. When we arrived, the cars involved were already on the hard shoulder and nobody was injured. I returned to the driver's seat while Bob made sure that details had been properly exchanged. The fuel gauge was in the red as Bob climbed back in.

'Bob, we ain't got enough fuel to get back.'

As I've said, Bob was a remarkably carefree guy, nothing, but nothing ever remotely troubled him. Sometimes I wished I could have been the same.

'We'll be fine Nick, when we run dry, we'll just get a breakdown.'

I couldn't begin to imagine the paperwork and piss-taking we'd endure if this happened, I started driving, *very* slowly. As I turned around at junction 16 and headed up the entry slip road, the needle had now dropped *below* the red zone.

'Bob this ain't going to work, we're going to run out of fuel any moment. I'm not waiting God knows how long for a breakdown, and the shit we're going to be in...'

'How much cash have you got?' Bob asked.

I patted my pockets.

'Just a one-pound coin, why?'

'Me too, let's see if we can make it to Keele services and put a couple of quid's worth in.'

I drove to the service area as slowly as was safe. The cashier looked incredulous as the two of us got out, carefully put about five pints of fuel into the big Jaguar and went on our way after handing over two coins.

I drove all the way back to CTG... er, TSS at 30mph, the car spluttered as I coasted down the access road, under the barrier and onto the pumps.

We were an hour late going home, had we gone with Bob's original plan it would have been much later still.

Like many things the escorting of abnormal loads has now been mainly handed over to the private sector, but we escorted loads of loads at the time.

Many of them were cranes; I couldn't understand how it was that we would escort a crane north to the county boundary at junction 16, only to exchange it for a seemingly identical crane in the load parking area from the same company and escort it south.

It was pretty straightforward but if things went wrong it could be catastrophic; it was sensible and preferable to have a chat-cum-briefing with the driver before moving off. Sometimes this wasn't possible, so you had to take a load on the move, hoping that the patrol handing the load over to you had fully briefed the driver.

Bob was driving as we took a gargantuan load on the move at junction 15 at Hanford. We were taking it to the abnormal load layby at junction 16 for handover to Cheshire. It was fully taking up two lanes of the carriageway. Moving along the carriageway was straightforward, apart from the queue of impatient drivers behind us. The difficult part was leaving the motorway.

The regular drivers knew of the established procedure at junction 16; as soon as they were clear of the carriageway, the escorting car would 'undertake' the load along the hard shoulder of the exit slip road and stop the traffic on the roundabout, in order for the load to cross and park on the designated area on the central island.

As we went down the inside of the behemoth, I became suddenly aware that it was still moving to the left.

'BOB!' He seemed to be momentarily oblivious to the impending disaster.

'**BOB!!**'

He jumped and veered to the left, but the load was still slowly heading towards us; the gap between the embankment and the load was narrowing and we had no escape route. I hit the siren to attract the driver's attention, but there was no response as the side of the load hit us, pushing us up the grassy slope and continuing down the slip road towards the roundabout, leaving us part-way up the embankment. Bob somehow managed to get the car back onto the tarmac and down to the layby, by which time the driver had managed to cross the roundabout and park up. He looked puzzled as our badly damaged Jaguar pulled up next to him, one of the huge tyres of his load carrying a partial mirror-image imprint of the Staffordshire Police crest from the driver's door. His load was so massive that while aware that he was under escort he'd never had sight of us at any time and hadn't felt or heard the collision.

It was actually his first time driving an abnormal load alone and he'd never been to junction 16 before. A flurry of paperwork followed, as well as Bob being on the end of the barracking that anyone was subjected to after a crash.

We resolved *never* to take a load on the move again.

I met some interesting people on the motorway. We stopped a Jaguar XJS, with the registered number A15 WUM, but it was spaced to appear as A I SWUM. The driver, Sharron Davies, displaying a very self-important attitude was issued with a VDR and sent on her way. The plate no longer exists, so maybe DVLA eventually took it off her.

Middle of the night, we passed an almost luminous pink Cadillac. Bernard Manning waved to us. A couple of years later he was the entertainment at a hotel less than a mile from where he'd spotted us. An angry audience trashed the place so badly that it closed down, never to reopen.

We stopped a Vauxhall Calibra for speeding. Unusually, Bob dealt with the driver through the passenger window; having sent it on its way he came back to the car,

'Think he gave me false details Nick, but I can't prove it...',

We were in a notorious radio black-spot so couldn't do the usual PNC check,

'...the guy said his name was Robert Fripp, how dodgy is that?'

Before I could interrupt, he continued,

'...and what's more, the passenger was the dead spit of Toyah Willcox.'

291

'Bob, it *was* her!'

'You're kidding!'

Bob's musical taste was confined to top-twenty stuff. As an almost lifelong devotee of King Crimson, how I *wish* it had been my turn to deal with the driver.

Parking provision at Hilton services was woefully inadequate, so much so that some LGV and car drivers would park on the hard shoulder leading out of the service area, actually on the motorway. Despite this being illegal we'd exercise a certain amount of discretion, particularly at quiet times. I found myself knocking on the window of a car parked there, fully intending to issue a fixed penalty notice if the driver failed the 'attitude test.' Jimmy White passed the test with flying colours.

Spring bank holiday, Monday evening; we were with a hard-shoulder breakdown on Keele bank. Traffic was extremely heavy, three solid lanes of traffic going uphill at 60mph, but everyone trying to go faster, absolute pandemonium. I saw a Lada in lane one which was clearly slowing down; it came to a halt alongside us in lane one. The passenger window rolled down and the driver leaned over to me,

'Excoosi mi, which is ze way to Leevairpool pliz?'

I was paying more attention to the line of traffic behind him suddenly having to brake, visualising an impending multi-vehicle shunt.

'MOVE, **NOW** you bloody **idiot**!'

My tone intentionally didn't give room for discussion, so he did. Having left the breakdown, we rolled onto Keele services for our break. As we got out of the car at the police post I saw the Lada driver angrily walking over to us.

'Yoo voz ver' rood to mee back zere. I only vonted to know ze way.'

After our conversation the gentleman walked away without any apology whatsoever, but with a memento of the occasion - an endorsable fixed penalty notice for stopping on the motorway.

On normal patrol we'd trundle along at 50mph in lane one; with the traffic for some reason slowing down and backing up behind us. The observer would be turned in the passenger seat to watch the traffic coming past, looking at excise licences, seat belts, vehicle condition and the general demeanour of the drivers.

It was strange how many drivers needed to scratch their ear or nose as they came past.

We'd stopped a speeder from Liverpool, his speed was far too high to qualify for a fixed penalty, so Bob and I were called to give evidence at Stafford Magistrates' Court.

He was representing himself. Abraham Lincoln was absolutely right when he said, 'He who represents himself has a fool for a client.'

We were in court for the opening of the case. The CPS lawyer made the opening statement along the lines of,

'Officers followed the defendant's car for a distance of one mile at a speed of a hundred and twelve miles per hour.'

The Merseyside moron interrupted,

'I was only doing a hundred and five.'

The clerk of the court looked at him questioningly,

'Is that the basis of your 'Not Guilty' plea?'

'Yeah like, I wasn't going as fast as the bizzies said.'

'But you admit doing over the speed limit of seventy, so you're guilty.'

'Yeah, I hold my hands up to that, like, but it's not as fast as it says on the summons like.'

He changed his plea eventually, so we didn't give evidence. The sentence and ban reflected the Magistrates' irritation at having had their time wasted by this Liverpudlian lamebrain.

One morning we followed a Mercedes sports car from junction 16 southbound, it was doing a hundred and forty miles-per-hour. Despite being followed with blue lights and headlights flashing it was six miles (but only just over two-and-a-half minutes) before the driver finally looked into his mirror and pulled onto the hard shoulder. The car and driver were German. Having less than the average number of arms, he'd been using the remaining one to steer the car, at double the speed limit.

As he had no address in the UK for a summons to be served, we had the power to arrest him. We took him before the Magistrates Court a couple of hours later; he was very heavily fined and disqualified from driving for six months.

His car was removed by a rota garage to their compound. I don't know – or care - how he got either himself or his car back to Germany. For one thing, he couldn't now legally drive to a Channel port. It would have been an extremely expensive experience for him, deservedly so.

Every day, people would say, 'Why don't you go and catch some real criminals?'

We did, and lots of them.

It was 6.45am. We had just left Doxey post after a brew and were heading for the top sector. I was driving and after passing a rather dilapidated Transit van we decided to stop it. Blue lights and 'STOP' sign on we pulled over to the hard shoulder. This needed care – you never knew how good the brakes were on a vehicle you stopped, so you stayed a good distance ahead until you were sure the other driver was actually coming to a halt. In view of the van's condition, I stayed well ahead of it.

The safety gap suddenly grew, and the van came to a complete stop about thirty yards behind us, directly under a bridge. As I reversed towards it at speed, the driver and passenger leapt out and ran off up the embankment. Bob, a member of the force cross-country team was out of the passenger door like a greyhound and across the fields.

We were close to the Yarnfield intersection, an unmarked junction for emergency and maintenance vehicles. I left the motorway and headed for the point where I thought the field would come out onto the country lane. As I drove along, I came across two Liverpudlians in a gateway, doubled over and gasping for breath. As I grabbed hold of one of them, Bob came out of nowhere, fresh as a daisy and collared the other.

The van contained jeans to the value of over £30,000, stolen in a ram raid in Birmingham an hour earlier.

Sportier versions of family cars, such as the Fiesta, Escort and Sierra were always worth stopping. Lifting the carpet by the driver's seat of a Ford would sometimes reveal a hole in the floor, where the VIN (Vehicle Identification Number, or for the real oldies, the chassis number) should have been but had been cut out. This would give more than reasonable suspicion that the car was either stolen, or subject of criminal activity. A hole in the floor would always lead to arrests and charges.

Stolen property, drugs, cars and criminals are moving on the motorway network all the time. Yes, we did catch 'real' criminals too.

We'd have people frantically approach us on service areas.

'We're on a coach and it's left without us!'

'Did the driver tell you what time to be back on the coach?'

'Yes, we were only five minutes late, and he's gone.'

'Sorry, there's nothing we can do. If the driver told you what time he was leaving, you should have been back. You'll have to contact the coach company.'

Then, incredibly,

'Well you've got a fast car, we can get in and you can chase after it.'

'If you think for one minute we're going to do that...'

Back to 'weighers' – a patrol from another shift had escorted a tanker to the weighbridge at Doxey. Apart from abnormal loads, the absolute maximum weight limit for a vehicle on UK roads at the time was thirty-eight tonnes. The tanker, normally used for powder, weighed almost three times that - it had been filled with bitumen. The driver said that he'd had to call breakdown companies four times on his way up the motorway to replace burst tyres, little wonder. Needless to say the tanker was prohibited and the company had to remove enough bitumen to make it legal. This was a logistical problem for the company as the tractor unit was no longer supplying power to heat the bitumen, so it solidified. The whole rig was parked at Doxey for weeks while the company worked out how to deal with the issue.

I was called in to see the Chief Inspector, John Reynolds. He said,

'You're applying for a promotion board this year.'

Thinking he was asking me a question I said,

'No boss, I'm perfectly happy here.'

'No Nick, it's not a question, it's a statement, you're applying for a promotion board, it's come from on-high, *very* on-high.'

I wasn't happy about this, I didn't want promotion any more, I'd come to Traffic to escape its clutches and would be happy to see out the remainder of my service exactly where I was. However, we still had the same Chief Constable and if I didn't do as I was told I could be subjected to an unwelcome move. I half-heartedly put in my application and was invited to attend the annual ritual humiliation at Stoke. I simply wasn't bothered, and I answered all their questions with even more honesty than last time. This frequently developed into heated discussion.

After being told to leave the room for a few minutes I was asked back in, told that I'd been successful and would be invited to appear before a Force Promotion Board in the near future.

WHAAAT?

How things had changed. I was complimented on my openness and my frank, forthright views, all things for which I'd been much criticised in the past and was told,

'Straight-talking people like you are the future of the service.'

I hadn't changed one bit, but the job had, for now at least. I wasn't happy though and felt railroaded. If I'd sat with my back to the board and not answered a single question I'd probably still have passed. I probably hadn't even needed to go.

The day of the Force board came a few weeks later. I was before (no longer acting) DCC Dave Rowley and two Chief Superintendents who I didn't know. I was very surprised by the informality. I wasn't asked any of the expected questions about force policy, which I hadn't bothered to read up on anyway. My personal views on the review and reorganisation of the force were asked for, and I *was* honest, as I wasn't bothered one way or another. Most of the half-hour was taken up with chat about holidays, hobbies and family.

The next week I made another visit to John Reynolds' office to be told that I'd been successful and would be promoted in the near future. I was really unhappy at the prospect of leaving a job I absolutely loved and where I'd never been happier in all my service. Promotion would mean returning to a Divisional station for at least twelve months. So many times in the past I'd craved promotion - now it was the very last thing I wanted.

I was on a four-week Traffic Patrol Officers' course, which would give me the authority to examine and weigh vehicles. There was one guy amongst us who was a relentless piss-taker; I'd known him for years, so was often his target. It was all good natured, but he couldn't help himself; our exchanges were a prominent feature of the group's banter and much commented on.

The day before the course ended I was walking across the yard to the canteen. Our new Superintendent, John Mottram, opened his office window and asked me to join him inside.

As I approached his office, 'Nick, Nick, come in, sit down. You're going to be doing some acting'.

Oh, no! Please, not more time back at Division!

'No, no, I can see what you're thinking, it'll be here, on Mark Judson's shift, Mick Tafano's been seconded away.'

I was hugely relieved at being able to stay, although I knew it wouldn't be for long. I was sorry not to be able to work with Bob for a while though.

I went for my meal and joined the others.

My piss-taking colleague asked,

'What did the boss want, you're in the shit aren't you? Listen everybody, Tucker's in the shit.'

'No, he's asked me to do some acting…'

and then the line I couldn't wait to deliver,

'…on your shift mate, I'm your Sergeant from Saturday.'

I wasn't the butt of his taking the mickey very often after that.

Traffic Patrol Officers' Course 1992 – I'm second in from the right

The same day a plain brown, very thick, heavy sealed envelope had arrived, simply hand-addressed *1441 Tucker*.

Intrigued, I opened it to find that it contained every single report, going back through my whole seventeen years where someone had something negative to say about me. As I've said, it was *very* thick.

I was really mystified and mentioned it to my own shift Inspector, John Lockett. He touched the side of his nose,

'Somebody's weeded your personal file mate before the Chief takes a look at it, promotion won't be long now. I'd drop it all in the shredder if I was you.'

Good advice, the shredder was very busy for a while and kept overheating.

I enjoyed my spell of 'acting', it was much easier than my previous spells, for a start there were no probationers to take care of, and as I've already said, everyone actually wanted to be there. Mark Judson was a decent Inspector who gave me a free hand to do things my way; his father had been at school with mine and had also been my Maths teacher twenty years previously.

What I hadn't realised was how much driving would be involved. When I'd been crewed with Bob, we drove for half a shift each, but I was now driving for the whole of it, often over two-hundred miles. I could be north of Keele and to have to travel to the southern end of Staffordshire's stretch of the M6, and sometimes very quickly. One night I found myself at 5.15am at junction 16, needing to be back at Stafford in three-quarters of an hour. The soft suspension did its best to rock me off to sleep, and three times I had to stop en-route and walk around the car to wake myself up.

I had a bit of a nightmare on my first day. I took out a Senator, we had two different models, the older, quick 12-valve, and the newer, very quick 24-valve which I was driving; they had different wheel sizes. The amount of kit in the boot meant we couldn't carry spare wheels, a supply was kept at Doxey post, the cars and wheel sizes were very clearly marked with tyre chalk. Punctures were fairly common, when driving along the hard shoulder it was very easy to pick up unseen debris. I was just north of junction 12 with a front nearside puncture; I'd radioed for a spare wheel and trolley jack to be brought to me, specifying that I needed a 24-valve wheel. The replacement wheel was properly marked as 24v and with a colleague's assistance the wheel was quickly changed. As I moved off there was an almighty crunch from the front nearside, the car lurched forward with a loud metallic scraping and a bang coming from the wheel that had been changed. The wheel had fouled on the brake caliper, causing major damage.

It transpired that, unbeknown to anyone at the time there were now two different sizes of 24-valve wheel too. The damage was extremely expensive, workshop manager John Cross, in fitting with his surname was - very; but the responsibility lay entirely with him and his people for not having known the difference.

1pm on an early shift and I was sent to a report of a lone female broken down on the southbound carriageway about half a mile north of the Yarnfield intersection, which I was about half a mile south of. Calls involving lone lady drivers were always treated as urgent. For me to reach her meant driving to junction 14, turning round, then ten miles north to junction 15, then six miles south to the location – a twenty-mile journey. Instead, I reversed the mile along the hard shoulder. The young lady, driving a Mini, had a flat tyre. There was no jack in her car.

Now that I'd joined her, I couldn't leave her alone; there were no other patrols available to bring me a trolley jack from Doxey post, so I coned off the Mini, and seated her in my patrol car.

Down to Doxey, collected the jack.

Up to Yarnfield, turned around.

Reversed half a mile along the hard shoulder again.

Jacked the car up, removed the wheel.

Put the spare wheel on, lowered the jack, job nearly done... The spare wheel was flat.

Having removed the spare wheel again, I left the car jacked up and took the lady with me to a garage in Stone, five minutes away where I blew the tyre up on the airline.

Back to Yarnfield.

Reversed the half mile again, replaced the wheel and sent her on her way.

Finished late.

A satisfied customer, did I get a letter of thanks to the boss?

No. Some people are so ungrateful. She didn't even give me my 10p for the airline back.

The hard shoulder of the motorway is a very dangerous place – not that the M6 in Staffordshire has much left these days, just ten miles of it from junction 15 to 16. Most fatalities and serious injuries happen there, not on the carriageway. So, every vehicle on the hard shoulder was potentially dangerous and had to be checked out. I changed many wheels in rather more straightforward circumstances than above, just so that people could be back on their way and out of danger.

I never ceased to be amazed by the number of people who ventured onto the motorway without any form of breakdown cover, the annual cost of which was around a quarter that of one garage call-out.

Mobile phones were in their infancy, most people could only summon help via the roadside telephones. Some wouldn't even do this.

We'd find abandoned cars on the hard shoulder in the middle of the night, with no lights on. After putting out cones and lights we'd continue on our way and find the driver heading for the next junction and the possibility of a nearby garage. Incredibly they'd always walk in the same direction they'd been driving, towards the next junction even if they'd just passed one. Once we encountered them, they'd have the expense of a breakdown callout and be reported for being a pedestrian on the motorway. A lot of 'breakdowns' were simply the result of running out of fuel, I had no sympathy at all for anyone stupid enough to do this.

People who did have mobile phones thought that the hard shoulder was the safest place for making and receiving calls. This was in the days before there were laws regarding mobile phone use in vehicles. However, stopping on the motorway to make calls was, as was made clear to them - dangerous, illegal, and after our intervention, costly.

Saturday was a day when football supporters took to the motorway, maybe calling at a pub or two before they set off on the journey, or along the way. We'd frequently find a car on the hard shoulder, its occupants in team colours on the embankment relieving themselves after their earlier session, in full public view. Inexcusable, motorways have service areas, not far apart An expensive toilet break, tickets handed out to each for being a pedestrian on the motorway. On one occasion none of them were able to watch their team after the driver failed a breath test.

If only they'd stopped at the services five minutes ago.

I stopped a speeder. drawing up behind the car, I went to the driver's window, already wound down.

'I've just followed you for a mile at speeds between 93-95mph, can you jump out and join me in the patrol car please?'

I returned to my car, cleared the passenger seat for him to sit down and started to write out the fixed penalty notice that I'd decided to give to him.

Bloody hell, he's taking his time!

I looked up from my pad.

My client had climbed into a wheelchair, lowered from a top-box and was wheeling his way towards me on the hard shoulder.

He only had one leg; I wanted the ground to swallow me and my patrol car, whole. I let him off after a lecture and helped him back to his car, while choking on a large slice of humble pie.

Early one morning, I was at Keele listening to a pursuit happening in the south of the county. The pursuit car's observer was doing the commentary and at one point said,

'…they've thrown a package out of the window.'

The pursuit ended with a crash into an unyielding wall some moments later.

'YF, pursuit ended, offenders made off'

'*(Call sign),* where shall I send the ambulance to? YF over.'

'There aren't any injuries YF, damage only.'

'But you said they'd thrown a *(racist word for a south-western Asian)* out of the window. YF over.'

'A pack-**age** YF.'

Nobody *should* have laughed at this misunderstanding, but...

I was briefing the shift one November afternoon and one of the bosses popped in,

'*[A senior ranking officer]* is having his retirement do in the bar tonight. Could you all stay away just for this one night?'

We were annoyed; we usually spent half an hour at the end of the shift having a much-needed wind-down before making our way home. We had as much right to use the bar as any other member of the force.

During the evening a thick fog descended, a real pea-souper the like of which we don't seem to have these days; this resulted in a spate of minor crashes. One, not so minor was a four car collision at the bottom of Weston Bank on the A518, just a couple of miles from our base. The scene was one of total devastation, pieces of vehicle wreckage extended as far as the eye could see, which admittedly wasn't very far. Surprisingly, nobody had been injured, but the road was completely blocked and clearing it safely would take some time. We were turning traffic around, the occupants of some of the approaching cars were people attending the retirement function. The alternative route was lengthy; with conditions were getting steadily worse, it was enough to make some of them give up and head for home. Irritation at being excluded from the bar may have caused some of the officers attending to tell the drivers that the function was cancelled due to the fog, but I didn't actually hear it being said...

We were getting ready to leave for home when someone came from upstairs,

'Mr *[senior ranking officer]* extends his compliments and invites you to join him for a retirement drink.'

We politely declined. Driving away, I looked up at the windows of the bar, there were very few people present.

My spell of acting Sergeant at TSS ended abruptly, for no apparent reason, I certainly hadn't done anything wrong, but I was told to return to my old shift the next Monday. John Lockett was in the office and said,

'Don't worry Nick, everyone gets a kick just before they're promoted.'

That was exactly what I was afraid of, but he was absolutely right.

I arrived at Weston Road on the Monday to rejoin my old shift. I hadn't even had chance to take my coat off before John Reynolds' ushered me into his office, beaming as he said,

'You're to see the Chief Constable at HQ, ten o'clock Friday morning, it's very good news Nick...'

It bloody isn't, I thought.

'...but we're going to be very sorry to lose you', he added.

Seeing the Chief was a best uniform job, whether I wanted promotion or not; such a meeting could end badly if I didn't present myself properly. So, in best bib-and-tucker, hair and beard neatly trimmed, I headed for Headquarters on the Friday. I sat at the Conference Room table with a dozen more soon to not be Constables, as our Chief announced that he was promoting each of us to Sergeant, addressing us in turn with our postings. This was the moment I'd dreaded most; if I was to leave the job which I loved, then please, please let it be Stoke, Longton, Newcastle, Kidsgrove or Burslem.

Anywhere but Hanley.

'Mr. Tucker, with effect from Monday 21st – Hanley.'

Promoted, to the very last place I wanted to go - a massive kick in the teeth.

It was my own Black Friday. A week before Christmas Day - I was devastated.

It was the first time I'd seen the Chief Constable in over seven years and the only the fourth since he was appointed fifteen years ago; I'd never see him again.

We had our shift's Christmas 'do' in Stone on the Saturday evening. It was a fantastic night, probably the best shift function I ever attended, but tinged with the sadness of a farewell. I'd had great bosses, made friends and had some wonderful, memorable times with them. We'd worked well as a close-knit team and got on really well together. My happiness and contentment had come to a sudden, crushing end. I was absolutely desolate at having to leave them and a job I absolutely loved.

It brought to mind a saying within the force – *Never look as if you're happy, you'll get moved.*

Before I'd been promoted, one of the security staff was organising a New Year's Eve celebration at Weston Road. He was plugging tickets for all he was worth, warning that they were nearly sold out. We had no other plans, and I was persuaded to buy a couple.

The tickets were numbered, mine were something like 212 and 213.

Ooh - should be a good do with that many sold!

It turned out he'd started numbering the tickets at 200. There were about twenty people there, it was absolutely bloody dismal.

We were back home long before Big Ben chimed; I'm sure most others were too. The organiser may have sung Auld Lang Syne as an unaccompanied solo.

20– Grounded

There was no way that I was going to join the fray at Hanley just four days before Christmas. So, conspiring with Alan Edwards, the office Inspector at TSS, I put together a backdated leave application which would delay my arrival at Hanley until 4th January. The festive season with my family would be welcome, and I could get my head ready to face the huge changes ahead of me. If there was any consolation, it was that I would be on the same shift I'd been unjustly forced to leave a few years before. There were only a couple of the original members left - including my former shift partner Don Holford in the Control Room - but the atmosphere of a shift remains the same for years, even though the people change over time – a sort of Trigger's broom.

Despite my promotion being unwanted, I was determined to act professionally and perform in my new post to the very best of my ability. It was what I was there for and what I was paid to do.

I decided to visit Hanley before my new shift's long weekend, after which I'd be joining them. I had an end-of-shift drink with a few of them and met my Inspector, Eddie Lewis. He had the enthusiasm of a newly appointed probationer, but with twenty years of experience. He was very approachable, and we took to each other straight away. He told me that as Patrol Sergeant, I'd have a free hand to run the shift as I wished, and that he'd support all decisions I made in their presence. Anywhere he felt I was wrong would be discussed in private, absolutely fine by me, that was how it should be. We were to have lots of private discussions, but none of them for that reason. He wouldn't be there on my first day, but by now I'd become quite used to starting out on my own.

I'd spent about half of my service as a PC at Hanley, my face was well known, and I knew nearly everybody there. Oddly though, it was the only station in the city where I'd never worn a Sergeant's stripes.

'Congratulations Nick, long overdue', echoed in my ears throughout my first afternoon.

There were two other Sergeants on the shift, Bill James, who I'd known for a long time but was off this week, and Paul Clarke, the Custody Officer who joined me on my first parade to introduce me to the team and helped with dishing out duties.

First job was a suicide at Abbey Hulton. Steve Morris, the stand-in Inspector for the afternoon asked me to take him to the scene. On my last shift I'd been a PC driving a high-performance Jaguar XJ6. As a Sergeant I climbed into the driving seat of an arthritic Austin Maestro 1.3, feeling thoroughly dejected. The sight of a middle-aged man hanging from a belt in his garage with a contorted face, blue tongue protruding from his mouth only served to deepen my mood.

The workload at Hanley was phenomenal; in the few years since I'd last worked there it had spiralled beyond control. The front line just wasn't coping, but through no fault of their own; they all worked extremely hard. There were now four IRVs being put out. Even six would only have eased the workload slightly, assuming we had the people available to drive them – which we hadn't.

Thefts of mobile phones had become fashionable, supplementing a raging epidemic of vehicle crime, which provided currency for the very many drug addicts who infested the patch.

My shift, between them was handling a caseload of around two-hundred reported crimes at a time; the pace of incoming complaints was so fast that there was absolutely no hope of investigating a single one of them.

Eddie had the right idea, he asked me to screen them all after they'd come back from being recorded in CID Admin. Those with little or no chance of being detected I passed to our front office staff, asking them to contact the victim by letter a week later, offering the usual platitudes and apologising that their crime had not been detected.

The crime report screening could take me most of the first shift after long weekend; I must have screened out over ninety-five percent of them. At least my overstretched team could have a chance to follow up the odd few reports I passed back to them. To their credit they did, and we had one or two satisfied victims, probably more than we would have done without operating this system. In years to come this would become official practice across the force, despite being very much frowned upon from on high at the time.

My second week at Hanley was nights. Eddie had already told me that on Friday and Saturday nights a team would be put out in the personnel carrier (or 'riot van' as they've become popularly known) for at least the first half of the shift; I'd be in charge of it.

For my own reasons, I decided that this week we would also operate a carrier on the Thursday night. Eddie took a look at the duty sheet before parade.

'I see you're putting out a carrier.'

'Yes boss.'

'I'm not going to interfere, you must have your reasons, but I don't see it myself.'

'I do, you'll find out.'

The night was incredibly busy, fights were breaking out all around the city centre, the streets were packed with revellers. We filled the cells with drunken louts.

As we were completing the handover paperwork at the end of the shift Eddie came to me.

'Bloody good job you put the carrier out Nick.'
'Yeah, I know, I told you didn't I?'
'Yes, but what did you know?'
'It was the first pot-bank pay day since before Christmas, they were bound to go out and blow it tonight, I've seen it every year.'

He never questioned my judgment again.

From experience, I knew that when moving to a new shift as a supervisor you need to make your mark on the team, quickly. A golden opportunity presented itself when at 11pm I spotted a young PC, driving alone through the city centre. On parade, I'd put her on foot patrol, partnered with another PC. Returning to the station I called her into my office, asking her to close the door.

I wanted to know why she was driving a car when allocated foot patrol. She explained that she had an enquiry to do a couple of miles away.

Had she asked anyone if she could take the car out?

No.

Had she made any other supervisor aware of the enquiry and the need to use a car?

No.

I gave her a bollocking, recorded it in my pocket-book and that was, officially at least, the end of the matter.

It was a trivial matter, but the PC concerned was a very popular member of the shift. Affronted by the dressing-down from this upstart new Sergeant, she told everyone. Despite her popularity, there had been a mood amongst the team that she pushed the boundaries too far, too often. Because of this, they considered the reprimand well deserved and not before time. They now also knew with certainty that their new Sergeant was on the ball and not to be messed with.

Eddie was very impressed, noting that I couldn't have chosen a better way or person with whom to make my presence felt.

During the early hours of the next night there was a ram raid in the city centre, an all-too-common crime at the time. Scrotes would steal a car, drive it into the plate glass window of a shop, grab as much merchandise as possible, load up and drive off – all in less than a minute. One of our patrols came across it just as they were making their getaway. A brief pursuit followed to Bucknall. Eddie was already in the area and very close by, he managed to intercept the pursuit and rammed the driver's door of the 'bandit' car. The thieves inside ran away into a row of rear gardens. I arrived very shortly afterwards, a dog handler and the force helicopter were en-route, but the offenders were long gone. At least we'd recovered the stolen property.

However, the matter of my Inspector crashing into the stolen car was of some concern, especially after his first words to me,

'I had to ram him to stop him getting out of the car.'

The recently introduced Code of Practice for police pursuits didn't outlaw ramming but took a dim view of it.

All crashes involving police vehicles had to be dealt with by at least a Sergeant, and I asked for the patrol Sergeant from Traffic Support North (TSN) to attend. The Duty Officer at Headquarters had different ideas, deciding that as I'd recently transferred from Traffic, I was the best qualified person available to deal with it.

I'd been working with my new Inspector for less than two weeks and now I was investigating him. My first responsibility after what he'd said to me was to suspend his driving authority. In all fairness to Eddie, he didn't object and after I'd formally cautioned him he said he'd make a statement, which he handed to me the following night.

I took one look at it and was astounded, his natural enthusiasm graphically translated itself into writing, including his well-intentioned, but somewhat unwise decision to ram the car. Had I submitted it unedited, our bosses would probably have hauled him over some very hot coals, even though nobody had been injured.

He complied with my (many) suggestions as to how his statement should actually read and the matter died a natural death.

The next night, a motorist in the city-centre blatantly drove through a red traffic light in front of me. After breathalysing him with a negative result, I dealt with him by fixed penalty, using exactly the same words and procedure that I'd have used on the motorway.

He made a complaint to Eddie that I'd been uncivil to him, clearly hoping that this would result in his ticket being waived – which it wasn't. It was a different world off the motorway, and I was still adjusting.

I decided to try to do something about the epidemic of vehicle crime, much of which was happening in broad daylight on the city-centre car parks. My overtime budget gave me enough funds to keep some volunteers on duty for three hours after an early turn. The plan was for us to go out in casual clothes with covert radios and merge with the public, particularly around car parks.

I was out there myself, in a side street just on the edge of the shopping centre when a man came barrelling towards me, with three others in pursuit yelling for him to stop. Before I could react, the man barged past me and I joined in the chase, shouting 'Stop, police!' He was wearing a brown leather jacket with a white hood pulled up over his head, and denim jeans, carrying a cloth cash bag which appeared to be full.

I was only a few yards behind him and lost sight of him momentarily as he rounded a corner into a deserted street. Then I heard reports over my radio of an armed robbery at Barclay's Bank a few moments earlier and made the connection.

A few seconds after losing sight of him, I found him hiding in a blocked entry between two houses, out of breath, still wearing the leather jacket and jeans. I didn't consider the 'armed' part of what I'd heard as I took him to the ground, told him that he was under arrest on suspicion of robbery and after a few moments was joined by uniform colleagues responding to the incident.

There was a lot of money in the bag, subsequently found dumped with an imitation pistol a short distance away. My prisoner was on the radar of Special Branch, as an active Provisional IRA sympathiser and fundraiser, probably the biggest arrest of my career.

We were in Crown Court a few months later and I was being grilled in the witness box by the defence barrister. He was trying to cast doubt on my identification, making a meal of the few (less than five) seconds when his client wasn't in my view. Glancing to one side I saw the court palantypist, just five feet away was none other than Mick Bills, long since retired.

'Sergeant, did the man you were chasing stay in your view the whole time?'

'No, your honour, he was lost to my view for just three or four seconds as he went around a corner.'

You always have to address your answers to the judge, regardless of who's asking the questions.

'But how can you be sure that my client, who you found around the corner was the man you were chasing?'

'It couldn't be anyone else, there were only the two of us in the street.'

'But you say your suspect was wearing a white hood?'

'Yes, that's correct.'

'But my client wasn't wearing a hood when you arrested him.'

'No, your honour.'

'Let us take a look at the clothing taken from my client at the time of his arrest.'

He handed me an evidence bag containing a pair of jeans.
'Are these the trousers my client was wearing?'
'Yes, they're similar.'
Another bag.
'Is this the leather jacket my client was wearing?'
'Yes, it could well be.'
'Does it have a hood?'
'No, your honour.'
A third bag.
'Is this the white tee-shirt my client was wearing?'
'Yes, it appears to be.'
'Does it have a hood?'
'It doesn't appear to, your honour.'
'Can you take it out of the bag please?'

I could see *exactly* where he was going with this and was ready.

I took it out of the bag.
'Take a good look Sergeant. Does the shirt have a hood?'
'No, your honour.'
'So, the only way he could've been wearing a white hood is if he'd pulled the shirt over his head. He'd have had to be built like Quasimodo. Surely, you're not suggesting that?'

Here I go!

'I'm not suggesting it your honour, learned counsel for the defence is.'

I heard Mick Bills gag, as a ripple of laughter went around the court.

'N-no f-further questions', the barrister spluttered and sat down.

As I left the witness box Mick Bills gave me a wink.

Quasimodo was jailed for seven years.

Solicitors figured large in my day-to-day work. Some were very good; even when defending a client, they would be friendly, helpful and professional in their dealings with us. Some were absolutely atrocious though and it was these that our regular 'customers' in the custody area would usually choose; often they did terrible harm to their clients' case.

One such solicitor was no stranger to the station, a scruffy man who excreted his verbal diarrhoea in whining, pleading tones. Although nobody else did, he liked the sound of his own voice.

One of his clients was in custody and had been charged, but we needed conditions attaching to his bail, so he had to be put before the court the next day. Custody Officers are now able to attach conditions to bail, but this was before a change in the law to allow it.

The next morning the man appeared in court. We had no objections at all to the granting of bail with straightforward conditions. The solicitor stood up and poured out verbal diarrhoea at great, droning length in support of his client. Eventually the presiding magistrate interrupted him,

'We've heard quite enough from you *[name withheld]*, your client will be remanded in custody for seven days.'

What an absolute bloody idiot! Even more of an idiot was his client, who on being arrested yet again a few months later requested the same solicitor,

'He'll get me off and out of here.'

As usual, he didn't.

Barely qualified 'legal representatives' were another bugbear. Their lack of legal knowledge could lead to them insisting that their client replied 'No comment' to all questions. Sometimes I could see a clear line of defence for a suspect, which a properly qualified lawyer would eagerly exploit. These legal representatives didn't know the law well enough to spot them though. They'd prevent the suspect from putting their version of events forward, for fear that their client could incriminate his or herself. This could, and often did lead to their client being charged, instead of being unconditionally released.

For a long time I'd become quite irritated by the attitude of some of the administration staff at Hanley, the huge majority of whom were very helpful and supportive. However, there was a clique amongst them who had the delusion that the police officers that they were employed to support, were actually there to support them. They made ridiculous requests for forms to be filled in, which they could easily have done themselves, a needless waste of a great deal of valuable operational time.

One day I was perusing a file in Hanley's Divisional Office when I overheard snippets of conversation referring to the *part-timers,* I knew what they were talking about, but decided to ask anyway,

'Who do you mean, the part-timers?'

'Why, your lot of course, you're hardly ever here.'

'Tell me, how many hours did you work last week?'

'Thirty-seven of course.'

'Do you want to know how many I worked?'

'Er…'

'Including unpaid overtime, I worked sixty-two. Is that part-time?'

'Er...'

I made it clear, so that I could be heard by the whole office, that I didn't expect front-line officers to be referred to in such disrespectful terms again, and that the *part-timers* were the reason they had jobs. It didn't make me very popular with them, but I wasn't the least bit bothered – supporting my people was paramount.

It wasn't long before I was very sorry to lose Eddie to a department at Headquarters, meanwhile we had an acting (yes, it was still happening) Inspector for a few weeks until a new Inspector was appointed. In keeping with Hanley's rapid turnover of staff, by now Bill James and Paul Clarke had moved elsewhere. I had one very capable acting (another...) Sergeant as my new colleague; until a replacement Sergeant was brought onto the shift a few weeks later there were now only two Sergeants rather than three on the team.

So, it came to pass that I went the way of all Sergeants at Hanley, Custody Officer in the dreaded dungeons. I had a tremendously competent and capable civilian assistant, Tom Evans, a retired army captain who attended to the prisoners' needs as well as maintaining the paperwork, video tapes and many other things; this left me able to concentrate on ensuring that the requirements of the Police and Criminal Evidence Act were properly complied with. He was invaluable in keeping the whole area running smoothly and rarely had to be asked to do anything – he just did it anyway..

It was a Saturday of long weekend, and I was doing overtime at a Stoke City match. I welcomed these as I was only out of the house for about five hours and would be better off to the tune of around £120. Malcolm Beech, another Hanley Sergeant saw me and chuckled, turning to laughter as he looked at me,

'What's so funny Malc?'

'You've got a new Inspector from Monday', he carried on laughing.

'Who?'

'You'll never guess! Who's the last person you'd want as your boss?'

I thought about it for a few seconds.

'Not.... M...'

.'.. yup!', by now beside himself with laughter.

One of our fellow Sergeants had performed six months as acting Inspector at Hanley, not particularly impressively by all accounts. The stint had been reported upon by the Superintendent, who, wanting to be rid of them had submitted a glowing report, seen by the Chief Constable. Perversely, if you wanted to be rid of somebody, it was a commonly used tactic to praise their performance; if you wanted to keep them, do the opposite. The Chief had apparently seen through this cunning plan; it was rumoured, quite probably true, that he'd been heard to say upon deciding to promote them,

'If he thinks this Sergeant is so good, he can have them as an Inspector.'

So, I had them as well. No wonder Malcolm was laughing..

I yearned to return to Traffic. Only a few weeks after my promotion, Sergeant posts on Traffic had been advertised. I'd applied, been interviewed and was successful. My former Superintendent, John Mottram was as eager as me for my return and assured me it was only a matter of time. But I had to endure the remaining months as a Sergeant on probation first; this unwelcome development was going to make those months feel very long.

My new Inspector was one of the nicest, friendliest, thoughtful people you could hope to meet. However, in post they were absolutely, completely, and utterly disastrous, the Inspector From Hell. Thoroughly incompetent and out of their depth, with no leadership skills; by a long way the very worst Inspector I ever worked for. I was undermined every single day; for example, I'd give orders which were then immediately countermanded in front of the team, without any prior discussion. The fact that they were of a different sex was irrelevant; I just tried to stay focussed on reaching the end of the year, when my escape may be possible.

One afternoon we had a very difficult female prisoner; irrational and violent, who wouldn't cooperate with anyone. Eventually after being forcibly searched by female officers she was unceremoniously dumped in a cell until she calmed down.

Enter Inspectre ~~Clouse~~ Clueless.

'What's going on, what's the matter with her?'

'You tell me, she just won't calm down, there's nothing I can do with her, I'm leaving her to wear herself out.'

I'd learned from experience that trying to calm violent prisoners usually exacerbates the situation; far better just to let them get on with it, provided of course that they can't harm themselves.

'This can't go on, the poor woman needs sorting out.'

'What do you suggest?'

'I don't know, she's *your* responsibility.'

That is s-o-o bloody useful Inspectre, now just fuck off out of here if that's all the help you are.

She must have read my mind, off she went; a quarter of an hour later she returned bearing a china mug with a hot drink.

'Ooh lovely, I'm parched.'

'Very funny Nick, it's for the lady in the cell...'

Fine, are you going to get drinks for all the other prisoners too?

'...it's herbal tea, it'll calm her down.'

Jesus wept! What fucking planet are you on?

'She's not having it. For one thing in her state there's no way she's having scalding liquid, and certainly not in a china cup which she can break and cause injury to herself or us.'

Go away, you fucking stupid idiot.

'She's having it, that's my decision.'

Oh, for fuck's sake!

I drew myself up to my full height, helped by me standing on a raised platform while she looked up at me, hands on hips I announced,

'It's NOT your decision to make. You've already said that she's my responsibility, quite right, I'm the one in charge here. Responsibility for the safety and wellbeing of detainees is entirely mine. Giving her that drink will be against my explicit instructions. I'm entering this conversation on the custody record, right now.'

Now fuck off.

Ignoring me, she seized the keys from Tom and let herself into the cell; 'discussion' over, I started to make my entry on the Custody Record. Then,

SCREAM!

SMASH.

SCREAM!

TINKLE.

SCREAM!

The Inspectre loomed in the doorway, white shirt bearing pink herbal tea stains.

'Sergeant, the lady needs to go in another cell, there's smashed china on the floor, it's dangerous.'

'I warned you what would happen, Inspectre. *You* can arrange cleaning up, your problem – it's all on the custody record and on videotape.'

To her credit she did sort it out, but I hadn't given her much alternative.

There were twelve cells at Hanley, including two female cells in a separate block, and two detention rooms for juveniles on the floor above. The only difference between a cell and a detention room was that a detention room had a wooden, rather than a steel door. A major flaw in the design of all the detention rooms and cells, meaning that their use was actually unlawful was that only one cell had a toilet in it. Detainees would be constantly asking to use the toilets. At busy times Tom could be kept fully occupied by prisoners wanting comfort breaks, and they quite deliberately took their time. Repeated representations to Headquarters over many years to upgrade the cells to the requisite standard had been ignored.

By the call button in one cell, some prisoner had written, *If you want a shit, press this button and one will come.*

It was a Friday night and Tom had the night off. I'd told the Inspector From Hell the previous night that I'd need cover from an experienced officer on the team, and from the moment the shift started. The IFH had refused outright, saying that all the uniform staff would be needed on the streets.

'You'll just have to manage by yourself for the one night.'

'So, you really expect me to be down there all by myself, on the busiest night of the week?'

'It's only one night.'

You absolute fucking moron. you want all the pissheads locking up, but you won't give me the resources to deal with them when they get here.

I was infuriated by this arrogant, but sadly typical lack of support for me. Not only that, but also her ignorance and disregard of the critical need for a properly run custody area. The smallest of mistakes made here could easily lead to acquittals at court. Big mistakes could have huge consequences.

When I started at 10pm the cells were completely full. Sometimes this was no problem as they could mainly be people who had been charged pending court appearance and just needed bedding down for the night, with hourly checks.

Not this time, all but two of the prisoners were 'live', arrested within the past few hours, awaiting solicitors and interviews, enquiries ongoing - a constant, rapidly changing situation.

As soon as I saw the scenario I phoned the Inspectre.

'I need an assistant down here straight away please, the cells are full, it's absolute chaos.'

I sensed the (not unexpected) reluctance in her tone.

'I'll send PC (*whoever, a raw probationer*) down to you, but it'll be after parade.'

'Inspector, I need someone, *right now*, someone who knows what they're doing, not somebody who's just back from Ryton'

'It'll be a good learning experience for them.'

'How the hell do you expect me to teach someone? I'm up to my neck in it down here? That's ridiculous.'

'Take it or leave it.'

She ended the call.

It was a further twenty minutes before my assistant arrived. I hadn't time to give even the most basic of instructions to him; he'd never set foot in a cell block before, let alone one full of prisoners pressing their call bells and shouting. He just stood there, mouth agape, without a clue as to what to do, and I had barely a second to tell him.

The phones were ringing off the hook, solicitors wanting to know about their clients and other stations wanting me to accommodate their prisoners. There were also families wanting visits. It was odd how somebody's arrest could trigger their family's urgent desire to visit them, even if they hadn't spoken for months, or even years.

I was absolutely swamped, feeling like I was drowning.

What if I reported sick now? I bloody well feel like it.

Burslem phoned asking me if I could take two of their prisoners,

'No, I'm full.' I put the phone down.

Shortly afterwards another phone call, the IFH.

'Why won't you take Burslem's prisoners?'

'You know perfectly well why, every cell is taken. My hands are completely full with live prisoners, it couldn't possibly be any busier down here. The only support I've had from you is one solitary probationer who hasn't a bloody clue what they're doing.

'Well, I've told Burslem you *will* take them, you'll have to go two to a cell.'

'You'll just have to bloody un-tell them then!'

Livid, I slammed the phone down.

What have *I done to deserve this absolutely bloody terrible boss?*

Two to a cell? Putting two complete strangers together in a locked room has the potential for dire consequences. If disagreement led to injuries, the custody officer would be subject of a far-reaching enquiry which could go on for months, or in a worst-case scenario, years. If this should happen tonight, my nightmare Inspectre would doubtless deny all responsibility – in all likelihood happily throwing me under the bus.

A death in custody, as well as being a tragedy, inevitably spelled the end of any ambitious Sergeant's career.

The bell at the back door rang. Three unexpected prisoners from Tunstall, although the arresting officers said they had phoned ahead – if they had then it wasn't to me. I was now in over my head, embroiled in the most stressful, impossible situation of the last seventeen years. My unassistive assistant had let them in and before I knew it, they were sitting down on the bench in the reception area. Call bells continued to ring, together with the clamour of shouting from the cell corridor.

It was to this scene of bedlam that the hero of the hour, Chief Inspector Dave Young, a decisive, no-nonsense, straight-talking boss came down the stairs on a routine late visit.

He quickly saw the situation, realised how inundated I was and beckoned me into a quiet(er) side-room.

'What the fuck's going on here Nick?'

I told him, in detail, with unguarded, honest criticism of my incapable line-manager, their failure to understand the situation and lack of support.

'Take a breather. Leave it with me.'

He headed upstairs.

Not long afterwards he returned with not one, but two experienced officers to assist. Clearly harsh words had been exchanged between him and the Inspectre From Hell. I didn't see or hear from her again that night.

Having ushered the Tunstall officers and their prisoners into the holding area and sending my two new assistants down the cell passage to attend to the prisoners' needs the Chief Inspector started going through the custody records with me.

In this calmer atmosphere we managed during the next hour or so to release several of the prisoners on bail to return the following day, then booked in the three Tunstall prisoners.. I now had space to accommodate any prisoners arrested during the rest of the night. I dread to think how that night would have turned out without the Chief Inspector's welcome intervention. Good bosses were worth their weight in gold but so thin on the ground, I certainly didn't have one at the moment.

Being a Custody Officer is easily the most stressful job in the service. Decisions, even those made in good faith can have a huge impact on the outcome of a case. During my stint at Longton I'd had a revolting eighteen-year-old lad in custody, accused of raping his younger sister. The evidence against him was incontrovertible. During a 'stand-off' arrest he'd slashed his wrists with a broken bottle and inflicted several deep cuts to his hands; he'd been handed to my custody after being discharged from hospital with several stitches.

He was very agitated and gave me immediate cause for concern, I needed to watch him very carefully. My first visit to his cell was after just ten minutes and there was blood all over the place. He'd bitten through his stitches and pulled them all out. I called for an ambulance, and he was escorted back to hospital. On his return he promised me that he would leave his stitches alone. An empty promise, as an hour later he had unpicked some, but not all of them.

324

There wasn't a lot of blood this time, the wounds had started to clot, so I decided to call out the police surgeon. My reasons were twofold, for him to look at the wounds, but more importantly to assess whether he was fit to be detained and interviewed. The doctor said that the cuts weren't of great concern, and after a lengthy consultation gave his opinion in writing that the lad could continue helping us with our enquiries.

Being still quite concerned, I spoke with his devastated parents, making certain that there were no underlying mental health issues.

Nonetheless, ensuring everything that could be done was in fact being done, I took the decision for him to have a social worker present as an 'appropriate adult' during interviews. I wasn't taking any chances.

A few months later at Crown Court I spent a very long hour in the witness box being cross-examined about my detailed entries on the custody record. Despite my having taken every possible step to ensure the welfare of this horrible young man, the defence managed to convince the judge that he should neither have been detained nor interviewed. This rendered the subsequent interviews and confession inadmissible.

Despite being manifestly guilty of an horrific crime, he walked free.

That's how a Custody Officer's actions and decisions can affect a case, even when correctly and conscientiously conducted.

As well as the effect that a Custody Officer's actions and decisions can have on a prosecution, the safety of detainees is entirely their responsibility. As well as drunks, many arrested were under the influence of drugs; it was all too easy to mistake serious illness for drunkenness or the effects of drugs. If it wasn't either of these, it was more than likely that there were mental health issues. More often than not a police surgeon would have to be called for a proper diagnosis, and to judge their fitness for further detention and interview. Sometimes I'd call for an ambulance instead. Nowadays most custody centres have full-time health professionals on their staff, years too late.

A particularly troubled and troublesome sixteen-year-old lad, no stranger to the police station had just been charged. He was handed over to me by the previous Custody Officer to remain in custody for the following day's remand court. The case officer was with him in the adjoining documentation room taking photographs and fingerprints. He put his head around the door to ask me something. The youth was out of his sight for no more than five seconds, during which time he downed the contents of a bottle of white spirit, kept in the room for cleaning the fingerprinting equipment.

I phoned the police surgeon,

'You don't want me Nick, you want an ambulance.'

After being escorted to hospital and stomach pumped, he was returned to my custody later in the afternoon, thoroughly searched for anything he could harm himself with and put in a detention room as he was too young for a cell. I ordered fifteen-minute checks on him.

Half an hour later the panic alarm sounded, and Tom shouted to me from the detention rooms upstairs,

'Sarge, **FIRE**!!'

I dashed upstairs to find Tom dragging this semi-conscious imbecile out of the room, flames were licking out of the mattress and the detention room and corridor were full of smoke. This time, as well as an ambulance, we had to call the fire brigade. The stupid lad had earlier found a lighter and concealed it far from the reach of sunshine.

On his return in the evening, I ordered him stripped naked and put in the detention room with no mattress, and just a blanket. If I hadn't decided upon the quarter-hourly checks he would have been dead, and it would be me who'd have carried the blame.

Naturally, the Inspectre took issue with my decision to remove his clothing,

'Don't you think that's a bit extreme?'

I'll tell you what's extreme, him setting fire to the bloody place!'

I stood my ground, reminding her once more that as far as the custody area was concerned, I was in charge.

Yes, Custody Officer was the most stressful job you could have, and with a clueless, incompetent, unsupportive line-manager it was next to impossible.

There was fun to be had though, sometimes. We had a once-in-a-blue-moon moment of every single cell and detention room being empty, half an hour from the end of an early shift. It was unusually quiet on the streets, with no prospect of detainees arriving any time soon.

I had an idea.

'Tom, let's wind the noon shift up.'

I grabbed a fistful of old custody records from the filing basket and put them in the slots on the board for each cell, marking up the board with fictitious names, offences and times, giving the impression that the cells were completely full.

As the clock made its way towards 2pm, anticipating the arrival of my noon shift counterpart. I rang both of the reception area phones from other phones in the block and let them ring out continuously, Tom went down the cell corridor to press the call buttons as often as he could.

I let my colleague in through the back door, to the apparent scene of absolute pandemonium. He took a quick look at the board,

'Fuckin' hell Nick, wish I'd phoned in sick! Hang on, I'll go upstairs to get some interview teams sorted and get the CID at it too.'

After a very quick tidy-up, Tom and I went up the stairs to book off, where we met the very flustered noon shift Custody Officer on his way back down to the cells.

'Wha.., eh? Aren't you going to do the handover?'

'Nothing to hand over mate, the cells are empty!'

'You bastards, I'll get you back for this...', his voice fading as we carried on walking.

He nearly did, a few weeks later I was woken by a 7am phone call one Sunday, a guy on the early turn with an offer of eight hours' double-time overtime if I could come in straight away. Sensing the catch in his voice and realising this was from the same shift whose Custody Officer we'd set up, I declined.

Occasionally a senior officer would read about something and have what they believed to be a 'great idea.' It would be implemented with great enthusiasm, but proportionally less common sense and forethought.

Nowhere was this more noticeable than in the case of a bright spark reading that psychological studies indicated that the colour pink could calm a violently disposed mind. Additionally, some stations in the UK already had a cell specially painted pink to house troublesome prisoners. This cretin, their name now lost in the mists of stupidity, decided to close down the custody area at Hanley for a week for redecoration. Hanley's custody staff moved temporarily to Stoke where the cell-block facilities, although good (and having toilets) were very limited compared to Hanley. We were busy, so it was a difficult week.

On our return to Hanley the entire block had been painted – PINK. The walls were pink, as were the ceilings and doors, cells and rooms. The big desk behind which Tom and I received and processed prisoners was painted, yes – pink.

To be fair to the psychologists, they were right, the pink colour did have an effect on prisoners. The moment they came in through the door and saw this sea of pink, they burst out laughing. It had an effect on us too, a couple of hours working in the blushing dungeons had your eyes swimming. It lasted just one a week before we moved to Stoke again; Staffordshire's taxpayers unknowingly funding another redecoration, but just one cell remaining 'in the pink' this time.

One afternoon, a very young PC from another shift accompanied by a social worker brought a man they had detained into the custody area for booking in.

'Can you tell me why this man has been detained?'

'Yes, Sarge, he's been detained for his own safety under section 136 of the Mental Health Act for the purpose of bringing him to a place of safety.

Hmm. Very well-rehearsed.

'Can you tell me where he was detained please?'

'Room *[whatever]* of the Grand Hotel in Hanley.'

Shi-i-I-T! Unlawful detention.

I told the detainee to sit down for a few moments and quickly ushered the PC and social worker into a side room, away from the cameras.

'You've detained this man unlawfully', I hissed at both of them, continuing,

'The power to detain is only in a public place, which a hotel room most certainly is not, the clock is ticking, and this man can sue the hell out of us.'

The social worker was on the point of tears,

'We've been trying to section this man for weeks. I'd have hoped for some cooperation.'

'You're welcome to our cooperation, not that we ever get much in return. We can't cooperate by breaking the law. I'm releasing this man from custody immediately,'

'Oh, *please*. Can't we just take him upstairs and sit him in a room until we can get a doctor?'

'Certainly not, I want him as far away as possible from this station, now!.'

'Your Superintendent will be hearing from my managers about this.'

'Don't worry, your managers will be hearing from my Superintendent about your having inveigled one of my officers into making an unlawful detention.'

It was obvious that the social worker was well aware of the legalities of the situation and had taken advantage of the inexperienced officer.

I went back to the man, and without going into detail and as pleasantly as possible told him that there had been a mistake and that he was free to go, if he wouldn't mind quickly giving me his personal details.

Half an hour later, just as expected, the Inspectre materialised, taking issue with my actions.

'Couldn't you just have overlooked it and gone through the procedure? We're supposed to help Social Services, the caseworker's really upset about this.'

'Overlook a blatantly unlawful detention? You're joking, it'd be me who'd have to answer for it in the discipline enquiry and any civil action, not you.'

Police stations are not a suitable or safe environment for people who are mentally disturbed and never have been; the police's power to detain them in a cell is archaic and inhumane. It's only now, over thirty years later that government is waking up to the fact.

The constant undermining and grinding conflict with the Inspectre From Hell were taking their toll on me, with a knock-on effect on my family life. It was affecting my health; I was unable to properly relax in my off-duty time, just dreading what horrors the Inspectre would inflict next. The doctor signed me off work for two weeks, citing stress and debility. I took all the time I could to unwind and spend quality time with my family and friends. After those two weeks, feeling slightly refreshed, I entered the fray again. Within half an hour it was as if those two weeks had never happened, the IFH was at it again. It seemed that everything I did was subjected to challenge and undermined by the very person who was supposed to support me.

I'd been on a regional Sergeants' Management Course for a month, a most welcome break from the Inspectre. Part of my action plan on returning was to get some more outside supervision under my belt; my colleague Sergeant obliged by swapping roles with me for a few weeks.

We had a female probationer who was simply not making the grade, I'd had concerns ever since I arrived at Hanley, as had the Area Training Department. She was a bright, outgoing thirty-year old, easy to get on with and very popular with her colleagues. However, the drive, confidence and common sense to do the job were completely lacking. I tried really hard, with my now proven routine of going to incidents with her and talking through them with her afterwards. I would highlight what she had done well, and where she could have done better, but it was all about the latter. I couldn't find a single positive thing to highlight. Nothing changed; I was having to put together a log of her failures, which grew daily. I was very disappointed that I couldn't find anything constructive to say other than how outgoing and well-liked she was.

I arranged for her to be attached to CID for a week to see if they could help her with statement taking, general enquiries and interviewing, but for her first shift in CID on noons she arrived in uniform, just as I was going off-duty from early turn. I'd finally seen enough, this was the end of the road. I took her to my office and spent two hours of my own time with her. I went through her entire history as a probationer, everything she'd done recently, as well as the record of the few months before I'd started with the shift. It wasn't easy, she was quite understandably in tears, and I felt more than a little sense of failure on my part.

I told her that I would be recommending her probation should be terminated in accordance with Police Regulations. However, still trying to be as helpful and sympathetic as I could, I suggested that it could help her future employment prospects if she wrote out her resignation there and then; meaning that any employment reference from Staffordshire Police would say that she left of her own accord, instead of being dismissed. She steadfastly refused; I had some admiration for her determination to stay – if only she could have shown the same in her work.

I prepared a well-evidenced report to support my recommendation, which took a great deal of time; it never went beyond the Inspectre's desk. She wouldn't support my evidence or recommendation, instead deciding to implement her own ham-fisted, unprofessional course of action.

She set the hapless lady impossible tasks; ensuring that she was sent – alone - to deal with difficult incidents and enquiries she hadn't a chance of resolving. She made her life utterly unbearable, it seemed to me to border on malicious, quite deliberately setting her up to fail.

Protests from me fell upon the usual deaf ears. Although the probationer was clearly unsuited to the job, this shabby, callous treatment of her was completely undeserved. She resigned in some distress after a very difficult few weeks.

I was absolutely appalled at my inept line-manager's conduct in the matter. Instead of the proper, lawful route which I'd worked so hard at recommending, her actions could have led to Staffordshire Police being taken to a tribunal. I'm quite sorry that it didn't happen. I suppose the one positive aspect was that her reference would show that she hadn't been fired.

I was still on probation myself until I'd completed a year as a Sergeant and could revert to PC if my performance didn't make the grade, although my Superintendent had assured me that confirmation of my promotion would be a formality. Despite the ongoing discord there was nothing at all about my performance that the Inspectre could criticise, apart from my opinion of her. My promotion was confirmed just before Christmas.

I phoned John Mottram at TSS, wishing him the compliments of the season, telling him that I was now available. He assured me that I'd not been forgotten and that he wanted me back in the fold.

In North Staffordshire, and across the force for all I know, the larger stations would have a weekday 9.30am meeting, popularly known as *Morning Prayers*. The Superintendent, Chief Inspector, Detective Inspector, Duty Inspector, Station Inspector and any others who considered themselves important enough would meet to go through the incidents of the previous twenty-four hours, highlighting mistakes and, rarely, acknowledging good work. On Mondays it was a long meeting as it would cover the weekend. The IFH usually took the Monday early-turn off, probably in anticipation, so I'd have to go in her place. During the meetings, as the lowest ranking present, I'd be made to feel responsible for every perceived mistake during that period, even whilst off-duty. It was never an enjoyable, or even constructive meeting; we called it the *Nine o'clock shudder*, because of our bosses saying, 'They shudder done this... he shudder done that...'.

One evening, having given time off to one of the controllers without any other qualified terminal operators on duty, the Inspectre instructed me to work the second half of a noon shift with Don in the Control Room. Three transfers, four secondments, three driving courses, promotion and attending a regional management course; and there I was, sitting in the same seat, eight years later, doing the same job and with the same partner. Nostalgic maybe, but I had an

333

inescapable feeling of having travelled a very long, circuitous route only to arrive back where I'd started.

Early in the new year, the tension with the Inspectre deepened. I found that I was taking on and being delegated more and more work which was entirely her responsibility. As the senior Sergeant on the shift I found myself having to constantly protect the team from her random, ridiculous, unworkable decisions. A particularly bruising exchange one morning, after she'd made another impossible demand of me, was the final straw. The Chief Inspector from Personnel was doing a brief operational stint at Hanley in preparation for promotion. We'd known each other for a long time, and I knew that I could speak freely and confidentially with him.

I tapped on his door and put my head round,
'Hi Nick, come in, come in...'.
Seeing the expression on my face,
'...shut the door mate, what's up?'
'Boss, I can't work with that fucking woman for one moment longer. She's bloody impossible.'
He leaned forward, a very interested look on his face,
'I've been expecting something like this, tell me more.'
So, I did, the whole bloody lot, leaving nothing out.

Within days I was given a very welcome transfer to Burslem. The IFH's days at Hanley were numbered too, shipped off to wreak her uselessness on the police officers and people at another station. She even had the brass neck to turn up at my leaving do, neither speaking to me nor signing my card. It was common knowledge that my move was to get away from her, as well as the reason she was leaving.

Despite grinding conflict with just one person, I was very sorry to leave behind one of the hardest working and dedicated teams I'd ever worked with.

21 – A Fresh Start

Back to Burslem. I felt a huge weight had been lifted from my shoulders. Yes, I was Custody Officer but with only four cells. Frequently I had no prisoners, or they were bedded down for the night, so I could spend time out on the patch, becoming more involved with the day-to-day work of the team. I'd known my new Inspector, John Barrett for a long time and had worked with him briefly at Weston Road.

I'd phoned Eddie Lewis for a 'catch-up' a few days previously and he cautioned me,

'For Christ's sake keep him away from the prisoners',

I didn't know what he meant - at the time.

My partner on the shift was Acting Sergeant Alan Bayles. He was completely on top of the job, promotion would come soon, and he had the potential to go far. This was my old shift, after a four-year absence, several of whom I'd worked with as a PC. They made me feel welcome and seemed to easily adapt to my new status with them; it probably helped that I'd been the senior PC with them before. I settled in very quickly; I knew the place and the people well and had always enjoyed working there. We were very lucky too to have some cracking bosses who really knew how to look after their people.

The problem with prostitution was still there, despite the 'main man' still being detained at Her Majesty's Displeasure, continuing to smoke weed to oblivion.

A major policing operation in Wolverhampton had displaced its prostitutes to Cobridge. They were hitch-hiking to the city, in some cases arriving and leaving in hired minibuses or even fifty-three-seater coaches. They were incorrigible, accepted arrest as an occupational hazard and went straight back on the streets after being arrested, charged and bailed; maybe just an hour's interruption to their business and sometimes we were arresting them twice a night.

The community were understandably up in arms by the sudden escalation of this blight on the area, but their leaders were aware that we were doing our utmost to control it and appreciated our efforts.

We'd always had concerns for the safety of the prostitutes; a local prostitute had been murdered by a 'client' just a few years before and prostitute murders were happening with alarming regularity across the country. The Yorkshire Ripper was not quite a distant memory.

Two 'working girls' were arrested and brought in on three consecutive nights. One was Emma Merry, a mischievous eighteen-year-old from Worcester, her name suited her, but she was clearly hardened to her career choice. Her 'colleague', Kirstie was of similar age and from the same town; an attractive, well-mannered, intelligent girl who seemed to be from a decent background. I was baffled as to what circumstances could have pushed her into this grim profession. They were both pleasant and compliant, in full knowledge that cooperation would speed their return to the kerbside. Constant arrests were something towards which they had a completely blasé attitude. As well as being heartily sick of the situation I was becoming very concerned for their safety, something to which they seemed to have no regard at all. I was desperately trying to think of sound reasons to detain them in custody and place them before the next court. As I released them for the third time on bail on the Thursday, I told them in no uncertain terms that I'd find a reason, however tenuous, for bail not to be granted next time I saw them. I emphasised that they risked spending the whole of the coming weekend in custody. To this day, I bitterly regret my decision to grant them bail on that occasion.

Part-way into the Friday night shift Kirstie arrived at the station, almost beyond hysterical. Emma had gone off with a client and not returned; someone had given her a lift to the place where Emma 'entertained' her punters, where she'd found her dumped corpse. John Barrett was off, so Alan and I found ourselves in charge of a murder investigation for the time being. My two prisoners were bedded down for the night, so fortunately I was free to give my full attention to the situation. Word of the killing had spread like wildfire among the prostitutes in the area, we had them all 'rounded up' and brought into the police station. The dozen or so that we found were, for once, grateful for our attention.

Whilst taking statements from them, it quickly emerged that the local prostitutes harboured concerns about one of the regular punters who could be violent and with whom they would not *do business*. They resented the competition from Wolverhampton, and wanting nothing to do with them, didn't share this information. So Emma, Kirstie and their associates didn't know about this man. Within a couple of hours, we were putting together a description of a suspect.

Everyone on the shift was fully occupied and everything was being done that needed to be. I was really proud to see that all of them had risen to the occasion – they were an absolute joy to work with, teamwork at its very finest. Neighbouring stations assisted with our routine incident workload. Headquarters alerted the usual circus of senior CID, Scenes of Crime, pathologist, and photographer.

The senior detective, a Detective Chief Inspector, arrived at the station about an hour later. He'd obviously been drinking very heavily. On reflection, I should have had him taken home and requested Headquarters to turn out another senior detective. This could have had far-reaching consequences, but at the time my hands and head were already fully occupied with events.

The bibulous boss contacted a couple of his colleagues who arrived and closeted themselves with him in the

Superintendent's office. From behind the closed door came the occasional sound of raucous laughter and the scent of Scottish snifters but no instructions for us. This was while Alan and I were running the situation, our team dealing with the scene and taking statements, together with a police station full of frightened prostitutes. I was furious when I went in to update them on our progress and very little interest was shown. A bottle and glasses were on the desk, receiving far more attention than I was.

As if this wasn't enough, another hysterical young woman arrived at the station reporting that she'd been raped. This was the last straw, we couldn't possibly deal with this, it required a trained female officer. I contacted Headquarters duty officer, the only suitable person within miles was at Hanley. It was the IFH, she came to Burslem to deal with it; my showing her into the interview room was the very last, very brief contact I ever had with her. Although I was in charge of the station I don't know how that particular enquiry turned out, I was just too pressed already.

Checking with Alan that all bases were covered, I turned my attention to Kirstie. I'd left her in an interview room with a hot drink, popping my head in every now and then to check on her. I took a statement from her, including a description of the car she'd last seen Emma getting into, and its driver. Although quite understandably extremely traumatised, we needed a statement from her as soon as possible; a more detailed one would be taken by the Major Investigations Team once she was in a more settled frame of mind.

Despite my long-standing loathing of her 'profession' I did feel sympathy for her, even giving her a hug at one point. As I'd surmised, she was from a decent background and well educated, having left school the previous year with good A level grades. She'd fallen into prostitution by associating with the wrong people, particularly Emma with whom she'd formed a close friendship. Having discovered the murder she was totally overwhelmed, completely out of her depth and wanted to get out of it, right now. She asked me to call her parents, not the easiest of phone calls for me to make in the middle of the night. They said they'd come to Burslem, I can't begin to imagine the conversation that followed when they arrived after I'd gone off duty..

I took the evidence files for herself and Emma, requesting that the CPS discontinue all charges against Kirstie; it was far easier to persuade the CPS to drop a case than to pursue it.

The Wolverhampton prostitutes were never seen again after that horrific night. The local ones drifted back very slowly over the next few weeks.

When I booked on the next night a suspect was in the cells at Burslem. He was bedded down for the night, although whether he could actually sleep is questionable. Interviews would follow the next day, Sunday, when I'd volunteered for a quick changeover to noons.

On my arrival for that shift, interviews and enquiries were in full swing. The Detective Chief Inspector (another one) in charge of the enquiry told me that my shift, Alan and I had done a 'bloody cracking job' on the Friday night.

I'd never seen anyone so tense as the man in the cell, sweat was pouring out of him and tension crackled like static electricity inside him. After a mid-afternoon chat with me in his cell, he asked to speak to the senior detective. I could tell that he was at the point of admitting the murder, so an interview was quickly arranged. However, once the interview had been set up he stalled at actually making the confession which was bursting to get out of him.

He never did admit the murder, but the forensic evidence was more than enough to secure a conviction.

As I've said, my decision to bail Emma the night before she met her death is one I have desperately regretted ever since; it caused me a huge amount of heartache and guilt-tripping at the time. I have to remind myself that it was her choice to continue with her trade.

I do hope that Kirstie found a better path in life.

During the same week I'd had a particularly obnoxious prisoner brought in. He was offering violence to the arresting officers and refused any details of himself, this never bothered me as there was no way anyone would be released until their identity was known. They came round eventually, there was no point in wasting time trying to persuade them, although some of my colleagues would make fruitless attempts. After being forcibly searched and bodily thrown into his cell he started banging on the door and shouting - again, not a problem, I left him to tire himself out and went down to the front office. Half an hour later I went to check on him and saw water coming from under the cell door. The pillock had blocked his toilet with paper although he seemed to have calmed down. I opened the cell door,
'My fuckin' cell's flooded, I want to move, NOW!'
'You're staying where you are, you flooded it, your fault, your problem.'
'I want to see the IN-*SPEC*-TOR, NOW!'
'Why?'
'I want to make a fuckin' COMPLAINT!'
'He'll see you when he's free, he's busy now.'
I closed the cell door. He started banging and shouting again.
John Barrett's office was a few yards down the corridor and he'd heard what was going on. With an irritated expression, he came out of his office to the gate,
'What the fuck's going on Nick?'
'Idiot in cell one John, he's flooded it and now wants to move. He's just being a total dickhead.'
'Let me see him.'
I let John through into the cell block and opened the door, the prisoner said,
'Are you the Inspector?'
'Yes.'

'I want to make a complai…'

I didn't see what happened, but the next thing I knew the idiot was lying in the water on the cell floor with John standing over him. The dripping detainee's request for a change of cell was declined.

I recalled Eddie's warning from a couple of weeks before.

I was enjoying myself again for the first time since my promotion, every day I looked forward to going to work. However, I had another failing probationer coming up to eighteen month's service, another lively young lady, a former police cadet with her father and other relatives also in the job. She was extremely popular with the shift and very willing to work hard. However, but not for want of trying, she didn't seem to have the slightest clue what she was doing. This was at odds with a previous impression I'd had of her; she'd been a cadet attached to another shift at Hanley, appearing confident and on the ball.

I did my best to bring her on, my normal routine of going out on patrol with her, attending incidents, dealing with the public, and then discussing it afterwards. To put it bluntly, she was alarmingly inept at absolutely everything, lacking in both confidence and focus. She too wouldn't consider resignation, so I compiled a detailed report concluding with the regrettable recommendation that her services be dispensed with.

However, I had an uneasy feeling that I was missing something.

My discomfort was justified. Just after my report had 'gone upstairs' she suddenly discovered that she was pregnant and due to give birth at any time. Although she was neither slim nor very overweight, there was no outward sign of this. However, as was everyone else, I was incredulous at her having gone to the very last days of a pregnancy without noticing. It could explain a great deal, so giving her the benefit of the doubt I put together a hurried addendum to my report. I recommended, successfully, that she be allowed to continue her probation for a further twelve months after returning from what had, very suddenly, become maternity leave.

John and I called at the scene of a suicide which one of the team was dealing with. A man in his thirties and his wife had an alcohol fuelled row at bedtime. After the woman had gone to sleep, her husband had climbed into the loft, tied a rope around a rafter, the other end around his neck and had jumped into the stairwell. When we arrived, he was hanging two feet from the hall floor, very dead and turning slowly from side to side. Suicides can sometimes be a very carefully disguised murder, so initially treated as a crime scene. When the photographer and scenes of crime officers turned up and started doing their bit, including cutting down the body, John suggested I take the stunned wife into the living room, out of the way.

These were awkward situations, of which I had considerable experience by now; you can't just sit there in silence. My usual strategy was to make conversation by looking slowly around the room, talking about objects and pictures there. The dialogue was going as well as could be expected in the circumstances. It had included the various holiday photos and a feigned appreciation of some of their pottery ornaments. However, I was rendered speechless for the next topic of conversation, when my eyes alighted on a framed certificate which had been awarded to the dangling deceased - for a bungee jump.

Assaults on officers had been increasing, alarmingly. The force still expected to go out on patrol alone, with just a wooden stick for self-defence, although mine had only ever once seen active service; plus handcuffs that were all but impossible to put onto an uncooperative service-user.

Finally, Headquarters started to take notice. Self-defence training became routine, and we were issued with rigid handcuffs, which were far easier to apply.

Our truncheons had always been concealed in a long pocket. They were taken from us and replaced with longer batons, which were to be openly displayed. CID officers and motorcyclists were issued with extendible Armament Systems & Procedures (ASP) ones which were easy to carry. The rest of us were expected to wear the rigid 'Arnold' nylon batons on a utility belt which also had space for our handcuffs. These were fine for foot patrol, but made getting in and out of a car, or being comfortable while driving all but impossible. It was too much; I just threw mine onto the back seat of the car ready for use should I need it, as I'm sure many others did.

It was a typical donkey mentality decision to make us wear these impractical batons; the rationale behind it was that openly displayed, they would deter an attacker – which they didn't, read on. It was to be long after I retired that all officers were finally, sensibly issued with the ASP batons, just as they should have been in the first place.

Assaults didn't decrease anyway, and a couple of years later we were trained and issued with CS spray canisters which whilst easy to carry on the utility belt, if used in a volatile situation could result in ourselves being overcome by the effect intended for our attacker. Accidental discharges were commonplace; the donkeys stated *accidental discharge is negligent discharge,* which was absolute bollocks, it could easily happen. Going into the storage cupboard to issue fresh canisters would make your eyes water. They leaked, although this was officially denied, and everyone's locker and uniform smelled of CS. Tasers and pepper spray seem to be the most commonly used self-defence methods nowadays, how I wish we'd had them years before.

After a reorganisation of responsibilities on the shift, and eight years after the last time, I was back at Biddulph, also having responsibility for the officers on the shift stationed Tunstall. This however would be only for a few weeks. There was no sign of a vacancy for me yet on Traffic, so I successfully applied for the vacant post of manager of Burslem's Divisional File Management Unit. Recalling Chapter 14, this department was responsible for the preparation and submission of evidence files to the CPS. Within a few weeks of my appointment it was renamed the Criminal Justice Support Unit. I'd had two competitors for the post, both of my fellow Sergeants on John Barrett's shift. I do hope John didn't take offence at this attempted exodus of all his Sergeants, as he was probably the very best Inspector I ever worked for.

22 – C.P.S. - Couldn't Prosecute Satan

On the face of it I'd dropped into the perfect job. No more shifts, I could work whatever hours I liked, as long as they met with regulations, I could grant myself time off and approve my own leave. For the first time I had my own office, which I didn't have to share; formerly a bedroom of a pair of semi-detached police houses in Biddulph which had been converted to office space. Added to that, my Divisional Commander, the outstanding Superintendent Peter Herward gave me free rein to run the department as I wished. He never interfered but phoned me a couple of times a week for an informal catch-up; I felt very well supported.

What could be better?

My new role would involve me heavily with the Crown Prosecution Service. Until their inception in 1986, police prosecutions were handled by local solicitors. The more cases they won, the more would be given to them.

The CPS was in the public sector, paying public sector salaries; thereby having to employ sometimes newly-qualified lawyers, prepared to do the job for less remuneration than the well-qualified ones in the private sector – and it showed.

Meanwhile, the formerly successful, but now redundant prosecuting solicitors turned to defence work; their superior experience and knowledge meant they could easily demolish prosecutions conducted by the CPS.

To add to the perfection, I was very fortunate to have a well-staffed department made up of first-rate people. Further agreements reached nationally with the CPS, where the senior police representatives must have been asleep again, required strict time limits for progress of evidence files through the system. After someone was charged with an offence, the completed file had to reach the CPS no less than two weeks before their first court appearance. For various reasons this had often not been achieved in the past. One reason I'd identified whilst operational was that whole files were returned to the case officer with queries, sometimes trivial. Shift patterns, leave or courses could result in a week or more passing before the file was received back in the department, by which time the file was already overdue with the CPS. An unnecessarily rigid framework of forms for case officers to include further added to the delay. The time limitations and forms mandated to be included with every file made the FMU/CJSU a very high-pressure environment to work in.

My start in the department was the by now expected jump into the deep end, prompted by a call from the Superintendent's deputy. An incident the previous weekend had led to three officers from the Division being suspended. After the usual glacial enquiry they were exonerated, but for now this had implications for all the cases in which they were involved. Compounding this, the three officers were among the most prolific and hard working in the Division. They figured in a significant number of cases which were progressing through the courts, all of which I now had to review. I had to consider the importance of their evidence to each case, whether it could be challenged and then discuss it with the CPS. After retrieving the copy files, they stood in a pile three feet high by my desk. The task took most of my first three weeks in post, in addition to my day-to-day work leading the department.

Once this was done I heaved a sigh of relief. It was now time to look at how things were working. As I'd be the link between the Division and the CPS it was in everyone's interests that we got on well, so I met with the Senior Crown Prosecutor to try to understand their issues and make them aware of ours.

My operational experience had made me well aware of the problems faced by front-line officers when submitting files. I decided that the future ethos of the unit should be that our sole requirement from case officers would be good quality evidence from which we'd build the appropriate file, thus reducing form-filling on their part to an absolute minimum. It was well received and rapidly paid dividends, within weeks our timeliness and quality figures had risen considerably, and our greatly improved performance was acknowledged by the CPS. We were able to maintain a solid reputation throughout the eighteen months that I was running the unit.

The CPS were devious buggers though, often downright unprofessional. It suited me to work most days from 8am to 4pm, with Friday 6am-2pm, so that I could start the day with a two or three quiet hours at my desk without distractions. They soon became familiar with my work pattern though. Almost every day, at 3.55pm my phone would ring,

'Hello Sergeant, it's (*insert name here*) from the CPS. I'm looking at a file I've got in court tomorrow and there are a few questions.'

I'd then have to go downstairs to fetch the copy file, then back to my office.

'OK, I've got our copy here. We sent this to you three weeks ago, is this the first time you've looked at it?'

'I'm afraid it is.'

This was exasperating, effectively our concerted efforts at timeliness were ultimately pointless.

'What IS the point of us having agreed time limits if you're not going to look at the files until the last minute?'

'Well, I need these questions answering or we may have to discontinue.'

This was tantamount to blackmail, and it happened almost daily. Knowing I was about to leave the office, they'd phone me in the hope of a quick answer, just to make life easier for them.

I became increasingly infuriated by this as time passed. Once, having received an impossible list of tasks on a file the evening before a first court appearance, I decided it was time for action. The next morning, I went to the remand court in plain clothes and sat at the back of the room. The CPS lawyer stood up and outlined the case, concluding with,

'… we have requested that the police carry out enquiries, but they haven't responded.'

So, this was the way they were doing things. The *bastards!*

I stood up.

'Excuse me your worships',

Introducing myself, I continued,

'We sent the file of evidence to the CPS over two weeks ago, their requests were only made by telephone late yesterday afternoon. It would have been impossible for us to comply. I can assure your worships that enquiries are being made as I speak.'

The CPS lawyer was crimson with rage and embarrassment but hadn't a leg to stand on. The inevitable complaint to my Superintendent earned me a pat on the back. The 3.55pm phone calls seemed to diminish from then on, but they developed a new tactic; that of intentionally making their unreasonable demands *after* I'd gone home.

I arrived at the office on a Monday morning to find that over the weekend some of my staff had been working overtime, preparing a transcript of a video interview which had been requested late in the afternoon the previous Friday. This was a flagrant contravention of an agreed national Code of Practice that transcripts of video interviews should never be made under any circumstances. A *certain* CPS lawyer wanted to read the transcript, either not having the time (believing their time to be far more important than ours), or more likely, being too damned lazy to watch the video tape. I was furious.

On another occasion one of their lawyers wanted to discuss a dangerous dog file with me. The law has since changed, but at the time, dogs were allowed one bite, the magistrates would make an order that the dog be kept under control. If the dog went on to bite again then an order may be made for it to be put down. This dog was on its first bite and despite incontrovertible evidence, the owner maintained that it was not their dog. After going around in circles for a few minutes the lawyer announced,

'I want you to organise an Identification Parade for the dog.'

After a heated discussion, during which I repeatedly questioned the lawyer's intelligence and legal knowledge, I finally announced, immediately before ending the call,

'You're a bloody idiot.'

The case went ahead. Some people vehemently argue the system before having to go to court, but back down when the day finally arrives. This was such a case, once at court the owner didn't dispute the identification, and the order was duly made. A big part of me wishes that we'd organised the parade, but it would have been the police, not the CPS, who'd have been the laughing-stock once it gained the inevitable press attention.

I made a point of reading all the statements on every file, it was time consuming, but I knew the strengths and weaknesses of the evidence in every 'live' case.

Some statements could be hilarious, particularly from the younger Constables, full of enthusiasm but inexperienced in both the job and with life. One of the Cobridge prostitutes had been assaulted by a 'client' who'd been charged. The lady of the night's statement, written by a callow nineteen-year-old began:

'I am employed as a prostitute in the Cobridge area of Stoke on Trent.

At (time) on (date), I was on duty at the corner of Elm Street and Waterloo Road...'

It gave me and the staff a good laugh, fortunately the punter pleaded guilty, so the statement was never read or challenged in court, thank goodness.

Less than three years before while at Hanley, I'd attended the scene of a murder in Abbey Hulton where a thug killed his partner's mother. I'd known of him for a long time and had dealings with him going back for well over a decade; he was a very unpredictable and dangerous man who spent a lot of his time 'pumping iron', as well as pumping illegal steroids into himself. I'd never seen so much blood in one place in my life; the attack had been absolutely vicious, with knife wounds all over the woman's body. Naturally he was sentenced to life imprisonment.

I was astounded when a file came across my desk concerning the same man. He'd been charged with GBH, after having been released on licence from his life sentence after little more than two years. Obviously, on being arrested he was recalled to prison. I cannot believe that a savage murderer like him, with multiple convictions for violence and disorder could be walking the streets such a short time into a life sentence, causing yet more serious injury to other people.

The justice system in this country is an absolute joke, the police do their utmost but are failed time and again. Quite unjustly, they are often blamed by that very system for failings that are completely outside their control.

Despite the relentless assaults of the CPS on my sanity, our unit's results were gaining attention. We were visited by one of Her Majesty's Inspectors of Constabulary, keen to know our working practices. File preparation was developing into a highly specialised area with several discussion documents being published around the Inspectorate's findings. Some of my ideas became part of national policy over the next couple of years.

I'd known our newly appointed Chief Constable since we'd both been Constables in the 1970s. When he returned to Staffordshire after a spell in another force he called in my office whilst on an introductory tour of the area. He said that he was very impressed to have heard of my results and that he would like to see me as an Inspector, and beyond, within the criminal justice area. The ball was in my court if that was the direction I wished to take. However, my frustration with the CPS's lack of professionalism, shameless disregard of agreed protocols and many other issues had reached boiling point.

We were at a crucial stage through the courts of a very unpleasant rape case. A team of detectives had devoted a huge amount of time and effort to bring a particularly nasty individual to justice.

The man had taken a decent young lady back to his flat and raped her at knifepoint, cutting her neck with the knife. Following arrest, the rapist's flat had been searched and amongst other things, a large quantity of cannabis vegetation had been recovered. He'd been charged with rape, and possession of a controlled drug with intent to supply. The case had already been sent to the Crown Court and the offender was on remand. A CPS lawyer, the *certain* one referred to earlier, a recurring object of my exasperation phoned me,

'I've been reviewing this case and I'm going to discontinue the rape charge.'

'WHAT? For Christ's sake, why?'

'There are issues surrounding consent, there's no evidence that she was unwilling.'

'At KNIFEPOINT?'

'We only have her word for that.'

'What about her injuries and the medical evidence?'

'You're wasting your time Sergeant, I'm going to discontinue, please tell the complainant.'

'I'll tell the complainant why you won't continue, because you can't be bloody bothered.'

'Do that SERGEANT, and you will find yourself in very hot water indeed.'

'I don't bloody care. Where's the justice for the girl?'

I slammed the phone down and made senior management aware, but the CPS wouldn't budge, I was absolutely incensed. Justice had abysmally failed this young lady, who at the time had no right to challenge this appalling decision, made by one person, with no reference to her or the courts.

Discontinuances were a diabolical travesty in the justice system. CPS lawyers could 'discontinue' cases almost at will, without giving sound reasons, without reference to their senior managers and certainly without having to ask the permission of the court, even if hearings had already taken place. No consideration whatsoever was given to the victim, and the CPS cravenly passed responsibility for informing the victim of *their* decision to the police. This, victims would quite understandably believe that it was the police, not the CPS who had failed them. Nothing was ever put into writing, just a notification of discontinuance, without giving reasons other than *insufficient evidence* or *not in the public interest*.

It was an outrageous situation; nowadays victims rightly have a statutory right to challenge CPS decisions, as should have been the case from the start.

A few days later the *certain* lawyer phoned me again – at 3.55pm. My hackles rose instantly, I was in no mood for speaking to them.

'I'm looking at the possession charge, in view of the *lack of evidence* in the rape case I'm going to discontinue the possession with intent charge too as on its own it appears rather trivial.'

'Trivial? What is it you can't be arsed with this time, and what's this *lack of evidence*?'

'Mind your attitude Sergeant, remember who you're talking to.'

'You're an equal so-called partner, so don't you dare talk down to me. What's your reason this time?'

'There's no evidence that it wasn't for personal use.'

'W-H-A-T? Have you ever *seen* that amount of cannabis vegetation? It would take over a hundred years for one person to smoke it, and that's if they never slept.'

'That is my decision, Sergeant. There is nothing that you or anyone else can do about it.'

She hung up. This was a violent scumbag who had raped a respectable girl at knifepoint, possibly destroying her life. He'd be released from remand with all charges dropped, all on the whim of one single lawyer.

He should have been serving a very long jail sentence.

Emboldened by the incompetence of the CPS, he could put two-fingers up to society and continue abusing women, dealing illegal substances and all the other criminality of his lifestyle. All this, with a newly acquired sense of impunity, freely handed to him by the justice system. He may even have sued us for wrongful arrest.

I was absolutely livid, I cannot remember having ever been so angry at anything that had happened during my service. I went home, drank half a bottle of whisky before my tea, and the other half straight afterwards. I'd had enough.

The prospects offered by the Chief Constable a few weeks before would mean higher rank and salary, but I'd still have to deal with the barrage of perverse demands and decisions of the CPS. It simply wasn't worth it, I valued my sanity.

Next morning, completely by coincidence, maybe, I had a call from the Chief Inspector in Personnel, nowadays *Human Resources*.

'Nick, there's a vacancy coming up for a shift Sergeant at Northern Traffic at the end of the month. It's yours if you want it, have a think about it and let me know by the end of next week.'

I said I'd let him know, but I already knew the answer.

Three weeks later I cleared my desk and was heading back to Traffic – what I'd yearned for since promotion almost four years ago.

I'd be working shifts again.

I'd be out in all weathers.

I'd have to request time off instead of giving it to myself.

But it was worth it, just to get away from the egregious Crown Prosecution Service after eighteen months.

23 – ♪♪ Happy Days Are Here Again ♪♪

The downside to Northern Traffic, more properly Traffic Support North was that it was based at Hanley police station. Although I had fairly recent bad memories of the place, I was looking forward to getting back on the road with a new team and spending as little time there as possible.

The group was squeezed into five rooms, bizarrely on the top floor of the building, ten flights of stairs away from our fleet of patrol cars in the yard. There was a lift, at the other, distant end of the building. It had manually operated gates, often accidentally left ajar on another floor, so for much of the time it was useless. We also had use of the former vehicle workshops on the lower ground floor, but as they were unheated they were only usable as office space in mild weather. It was a ridiculous situation which nobody seemed to have the will to change. We needed a visible presence on the rural trunk roads around Leek and Newcastle, not in the snarled-up city centre. Being based on the top floor of a city-centre office block was comparable to a trawler fleet being run from Wolverhampton.

The force had a policy called 'Tenure of Post'. Anyone in a specialist role was forced to return to at least one year of Divisional front-line policing after a set number of years, ten in the case of 'T' Division - Traffic. It was a criminal waste of skilled people, trained and qualified at considerable cost to the public purse, tantamount to a car manufacturer moving its most skilled engineers and designers to a year's manual work on the production line. Compounding this, our former Chief Constable had refused to promote anyone into a specialist post, regardless of their qualifications, experience or ability. I'd been trained by the force as a specialist Traffic officer. Promotion by that same force rendered me, and the force, unable to make full use of the skills and qualifications I'd gained, as well as the force's outlay in training me, for almost four years. I relished the thought of being able to make proper use of my training again. However, I was replacing a Sergeant who was far more qualified for the post than me; his time numbered by this irrational, wasteful policy.

Fortunately, I'd be unaffected by this rule before my planned retirement in nine years' time; at least I thought so.

Inspector Pete Shone was in charge of the sixty or so officers in the group, I was responsible for a shift of about a dozen of them. Pete was promoted a few weeks later, to be replaced by none other than John Barrett.

I had an informal welcome meeting with my new Divisional Commander, Superintendent Peter Lawton, replacing John Mottram who was now retired. He noted how eager I must have been to come to my new post, back on shifts and out in the cold after the comparative luxury of a warm solo office and every weekend off for the last eighteen months.

I told him that the CPS had made my office a very cold, uncomfortable place to be.

My team were, without exception amazing, hardworking people, with service ranging from four to fifteen years. We were now running ARVs around the clock, one from each of the three Traffic groups; the TSN ARV being crewed in rotation by four members of my team who were AFOs. Due to their role, I'd need to pay particular attention to their welfare, being continually satisfied that they were in the right frame of mind for deployment to firearms incidents, which were steadily increasing in frequency.

I was again leading people who had strived to be where they were, they enjoyed their work and there was very little discontent – the principal, and probably only complaint being our unsuitable accommodation.

Our vehicle fleet consisted of several Vauxhall Omega MV6 patrol cars, one of them unmarked, a few (rather tired by now, but still much preferred to the Omega) Vauxhall 24-valve Senators, a rather tired Jaguar XJ6, a Land Rover Discovery V8 (which everyone hated), a Land Rover and a LDV Sherpa Incident Van, plus a fleet of BMW motorcycles. We later had a Volvo V70 T5, which was a far more suitable replacement for the Senator than the Omega, everybody wanted to drive it. I later had a couple of these Volvos of my own, fantastic cars to drive but the running costs were prohibitive for a private individual who enjoyed spirited driving; I was lucky if a pair of front tyres lasted 4000 miles, and as for the fuel consumption…

After briefing the shift and allocating duties for the first time, I grabbed the keys to an Omega and gleefully headed out onto the road. Although being a very fast, comfortable car which handled well, the Omega was a disappointing replacement for the Senator, which to date, arguably remained the best police patrol car of all time. Build quality was poor. Kit shifting around in the boot could produce dents in the single-skinned rear wings. At around 70,000 miles the driver's door check mechanism would break (the driver's door of a patrol car is opened and closed many more times than a similar privately owned one), then crash open against the front wing, causing a lot of expensive damage. Omegas would face certain death at around 120,000 miles (roughly two years' use), when a piston would make a break for freedom and spontaneously throw itself out of the side of the engine block.

My first day was yet another rude introduction.

It wasn't long before I was sent to the scene of a police vehicle collision, although the patrol car hadn't actually collided with anything. Mick, the driver had been responding to an emergency call using lights and siren. As vehicles pulled over for him, he overtook them, but one fool decided to follow in his wake - in an arthritic diesel Land Rover of all things. One of the cars that had slowed down accelerated to resume their journey and didn't see the errant Land Rover, leading to an inevitable crash.

Mick was completely blameless, but as his actions had initiated the circumstances of the crash it had to be dealt with as a police vehicle collision. On my recommendation, the idiotic Land Rover driver was prosecuted for dangerous driving.

At the same time, not far away, a child had stepped out in front of a car and sustained injuries that were potentially fatal. The driver was not at fault, but we still had to mount a full-scale enquiry in case the Coroner became involved which fortunately he didn't; the child made a good recovery.

During my first year at TSN, the whole group was concentrating on being highly visible, clamping down hard on the 'fatal four', speeding, seat belt use, drink-driving and mobile phone use. While the latter wasn't yet a specific offence, we could report a driver for the subjective offence of not being in proper control of the vehicle.

Speed camera use was still developing. We reported thousands of motorists for the fatal four, with a zero-tolerance policy on all of these. It worked spectacularly; by the end of the year road casualties on our area had almost halved by comparison with the previous year.

Lives saved, and life-changing injuries prevented.

It quickly became clear to me that at TSN we were dealing with a significantly higher number of serious RTAs (soon to be renamed RTCs as 'Accident' implied that the *Collision* was unavoidable) than my previous Traffic posting at CTG/TSS. The majority of these were in rural areas around Newcastle, Leek and Cheadle, which I endeavoured to give as much visible policing and enforcement as possible. It was pointless having patrol cars roaming the congested city roads where the likelihood of serious injury from a collision, while still possible, was not as likely.

However, not long after I'd started at TSN, we did have a fatality in the city centre. About 5am on a summer morning, the body of a man was found in the middle of a pedestrian crossing on the Potteries Way. It was clear that he'd been struck by a vehicle, but there was no vehicle at the scene. We were baffled and made appeals for witnesses.

I decided to visit the City Council's CCTV facility the next day to see if anything had been captured by their cameras. Recordings were in time-lapse mode, approximately one shot every second if I recall correctly. Although they hadn't recorded the actual collision, we had a shot of the man standing at the crossing, with a motorcycle approaching it, then one of the man lying in the middle of the road, with the motor-cycle gone from view.

I decided to see if I could track the biker's course around the city centre and found shots of him at various points around the ring road. I came away with some stills from the sequence.

The group's motor-cyclists were passionate about motorcycling. I showed them the stills, and despite the rather fuzzy quality of the shots, they were able to identify the make and model of the bike. Not only that, but there was only one of them they knew of locally and they knew who owned it.

The owner was brought in for questioning, and the bike seized for forensics. He admitted having been the rider, and body tissue from the unfortunate man was found on his bike. From the time-stamps on the stills, combined with accurately measuring the route taken around the city centre that morning, we calculated that his average speed had been more than double the speed limit.

He was charged with and jailed for causing death by dangerous riding, failing to stop and failing to report the accident, all from a few fuzzy bits of video and some tissue samples.

It was a summer Saturday lunchtime, and we were called to deal with a crash on the A53 north of Leek, a frustratingly regular occurrence.

A 38-tonne tanker driver was returning empty to his base at Buxton, having illegally bypassed its speed limiter, which was easily done at the time. He stupidly took it upon himself to overtake a line of five moving cars, crossing a lengthy section of double white lines. He collided almost head-on, on the wrong side of the road with an oncoming people-carrier. The five overtaken cars, probably following too closely, became embroiled in the same crash.

It was an act of criminal recklessness and a miracle that nobody had been killed. Fifteen people were taken to hospital with a variety of injuries.

This was just about the most serious instance of irresponsibly reckless driving that I'd ever seen, I was appalled by it. The case officer naturally reported the driver for dangerous driving, but a few weeks later was contacted by the CPS, suggesting the charge be reduced to one of due care. When told that *Sergeant Tucker will not agree to this* the lawyer backed down - it seems that I'd made a noticeable impression upon the CPS after all.

The contemptible driver, unemployed since only minutes after the crash, was handed a well-deserved term of imprisonment and a lengthy disqualification.

There was an obsession on the part of our higher powers with **figures**. Everyone had to submit monthly returns of how many cars they'd stopped, how many fixed penalty notices, endorsable and non-endorsable were issued, speeders dealt with, tachographs inspected, words of advice given, the list goes on. I simply could not be bothered with this preoccupation. Having had my teams monthly sheets I was expected to examine their pocket-books fixed penalty records to check that the numbers corresponded. Whilst asking for monthly returns from my shift, I told them, with a wink, that I was far too busy to check that they were correct and never did. I knew for myself whether my people were working hard, which they were, and then some – I certainly had no need to check.

First thing every Monday morning we had to conduct checks of the speedometers of the patrol cars on the rolling road. At CTG/TSS the rolling road was at ground level, sunk into the floor. However, at Hanley, the rolling road was on a narrow platform, approximately two feet high.

It could be quite a nerve-racking experience for the Sergeant standing by the rolling road's speedometer, checking accuracy at speeds of 30, 50 and 70mph. Having a car and its driver perched in the air, just inches away, engine revving and travelling, albeit stationary, at motorway speed made you feel pretty vulnerable.

Driving up the narrow ramp onto the machine demanded accuracy, there was no room for error as the ramp fell away vertically at both sides. One of my team made a slight error mounting the ramp one morning, and the car fell off the side. This was in the days before digital and phone cameras, but within three seconds flashguns were firing away, capturing images not only of the stricken car, but also the embarrassed look on the driver's face.

Between us all, we bodily lifted the car back onto the ramp. Fortunately no damage had been caused, other than to the driver's dignity. Thanks to while-you-wait printing, a selection of the photos was on show in the office within the hour.

I made mistakes, the man who never made a mistake never did anything, so they say.

The biggest one gridlocked a swathe of North Staffordshire on a busy Friday morning. We had an abnormal load to escort from the county boundary with Cheshire at Kidsgrove, to the boundary with Derbyshire, at Doveridge. The route for the load, high as well as wide, was circuitous and complex and would take several hours to navigate; it was quite commonly used. However, some transport firms' route planners hadn't taken into account that the new dual-carriageway from the A500 to Blythe Bridge and onward into Derbyshire had recently opened, and it was a game-changer.

I had an idea. We could take the A50 instead of the long route and have the load parked up at Doveridge within an hour-and-a-half. Every patrol car carried a manual detailing the height of every overbridge on the route, which I checked, all had sufficient clearance for the load.

Great, let's do it!

I contacted the Duty Officer at Headquarters with my plan, he agreed - with the proviso,

If it goes wrong, on your head be it....

Unfortunately, it did, and it was.

We took the load along the A34, then onto the A500 at Talke, instead of using the southbound A34 through Newcastle. The intention was to head towards the A50 at Stoke, then straight through to Doveridge. After a couple of miles, as the load went under Porthill interchange I heard a sickening crunch as the top of the load became wedged underneath the overbridge.

Oh bollocks!

The driver, quite understandably, was furious with me.

While we waited for a recovery firm to let down and reinflate the tyres to enable further movement, I showed him my list of bridge heights which clearly showed that his load

362

should have gone under the bridge with plenty of clearance. This defused his rage somewhat, but not my acute embarrassment.

It later turned out that the road had been resurfaced a year or two previously, but to a greater height; the County Highways Department had failed to update us.

Needless to say, I took a lot of stick for this calamity, but my bosses understood that I'd acted in good faith on incorrect information. However it didn't stop my colleagues, and some of my friends outside the job from taking the mick for months afterwards.

Comments!!

.... DOH!!!

OPERATION RAINBOW CHECK REVEALS SUSPECT DEVICE UNDER FLYOVER.

SGT. TUCKER OVERSEES THE DELIVERY OF ANOTHER TIN OF SAUSAGES TO STORE CANTEEN.

.. SO TELL ME PADDY, THE TAPE YOU USED WAS IT METRIC OR IMPERIAL?

FRED HALFPENNY TURNED OUT AS PART OF SPECIALIST LAUGHTER SQUAD.

ROOSTING PIGEON DROPPINGS HAZARD ON CITY BRIDGES (EVENING SENTINEL JUNE 8)

SGT TUCKER SPEARHEADS DECISIVE ACTION TO UNSETTLE THE PIGEONS

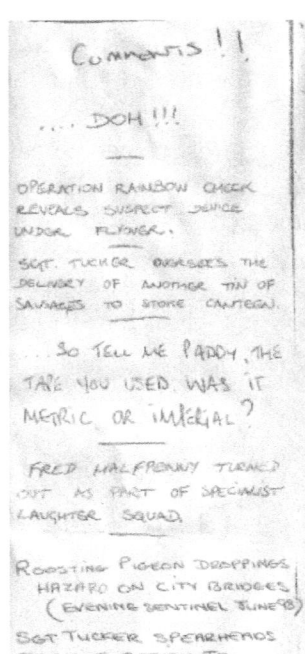

Bridge too far for A500 lorry

TRAFFIC jams over two miles long formed when a lorry became stuck under a bridge on the A500 today.

The vehicle, which weighed 30 tonnes and was around five metres high, was wedged under the bridge at Porthill just after 11am.

Police closed the southbound lanes at the junction and long queues formed as vehicles were diverted up a slip road, over the interchange, and down the exit sliproad, back on to A500.

A police spokesman said: "Routes are plotted for these sorts of abnormal loads but it is possible that the dimensions of the vehicle were not appropriate."

Police set up a diversion and were planning to let down the tyres on the truck and reverse it, then go round the roundabout and take it on an alternative route."

Passer-by Brian Underwood, of Porthill said: "It was absolute chaos."

"ANYWAY, IT'S NOT A TRAFFIC MATTER, JULIET ALPHA SIX FOUR CAN TURN OUT TO IT."

It's a crash Test, Dummy

I was only taking him home to kids grave for a cup of tea

SGT T "I'LL HAVE 2 BACON BUTTYS AND A COFFEE PLEASE"
"SORRY MATE THATS FURTHER DOWN THE ROAD"
like Frank Sinatra " I took it my way"
PORTHILL FLYOVER WAS TRANSPORTED UNDER ESCORT BY SGT TUCKER TO BOX YDS. HE INTENDED MOVING BOX YDS TO AUDLEY
SGT T's LATEST PURCHASE FROM BARGAIN BOOZE
"WHO ME"? I'M JUST WALKING THE DOG

I've always enjoyed a drink and would visit my local a few times a week for a couple of pints and a natter; the landlord and his wife were good friends and there was a warm, welcoming atmosphere. There was one guy, Bob, who came in every night not long before closing time and have four pints of Marston's Pedigree lined up on the bar.

He'd drink them like shots, then ask for more. He'd drink a minimum of six pints every night, didn't mix with the regulars and wasn't particularly well liked.

Until my friend Ron, the landlord told me, I was unaware that this guy was driving home. It was very much a 'local' pub where the regulars knew each other well, everyone knew what I did for a living. Now that I was, in their eyes, one of the 'bosses' on Traffic, they naturally expected me to do something about him; it was my sworn duty anyway.

It wasn't difficult, I told one of my patrols to lie in wait for him on his route home, he was stopped and failed the breathalyser. One evening, it was reported in the local paper that he'd been disqualified at court the previous day.

I suspected, correctly, that Bob would be undeterred by the ban.

As I passed another pub the same evening, I spotted his car on the car park, less than five minutes' walk from his house. I had two of the team lie in wait again, and predictably he failed another breath test; he was arrested for this, disqualified driving and no insurance. After I'd spoken on the phone to the custody officer at Kidsgrove, Bob was kept in custody for the next day's court. The same magistrates who'd handed him his ban two days previously were unimpressed. So much so that he spent the next few weeks in prison and had his disqualification extended.

There are two postscripts to this story.

Firstly, whilst calling in the area Control Room some months later, I saw on the incident log that Bob, a one-man-band electrician and disqualified driver had reported the theft of tools from his van overnight. I handed the ball to Kidsgrove to deal with this persistent lawbreaker, he really was taking the piss.

Secondly, fast-forward four years. I'd been retired for a little over a year. My friends had moved to another pub not far away. I'd followed them, as had many of the regulars, including Bob.

One night I was standing next to Bob at the bar and engaged in idle chat. Like everyone else he knew what I'd done for a living - but not what I'd done for *him*.

'I know you were a copper Nick, but you were one of the good 'uns. There was some bastard, I don't know who a few years back. He was out to get me and did a proper number on me. I went prison 'cos of him! What a bastard, if I ever got hold of him...

'...another pint?'

I politely declined whilst chewing through my tongue.

It's incredible that he hadn't worked out for himself who his nemesis actually was.

Long Service and Good Conduct (ha-ha) Medal Presentation 1998

24 – All Good Things

I was enjoying work tremendously. The team were fantastic, we worked well together, and morale was high. I'd like to think they enjoyed being led by me, I certainly felt loyalty and respect from them. On top of that I had a great boss in John Barrett, as well as a good working relationship with Ken Horton, my shift Inspector at TSS, and my opposite-number Sergeants in the Division. We also had exceptionally good senior Divisional bosses in Chief Inspector Janet Whalley, and, by now Superintendent, Steve Lovegrove. However, change was on the horizon, and lots of it.

A new radio system – Starnet – had been under development for a few years. Like all new things, a project team, including police officers seconded away from the front line worked at it for over two years. It was revolutionary compared to what we already had. Although we had newer, more technologically advanced radios, the actual radio network hadn't changed in a generation. Traffic and rural patrols were in contact with Headquarters Control Room over VHF radio, urban patrols used UHF which remained as patchy and unreliable as it had been over twenty years ago. The Starnet system would utilise VHF frequencies on cellular radio, very similar to having mobile phones on a private network.
There would be two Control Rooms, the existing one at Headquarters would cover the southern half of the county and the motorway – call sign changing from YF to YS, a new one under construction at Hanley would be responsible for the north, callsign YN.
Very imaginative, N for North, S for south, probably took a month-long sub-project for that alone.

We'd had new radios fitted to our cars, these as well as new personal radios were ready for the changeover – *after* we'd been trained to use them. Their operation would be completely different, they couldn't be eavesdropped by the bad guys, one patrol could call another without asking the Control Room for 'talk-through', and the system was divided into 'talkgroups', roughly corresponding to police station areas.

The key to anything working properly is training.

There wasn't any.

I came on duty one night to discover that the new system had been abruptly implemented, with no warning, and the same amount of planning.

A flustered member of the Starnet team spent a very hurried fifteen minutes, maybe less, 'training' us in the use of the new radios.

Communication is absolutely vital in operational policing. Training and understanding in its use and protocols was essential for the safety of front-line officers. The woefully inadequate, cursory training given was potentially dangerous.

It was decreed that with immediate effect, patrols from TSN we would deal with the Northern Area Control Room (NACR), instead of Headquarters (SACR).

My patrols would set their radios to the talkgroup(s) for their patrol area. This would mean that none of them would be aware of what the rest of the team was doing.

As well as not being in touch with each other, we'd be similarly unaware of our TSS colleagues, with whom we frequently needed to collaborate.

I asked how on earth I was supposed to undertake my responsibility for supervising and being in constant contact with my team.

How would I know where and what each of them was doing?

How I could be in contact with my opposite numbers at TSS and my shift Inspector?

Finally, and really important, how were my shift supposed to contact me?

The dismissive reply was,

'Well, you just set your radio to scan all the local talkgroups as well as the motorway.'

'That's more than ten talkgroups. Can you imagine how much radio traffic I'm going to be listening to, how much I'm going to have to filter out and how much I'm going to miss as well? It'll be impossible.'

This was far-and-away the most bone-headed, ill-considered cock-up that I had come across in all my service. The project had been ongoing for years, but it seemed scant consideration had been given to the fundamental operational needs of the system. I was unrelentingly vociferous in my criticism, never having had to be more so, I had the shift equally vocal in support. Within half an hour it was conceded that *for now*, all Traffic Division patrols would continue to communicate via Headquarters Control Room.

It felt like I'd scored a victory. What I didn't see at the time was that added to the renaming of the traffic groups four years ago, this was another small but insidious step towards the eventual death of Traffic. We were being slowly sidelined.

In earlier days, Assistant Chief Constables had generally been long-serving people who'd risen through the ranks in the same force; they knew the force, its area and people inside-out. No longer though. The ACC rank had become a year to eighteen months of making one's presence felt in one force, like a butterfly (wasp or sheep tick would be more fitting); another line on the CV, before moving on to another force. More often than not they'd leave their previous force totally screwed up by schemes which were difficult, if not impossible to reverse.

We had a new ACC typical of the 'butterfly' ACC rank. He had an air and appearance of arrogance that made you instinctively want to slap him – bloody hard too. His fixed term contract in Staffordshire wasn't renewed as he allegedly *conducted Ugandan discussions* (as Private Eye would put it) in office time, so he flitted on. Despite this and taking a wrecking ball to other forces, nothing stood in the way of his career progress. He made names for himself wherever he went, but none of them were remotely polite or respectful.

He was to wreak his particular brand of havoc upon Staffordshire, particularly on our Division. It was clear that he had an issue with Traffic policing in general from day one, maybe due to an unhappy encounter earlier in life. He was hell-bent on our demise.

As I've already said, a lot of people, usually misbehaving motorists, ask 'Why don't you go out and catch some proper criminals'. They don't appreciate that criminals use motor vehicles, just like everybody else. Some senior police ranks are apparently oblivious to this as well, particularly those whose rapid ascent of the greasy pole has left them with limited operational experience.

Local intelligence reports would feed us the vehicles the bad guys used, which were always good for a routine, very often productive stop.

As well as securing a year-on-year reduction in road casualties, we had a prolific arrest rate for crime. So much so that our arrest figures were outperforming those of our uniform and CID colleagues on the Divisions.

This had become embarrassing to Divisional commanders. Their people were by now so crippled by a burgeoning workload that they had precious little time to investigate crime and arrest people. So, obviously, they were naturally quite amenable to the ACC's scheming.

Attempting to stave off what my colleagues and I saw as an impending travesty, I tried to move our focus solely to traffic related matters, heavily emphasising our role and proven considerable success in casualty reduction.

I spent some weeks during off-duty time producing a discussion paper detailing where and when serious collisions were occurring, using year-on-year statistics, and suggesting changes to patrol sectors so that we could respond proactively to these patterns. Furthermore, I proposed a service level agreement with Divisional Commanders whereby all responsibility for traffic related matters would be placed in our hands. As it was, Divisions were still having to deal with traffic issues as well as their many other responsibilities; my proposal intended to reduce their workload so that they could concentrate on crime.

Blythe Bridge police station had become vacant and would make an ideal base for our operations, close to the A50/A500 corridor as well as the rural areas around Leek, so I further proposed that we investigate the possibility of moving there.

Both my proposals were well received, but only within our own Division.

Greater, darker forces were at work in the background. Alarmingly, some of our own people were joining in with the ACC From Hell's conspiracy; maybe hedging their bets and hoping for favourable postings when Traffic's demise happened.

I tried vehicle stop-checks at various locations, occasionally with involvement from Divisional staff so that they could see at first-hand what we were doing day-to-day. Although they were successful, it was becoming increasingly clear that we were fighting a losing battle for survival against a fait-accompli.

The first heavy-handed swing of the ACC's axe came. Henceforth, traffic patrols would be the first line of deployment for newly defined *Immediate Response Incidents*.

We were no longer to involve ourselves in casualty reduction, and certainly not go after speeders. *That's what we have the speed cameras for*, he'd defiantly stated, showing a cynical disregard for their inability to catch any of the other three fatal four, or disqualified drivers, or criminals on the move. We were attending upward of twenty such incidents per shift, so traffic patrolling and enforcement, even if we were allowed to do it became impossible. Divisional staff breathed a sigh of relief as the huge burden was lifted from them; our feelings were quite different.

Then the second, fatal swing of the ACC's axe. In short order, TSS ceased to exist, the force shed its responsibility for the M6 and M54 by seconding a small number of staff to the multi-force Central Motorway Policing Group (CMPG). Traffic Division was no more, as its remaining skilled people (apart from a few motorcyclists) were returned to Divisional policing, purportedly to share their expertise across the operational shifts.

It must have been absolutely sickening for those involved. I wasn't one of them as I'd been fortunate enough to have taken early retirement just a few weeks before it happened. The sharing of skills was fleeting, the former Traffic Division officers moved on as quickly as they could to other roles or retirement. No further specialist traffic related training took place, so enforcement (other than by speed cameras) slowly ground to a halt. Other than for very serious collisions, the former expertise of Traffic officers in investigating crashes was lost. It's probable that many incidents of poor driving leading to life changing injuries were not as rigorously investigated as they should have been.

The abolition of traffic policing nationally was an act of criminal negligence, it led to driver conduct on our roads becoming increasingly aggressive and inconsiderate of other road users, many drivers breaking the law with near impunity.

As I write, quarter of a century later, someone has had the latest 'great idea', dedicated Traffic policing has been reintroduced in Staffordshire, rebranded as the *Road Crime Team*. CMPG has been disbanded, and Staffordshire officers are patrolling the motorway again, just as they always should have.

Plus ça change.

Retirement came five years earlier than I expected. Everyone has a breaking point, but they're never aware of when and where it may happen. One evening in May 1998 I arrived at the scene of a double fatal crash, yet another one on the A53 north of Leek. It was a scene of carnage that haunts me to this day. A drunken driver was dead, face splattered on the windscreen as a result of a head-on collision which he'd caused; he had killed his teenage girl passenger in the collision. She was the same age and of quite similar appearance to my own daughter; on sighting the body, my first sickening thought was that it was actually her. The driver's daughter had sustained life-changing injuries. None had been wearing seatbelts. Life, for me, was never the same again despite concerted efforts to keep going over the next couple of years, I was just too fragile to carry on. My breaking point had been well and truly reached.

As well as my career, it ended my first marriage.

25 - Reflections

Uniformed police officers are a precious resource. They're the backbone of the service and it is they - not high-ranking officers or various specialists - who are by far its most important people. Without the uniform front-line, policing and public order would collapse completely. It has always irritated me, or infuriated would be a better word, that they are treated with such disdain by the public, the media and even their own leaders.

A few years ago, a senior member of the Government openly referred to uniform Constables as 'plebs'. This was a shameful insult which gave a stark insight into the mindset of politicians where police officers were concerned. While it did very little damage to this person's career, it chimed resoundingly with the unthinking masses and their perception of police officers.

Members of the public, when being dealt with by a uniform Constable would frequently ask,
'Can't I see someone higher?'
They neither realise nor understand that the officer has multiple skill-sets and is very highly trained, at the expense of the taxpayer.
Once, when asked this belittling question at Hanley's enquiry counter, I stood on a nearby box.
'Will this do?'
(It earned me a short-lived complaint and words from the Inspector).

I'm an avid reader of crime novels and watch crime dramas on TV, but only for fun as they bear very little resemblance to real-life. With few exceptions, authors portray uniform officers as unskilled functionaries; the term 'woodentops' being scornfully used to imply their being of low intelligence, suited only to menial tasks. CID officers are often depicted as senior to, and of higher status than their *equal* uniform counterparts. I've even read books in which uniform Constables have addressed Detective Constables or Sergeants as 'Sir' rather than *mate* or *Sarge*.

Unfortunately, many less well-informed (okay, thick) TV viewers see dramas as realistic illustrations of real life, which they're not.

For example, when TV detectives are interviewing a suspect, there's often a uniform Constable standing impassively at the door – this is pure fantasy, it *never* happens! Even more, sometimes, the interview will conclude with the detective officer saying,

'Okay Constable, take him back to his cell', as if they are some kind of servant at their beck and call.

If a detective officer had asked me to provide one of my officers for this kind of work, they'd have received a very brief, impolite response.

These, and other glaring, poorly researched inaccuracies on the small screen give the public a completely false idea of what goes on in the *real* police service.

Just in case you're wondering, I don't have any issue at all with CID officers, I'm just using this as an illustration.

The very worst though is the regard in which senior management hold their front-line uniform people. While publicly vaunting their vital importance, misdeeds in a specialist role such as CID or Traffic are punished by a deliberately ignominious transfer to the very front-line uniform duty which they hold so dear. The term **reverted** *to uniform duties* was the language used in the Force Orders of my day. This attitude from above corrodes the morale of all uniform patrol officers, receiving a clear message that in reality their leaders look upon them as the lowliest, least

375

deserving people in the whole service. *Cannon fodder* isn't all that wide of the mark.

In Staffordshire this indignity was reinforced by the Tenure of Post policy, which returned skilled, experienced specialist officers to the 'shop floor.'

It's on this shop floor where vital, spur of the moment, sometimes life-or-death decisions are made, where multiple, complex skills and abilities are paramount. Specialist investigators will normally arrive at a crime scene after it has been fully contained. People may have been arrested; evidence will have been protected and threats to safety, life and property neutralised, all by their unform colleagues. Those first actions are of utmost importance to any major investigation, invariably performed by very competent, capable people in uniform – the handling of the Emma Merry murder case being a prime example.

I happily walked away in July 2000 from the job I'd done for just over 24½ years. Although I've regretted my career choice from time to time, not for one moment have I ever regretted leaving it, apart from the loss of the very strong daily camaraderie that existed between colleagues.

I had an exit interview on my final Friday with the Chief Constable, who, as I've said, I'd known for a long time; it was very cordial.

We talked at length about how the job had changed, reminisced about old colleagues and discussed how the future was looking.

Naturally I criticised the demise of Traffic, saying how disappointed I was, he had little to say.

A few months previously, we'd had a Staff Perception Survey across the whole force, seeking officers' opinions on how the force was being run. Knowing that retirement was on the horizon I'd been very honest!

The Chief said,

'I was very hurt by some things you said in the perception survey Nick.'

'I thought it was anonymous John.'

'It was Nick, but I recognised your handwriting.'

We both laughed.

As I walked to the exit doors of the 'top corridor', the ACC From Hell came out of his office, coming face to face with me or more accurately, his eyes to my chin.

'Morning.'

'Good morning, you are…?'

'I'm Sergeant Nick Tucker of Traffic Support North.'

'Not for much longer though are you? Traffic's being disbanded', he sneered.

'Yes, all thanks to the likes of you.'

His face darkened. Then, with even more of a sneer,

'It's progress, the future.'

'If that future's people like you, then the job is truly fucked. Sir.' (Mentally I spelt it c-u-r)

'Who do you think you're speaking to? This is disciplinary…'

'You'd best get a move on then *sir* (similarly spelt), from Monday it'll be 'Mr Tucker, *sir*' to you.'

I'd had my say, I believe I was right too. People like him have destroyed the service over the last quarter-century, possibly even more so than the beasts of burden of the past. He and his kind infest the public sector and are constantly rewarded quite handsomely but undeservedly for repeated failures and questionable decisions.

He probably doesn't even remember the encounter, to him I was probably nothing more than an irrelevant dinosaur.

My best times in the job, where I'd gained the most job satisfaction were on Traffic, where I wish I'd been able to spend a great deal more time, although even when not in a jam-sandwich I had many 'encounters' with the motoring public in Staffordshire. I absolutely loved working on the motorway. Admittedly not a job for everyone, but I was in my element until that was ended by my unwelcome promotion.

As far as working on Division was concerned, I was certainly at my most contented at Burslem, busy enough to stop boredom settling in, but not so much that I couldn't do the job properly and act on my own initiative. Hanley, by contrast was so busy that all you could do a great deal of the time was to do enough to avoid folk calling us again within the next twenty-four hours, complaining of the same issue that you'd tried your best, but not had time to properly resolve. It was incredibly frustrating; job satisfaction for me was feeling that I'd made a difference, however small, it didn't happen often enough at Hanley.

Policing is a profession that demands and takes a great deal from you, giving little or nothing in return.

You become accustomed to people lying to you; not just offenders but anyone trying to embellish their side of the story. It causes you to develop a natural cynicism which eats away at you, to the point where you look upon every other human being as a liar.

Being a police officer makes you unconsciously attempt to dominate in all situations, even when relaxing at home. Add irregular hours to the mix and the job can put a huge strain on families and marriages.

The effect on your children of not coming home at the expected time is very unsettling; mine wouldn't sleep soundly if I was out of the house all night. They're unusually affected by your career choice; no schoolchildren are concerned with the occupations of their classmates' parents, unless that occupation is a police officer.

Your conduct, whether on or off-duty is subject to scrutiny. You cannot take part in politics, or make your political views widely known, which can be a very frustrating restriction of your freedom. At one time I found myself leading a local campaign regarding C of E primary education in my neighbourhood. Because it involved press, politicians and senior church figures, I was told in no uncertain terms that my actions may have a damaging effect on my *position in society*, by a senior bishop no less. I was treading a very fine line, being regularly quoted in local media - any public issue is also a political one or can be made into one. My only concern with was mine and my friends' children's education, but being a police officer limited my freedom to act or speak as I wished. Regaining that freedom upon retirement was an incredibly refreshing, liberating feeling.

Apart from the armed services, there can be few other jobs which affect family life so profoundly. I always prioritised my family over my job, sometimes it didn't help my career along. Maybe I'd sworn to serve the Queen, but my family was the most important thing to me.

Bill Norman's death, a few years ago gave me pause for thought. Every single boss and supervisor I had in my first two years at Newcastle were no longer with us. Some of them (I'm sure at least one is probably clear) I would gladly dance, or worse, on their grave, but as each one passed it gave me a moment to reflect on what they had done for me and what I'd learned from them, be it good or bad.

Few of my 1976 Newcastle C Shift colleagues remain. My tutor, John Clowes was heartbreakingly, savagely beaten in his home by an intruder, never to properly recover. My friend John *Noddy* Noden, an outstanding, superb detective died suddenly, far too young, just as the chimes of the millennium struck. Others, the 'Panda Romeo' included have all passed on.

Social media has helped me to connect with some from my class at Ryton. Again, not all of them are still with us, and naturally not all of them remained in the job. A handful of the twenty guys with whom I set off for Ryton in January 1976 have gone before, but most of us are still enjoying good health, having passed through the many years from fresh-faced recruits to our eighth decade. The time goes so quickly.

I've already said that the job has changed beyond recognition. I firmly believe that 1984 was a watershed for policing, when police forces (*services,* as they now prefer to call them) became de facto agents of the government of the day, not the Crown, which all police officers had sworn to serve.

Political control has been exacerbated by the pointless, costly vanity project of replacing long-established, effective Police Authorities with elected Police and Crime Commissioners, whose so-called mandate comes from a tiny percentage of a largely uninterested electorate.

Although anyone can stand for election, well-intentioned independent candidates usually fail as they have limited campaign funds available compared to those who are politically aligned. Thus, those successfully elected to these positions have been chosen by and are closely allied to a political party, having to toe its line. Once elected, all policing priorities and objectives are then based on their party's policies, wholly eradicating the independence of the Office of Constable under the Crown.

It's little wonder that so few people now apply to be a Chief Constable, accountable to a single political master and their party, instead of reporting to, whilst being independent from, a balanced committee of elected councillors and appointed magistrates.

Today, every action by the police can be subjected to intense public scrutiny, exacerbated out of all proportion by the malign influence of out-of-control social media. Front-line officers seem unable to exercise their lawful powers without being recorded by multiple phone cameras, either thrust in their face or at a distance. Although I always endeavoured to act beyond reproach, I would have hated to have dealt with this scourge during the time I served. I feel desperately sorry for those who now have to endure out-of-context footage being shared indiscriminately, in addition to sometimes being used as the basis for complaints.

Would I join again if I could rewind my life? I had some great times, but I don't think so.
I'm profoundly relieved that none of my family decided to follow my career path.
Would I encourage anyone to join? No, I'd actively discourage them in the present climate, I have done so several times when people have asked me my views.

What's desperately needed, and has been for years, is a Royal Commission to establish, once and for all, exactly what the role, powers, status and working conditions of the police should be in our future society. For now, until it has leaders prepared to actually lead, *from the front*, with wholehearted support from politicians and the media, it will only become worse. To use an expression familiar to both retired and presently serving officers –
T.J.F.
The Job's F***ed

Finally, to quote Bill Norman, half a century ago,

If you can't stand a joke, you shouldn't have joined!

Nick Tucker is retiring

Friends and Colleagues, past and present are invited to a celebration at

**The Red Bull
Congleton Road
Church Lawton**
(on the main A34 through Butt Lane)

8 pm onwards on Saturday 15th July
Food provided

(Supt's and above welcome in phone box outside)

End notes

I hope you've enjoyed reading my book.

I've managed to publish it on the very date that I have been retired as long as I served.

I started it late in 2015 but a couple of years later Staffordshire Police began a concerted effort to review the pensions of myself and many others, causing a great deal of stress to all of us. Because of this I lost interest and a hiatus of several years followed. My interest was reignited last year in 2024, resulting in what you've just read

As I've written about one memory, loads more memories, thought to be long forgotten have come flooding back. If I wrote about everything I remember, this book would probably be twice as long, if not more. Therefore, it should be considered to be edited highlights.

If you're a former colleague, and I haven't mentioned your name then I apologise. It doesn't mean that I've forgotten about you or the part you played in my time in the job.

I've always loved to write, but this is the biggest project to date. I'm just entering my eighth decade, I'm hoping to start a crime novel at some point. Whether I manage to complete it before I reach my expiry date is another matter!

Could I ask one last thing? If you've enjoyed the book, please leave me a review on Amazon, it really does help.
Thanks again

Printed in Dunstable, United Kingdom

67096129R00218